Sport Management

Books in the Sport Management Series

Sport Management
Principles and Applications

Second edition

Russell Hoye

Aaron Smith

Matthew Nicholson

Bob Stewart

Hans Westerbeek

Routledge
Taylor & Francis Group

LONDON AND NEW YORK

First Published by Butterworth-Heinemann
This edition published 2011 by Routledge
2 Park Square, Milton Park, Abingdon, Oxon OX14 4RN

Simultaneously published in the USA and Canada
by Taylor & Francis Group, 711 Third Avenue, New York, NY 10017, USA

Routledge is an imprint of Taylor & Francis Group, an informa business

Notice
No responsibility is assumed by the publisher for any injury and/or damage to persons or property as a matter of products liability, negligence or otherwise, or from any use or operation of any methods, products, instructions or ideas contained in the material herein.

British Library Cataloguing-in-Publication Data
A catalogue record for this book is available from the British Library

Library of Congress Cataloging-in-Publication Data
A catalog record for this book is available from the Library of Congress

ISBN: 978-0-7506-8755-3

Typeset by TNQ Books and Journals Pvt Ltd
(www.tnq.co.in)

Contents

Part 1 The Sport Management Environment

Series Editor

Dr. Russell Hoye is an associate professor in the School of Sport, Tourism and Hospitality Management, La Trobe University, Victoria, Australia. Russell has been involved in sport management education since 1993, working in Australia at La Trobe University, Griffith University and Victoria University, and in China, with The University of Hong Kong and Tsinghua University. He is a board member of the Sport Management Association of Australia and New Zealand (SMAANZ). He was the guest editor for the inaugural special issue of *Sport Management Review* on professional sport in Australia and New Zealand published in 2005.

Russell's areas of expertise include corporate governance, organisational behaviour, volunteer management and public sector reform within the sport industry. He has acted as consultant for the Australian Sports Commission, Sport and Recreation Victoria and a number of local government and non-profit organisations. His research interests focus on examining how governance is enacted with sport organisations and how volunteers engage with and are managed by sport organisations. He has published papers on these topics in journals such as *Nonprofit Management and Leadership, Sport Management Review, European Sport Management Quarterly, Society and Leisure, International Gambling Studies, Third Sector Review, Sporting Traditions, Managing Leisure, Football Studies, Annuals of Leisure Research* and the *Australian Journal on Volunteering.*

Preface

We noted in the preface to the first edition of this book that our desire to write it stemmed from our frustration at the lack of an introductory text in sport management that provided the right balance between management theory and contextual analysis of the sport industry. The success of the first edition, as illustrated by its adoption in many educational institutions across Australia, Canada, New Zealand, the UK and Europe, suggested that many academics shared our frustration. Our intention with the second edition of this book remains unchanged. We are not seeking to replace the numerous introductory texts on management theory or to ignore the many books that examine the international sport industry. Rather, our aim is to provide in a single text sufficient conceptual detail for students to grasp the essentials of management, while highlighting the unique aspects of management in a sporting context.

The book provides a comprehensive introduction to the principles of management and their practical application to sport organizations operating at the community, state/provincial, national and professional levels. The book is primarily written for first and second year university students studying sport management courses and students who wish to research the commercial dimensions of sport. It is especially suitable for students studying sport management within business focused courses, as well as students seeking an overview of sport management principles within human movement or physical education courses.

The book is divided into two parts. Part one provides a concise analysis of the evolution of sport, the unique features of sport and sport management, the current drivers of change in the sport industry and the role of the state, non-profit and professional sectors of sport. Part two covers core management principles and their application in sport, highlighting the unique features of how sport is managed compared to other industrial sectors. In response to feedback from prescribers of the first edition, we have included two new chapters on marketing and financial management. Part two, therefore, includes chapters that examine strategic management, organizational structure, human resource management, leadership, organizational culture, financial management, marketing, governance and performance management.

To assist lecturers and instructors, all chapters include an overview, a set of objectives, a summary of core principles, a set of review questions, suggestions for further reading and a list of relevant websites for further information. In addition, Chapters 2 through 13 each contain three substantial examples we have dubbed 'In Practice' that help illustrate concepts and accepted practice at the community, state/provincial, national and international levels of sport.

For this second edition, we have added a case study at the end of each chapter, which can be used by lecturers and instructors for classroom discussion or assessment. For those academics who prescribe the book as essential reading for students, a comprehensive website is available that contains:

- PowerPoint slides that summarize each chapter

- Teaching notes to accompany each case study

- Tutorial activities to accompany each chapter

- Testbank of questions for use in Blackboard/WebCT environments.

We would like to thank Eleanor Blow, Commissioning Editor at Elsevier: Butterworth-Heinemann and her predecessor, Francesca Ford, for their support for the book. We would also like to thank our colleagues and students for their valuable comments on the first edition of the book. Finally, we would like to acknowledge our respective partners and families for understanding our need to devote our time and energy toward this second edition.

Russell Hoye
Aaron Smith
Matthew Nicholson
Bob Stewart
Hans Westerbeek

List of Tables

List of Figures

List of in Practice Examples

List of Case Studies

The Sport Management Environment

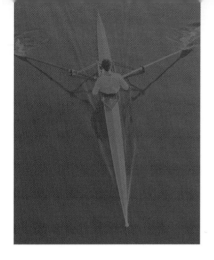

CHAPTER 1

Sport Management

OVERVIEW

This chapter reviews the development of sport into a major sector of economic and social activity and outlines the importance of sport management as a field of study. It discusses the unique nature of sport and the drivers of change that affect how sport is produced and consumed. A three-sector model of public, non-profit and professional sport is presented, along with a brief description of the salient aspects of the management context for sport organizations. The chapter serves as an introduction to the remaining sections of the book, highlighting the importance of each of the topics.

After completing this chapter the reader should be able to:

- Describe the unique features of sport

- Understand the environment in which sport organizations operate

- Describe the three sectors of the sport industry

- Explain how sport management is different to other fields of management study.

WHAT IS SPORT MANAGEMENT?

Sport employs many millions of people around the globe, is played or watched by the majority of the world's population and, at the elite or professional level, has moved from being an amateur pastime to a significant industry. The growth and professionalization of sport has driven changes in the consumption, production and management of sporting events and organizations at all levels of sport.

Managing sport organizations at the start of the 21st century involves the application of techniques and strategies evident in the majority of modern business, government and non-profit organizations. Sport managers engage

3

in strategic planning, manage large numbers of human resources, deal with broadcasting contracts worth billions of dollars, manage the welfare of elite athletes who sometimes earn 100 times the average working wage and work within highly integrated global networks of international sports federations, national sport organizations, government agencies, media corporations, sponsors and community organizations.

Students of sport management therefore need to develop an understanding of the special features of sport and its allied industries, the environment in which sport organizations operate and the types of sport organizations that operate in the public, non-profit and professional sectors of the sport industry. The remainder of the chapter is devoted to a discussion of these points and highlights the unique aspects of sport organization management.

UNIQUE FEATURES OF SPORT

Stewart and Smith (1999) provide a list of ten unique features of sport which can assist us to understand why the management of sport organizations requires the application of specific management techniques. A unique feature of sport is the phenomenon of people developing irrational passions for sporting teams, competitions or athletes. Sport has a symbolic significance in relation to performance outcomes, success and celebrating achievement that does not occur in other areas of economic and social activity. Sport managers must learn to harness these passions by appealing to people's desire to buy tickets for events, become a member of a club, donate time to help run a voluntary association or purchase sporting merchandise. They must also learn to apply clear business logic and management techniques to the maintenance of traditions and connections to the nostalgic aspects of sport consumption and engagement.

There are also marked differences between sport organizations and other businesses in how they evaluate performance. Private or publicly listed companies exist to make profits and increase wealth of shareholders or owners, whereas in sport, other imperatives such as winning premierships, providing services to stakeholders and members, or meeting community service obligations may take precedence over financial outcomes. Sport managers need to be cognizant of these multiple organizational outcomes while, at the same time, being responsible financial managers.

Competitive balance is also a unique feature of the interdependent nature of relationships between sporting organizations that compete on the field but cooperate off the field to ensure the long-term viability of both clubs and their league. In most business environments, the aim is to secure the largest market share, defeat all competitors and secure a monopoly. In sport, clubs and teams need the opposition to remain in business, so they must cooperate to share revenues and playing talent and regulate themselves to ensure the uncertainty in the outcome of games between them, so that fans' interest will be maintained. In some ways, such behaviour could be construed as anti-competitive.

The sport product, when it takes the form of a game or contest, is also of variable quality. While game outcomes are generally uncertain, one team might dominate, which will diminish the attractiveness of the game. The perception of those watching the game might be that the quality has also diminished as a result, particularly if it is your team that loses! The variable quality of sport therefore makes it hard to guarantee quality in the marketplace relative to providers of other consumer products.

Sport also enjoys a high degree of product or brand loyalty, with fans unlikely to switch sporting codes because of a poor match result or the standard of officiating. Consumers of household products have a huge range to choose from and will readily switch brands for reasons of price or quality, whereas sporting competitions are hard to substitute. This advantage is also a negative, as sporting codes that wish to expand market share find it difficult to attract new fans from other codes due to their familiarity with the customs and traditions of their existing sport affiliation.

Sport engenders unique behaviours in people, such as emulating their sporting heroes in play, wearing the uniform of their favourite player or purchasing the products that celebrity sports people endorse. This vicarious identification with the skills, abilities and lifestyles of sports people can be used by sport managers and allied industries to influence the purchasing decisions of individuals who follow sport.

Sport fans also exhibit a high degree of optimism, at times insisting that their team, despite a string of bad losses, is only a week, game or lucky break away from winning the next championship. It could also be argued that the owners or managers of sport franchises exhibit a high degree of optimism by touting their star recruits or new coach as the path to delivering them on field success.

Sporting organizations, argue Stewart and Smith (1999), are relatively reluctant to adopt new technologies unless they are related to sports science, where on-field performance improvements are possible. In this regard, sport organizations can be considered conservative and tied to traditions and behaviours more than other organizations.

The final unique aspect of sport is its limited availability. In other industries, organizations can increase production to meet demand but, in sport, clubs are limited by season length and the number of scheduled games. This constrains their ability to maximize revenue through ticket sales and associated income. The implication for sport managers is that they must understand the nature of their business, the level of demand for their product and services (whatever form that may take) and the appropriate time to deliver them.

SPORT MANAGEMENT ENVIRONMENT

Globalization has been a major force in driving change in the ways sport is produced and consumed. The enhanced integration of the world's economies has enabled communication to occur between producers and consumers at greater speed and variety and sport has been one sector to reap the benefits. Consumers of elite sport events and competitions such as the Olympic Games, World Cups for rugby, cricket and football, English Premier League Football, the National Basketball Association (NBA) and Grand Slam tournaments for tennis and golf enjoy unprecedented coverage. Aside from actually attending the events live at a stadium, fans can view these events through free to air and pay or cable television; listen to them on radio and the Internet; read about game analyses, their favourite players and teams through newspapers and magazines; receive progress scores, commentary or vision on their mobile phones; and sign up for special deals and information through online subscriptions using their e-mail address. The global sport marketplace has become very crowded and sport managers seeking to carve out a niche need to understand the global environment in which they must operate. Thus, one of the themes of this book is the impact of globalization on the ways sport is produced, consumed and managed.

Most governments view sport as a vehicle for nationalism, economic development or social development. As such, they see it as within their purview to enact policies and legislation to support, control or regulate the activities of sport organizations. Most governments support elite training institutes to assist in developing athletes for national and international competition, provide funding to national sporting organizations, support sport organizations to bid for major events and facilitate the building of major stadiums. In return for this support, governments can influence sports to recruit more mass participants, provide services to discrete sectors of the community or have sports enact policies on alcohol and drug use, gambling and general health promotion messages. Governments also regulate the activities of sport organizations through legislation or licensing in areas such as industrial relations, anti-discrimination, taxation and corporate governance. A further theme in the book is the impact that governments can have on the way sport is produced, consumed and managed.

The management of sport organizations has undergone a relatively rapid period of professionalization over the last 30 years. The general expansion of the global sports industry and commercialization of sport events and competitions, combined with the introduction of paid staff into voluntary governance structures and the growing number of people who now earn a living managing sport organizations or playing sport, has forced sport organizations and their managers to become more professional. This is reflected in the increased number of university sport management courses, the requirement to have business skills as well as industry specific knowledge or experience to be successful in sport management, the growth of professional and academic associations devoted to sport management and the variety of professionals and specialists that sport managers must deal with in the course of their careers. Sport managers will work with accountants, lawyers, taxation specialists, government policy advisors, project management personnel, architects, market researchers and media specialists, not to mention sports agents, sports scientists, coaches, officials and volunteers. The ensuing chapters of the book will highlight the ongoing professionalization of sport management as an academic discipline and a career.

The final theme of the book is the notion that changes in sport management frequently result from developments in technology. Changes in telecommunications have already been highlighted, but further changes in technology are evident in areas such as performance enhancing drugs, information technology, coaching and high performance techniques, sports venues, sport betting and wagering and sporting equipment. These changes have forced sport managers to develop policies about their use, to protect intellectual property with a marketable value and generally adapt their operations to incorporate their use for achieving organizational objectives. Sport managers need to understand the potential of technological development but also the likely impact on future operations.

THREE SECTORS OF SPORT

In order to make sense of the many organizations that are involved in sport management and how these organizations may form partnerships, influence each others' operations and conduct business, it is useful to see sport as comprising three distinct sectors. The first is the State or public sector, which includes national, state/provincial, regional and local governments and specialist agencies that develop sport policy, provide funding to other sectors and support specialist roles such as elite athlete development or drug control. The second is the non-profit or voluntary sector, made up of community-based clubs, governing associations and international sport organizations that provide competition and participation opportunities, regulate and manage sporting codes and organize major championship events. The third sector is professional or commercial sport organizations, comprising professional leagues and their member teams, as well as allied organizations such as sporting apparel and equipment manufacturers, media companies, major stadium operators and event managers.

These three sectors do not operate in isolation and, in many cases, there is significant overlap. For example, the State is intimately involved in providing funding to non-profit sport organizations for sport development and elite athlete programmes and, in return, non-profit sport organizations provide the general community with sporting opportunities as well as developing athletes, coaches, officials and administrators to sustain sporting participation. The State is also involved in commercial sport, supporting the building of major stadiums and other sporting venues to provide spaces for professional sport to be played, providing a regulatory and legal framework for professional sport to take place and supporting manufacturing and event organizations to do business. The non-profit sport sector supports professional sport by providing playing talent for leagues, as well as developing the coaches, officials and administrators to facilitate elite competitions. Indeed, in some cases the sport league itself will consist of member teams which are technically non-profit entities, even though they support a pool of professional managers and players. In return, the professional sport sector markets sport for spectators and participants and, in some cases, provides substantial funds from TV broadcast rights revenue. Figure 1.1 illustrates the three sectors and the intersections where these relationships take place.

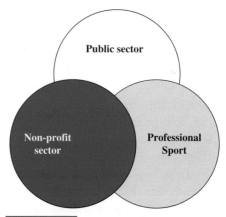

FIGURE 1.1   *Three sector model of sport.*

WHAT IS DIFFERENT ABOUT SPORT MANAGEMENT?

Sport managers utilize management techniques and theories that are similar to managers of other organizations, such as hospitals, government departments, banks, mining companies, car manufacturers and welfare agencies. However, there are some aspects of strategic management, organizational structure, human resource management, leadership, organizational culture, financial management, marketing, governance and performance management that are unique to the management of sport organizations.

Strategic management

Strategic management involves the analysis of an organization's position in the competitive environment, the determination of its direction and goals, the selection of an appropriate strategy and the leveraging of its distinctive assets. The success of any sport organization may largely depend on the quality of their strategic decisions. It could be argued that non-profit sport organizations have been slow to embrace the concepts associated with strategic management because sport is inherently turbulent, with on-field performance and tactics tending to dominate and distract sport managers from the choices they need to make in the office and boardroom. In a competitive market, sport managers must drive their own futures by undertaking meaningful market analyses, establishing a clear direction and crafting strategy that matches opportunities. An understanding of strategic management principles and how these can be applied in the specific industry context of sport are essential for future sport managers.

Organizational structure

An organization's structure is important because it defines where staff and volunteers 'fit in' with each other in terms of work tasks, decision-making procedures, the need for collaboration, levels of responsibility and reporting mechanisms. Finding the right structure for a sport organization involves balancing the need to formalize procedures while fostering innovation and creativity and ensuring adequate control of employee and volunteer activities without unduly affecting people's motivation and attitudes to work. In the complex world of sport, clarifying reporting and communication lines between multiple groups of internal and external stakeholders, while trying to reduce unnecessary and costly layers of management, is also an important aspect of managing an organization's structure. The relatively unique mix of paid staff and volunteers in the sport industry adds a layer of complexity to managing the structure of many sport organizations.

Human resource management

Human resource management in mainstream business or sport organizations is essentially about ensuring an effective and satisfied workforce. However, the sheer size of some sport organizations, as well as the difficulties in managing a mix of volunteers and paid staff in the sport industry, make human resource management a complex issue for sport managers. Successful sport leagues, clubs, associations, retailers and venues rely on good human resources, both on and off the field. Human resource management cannot be divorced from other key management tools, such as strategic planning or managing organizational culture and structure and is a further element that students of sport management need to understand to be effective practitioners.

Leadership

Managers at the helm of sport organizations need to be able to influence others to follow their visions, empower individuals to feel part of a team working for a common goal and be adept at working with leaders of other sport organizations to forge alliances, deal with conflicts or coordinate common business or development projects. The sport industry thrives on organizations having leaders who are able to collaborate effectively with other organizations to run a professional league, work with governing bodies of sport and coordinate the efforts of government agencies, international and national sport organizations and other groups to deliver large-scale sport events. Sport management students wishing to work in leadership roles need to understand the ways in which leadership skills can be developed and how these principles can be applied.

Organizational culture

Organizational culture consists of the assumptions, norms and values held by individuals and groups within an organization, which impact upon the activities and goals in the workplace and in many ways influences how employees work. Organizational culture is related to organizational performance, excellence, employee commitment, cooperation, efficiency, job performance and decision-making. However, how organizational culture can be defined, diagnosed and changed is subject to much debate in the business and academic world. Due to the strong traditions of sporting endeavour and behaviour, managers of sport organizations, particularly those such as professional sport franchises or traditional sports, must be cognizant of the power of organizational culture as both an inhibitor and driver of performance. Understanding how to identify, describe, analyse and ultimately influence the culture of a sport organization is an important element in the education of sport managers.

Financial management

Financial management in sport involves the application of accounting and financial decision-making processes to the relatively unique revenue streams and costs associated with sport organizations. It is important for sport managers to understand the financial management principles associated with membership income, ticketing and merchandise sales, sports betting income, sponsorship, broadcast rights fees and government grants and subsidies. Sport managers also need to understand the history of the commercial development of sport and the ways in which sport is likely to be funded and financed in the future, in particular the move to private ownership of sport teams and leagues, sport clubs being listed on the stock exchange, greater reliance on debt finance and public–private partnerships.

Sport marketing

Sport marketing is the application of marketing concepts to sport products and services and the marketing of non-sports products through an association with sport. Like other forms of marketing, sport marketing seeks to fulfil the needs and wants of consumers. It achieves this by providing sport services and sport-related products to consumers. However, sport marketing is unlike conventional marketing in that it also has the ability to encourage the consumption of non-sport products and services by association. It is important to understand that sport marketing means the marketing of sport as well as the use of sport as a tool to market other products and services.

Governance

Organizational governance involves the exercise of decision-making power within organizations and provides the system by which the elements of organizations are controlled and directed. Governance is a particularly important element of managing sport organizations, many of whom are controlled by elected groups of volunteers, as it deals with issues of policy and direction for the enhancement of organizational performance rather than day-to-day operational management decision-making. Appropriate governance systems help ensure that elected decision-makers and paid staff seek to deliver outcomes for the benefit of the organization and its members and that the means used to attain these outcomes are effectively monitored. As many sport managers work in an environment where they must report to a governing board, it is important that they understand the principles of good governance and how these are applied in sport organizations.

Performance management

Sport organizations over the last 30 years have undergone an evolution to become more professionally structured and managed. Sport organizations have applied business principles to marketing their products, planning their operations, managing their human resource and other aspects of organizational activity. The unique nature of sport organizations and the variation in missions and purposes has led to the development of a variety of criteria with which to assess the performance of sport organizations. Sport management students need to understand the ways in which organizational performance can be conceptualized, analysed and reported and how these principles can be applied in the sport industry.

SUMMARY

Sport has a number of unique features:

- people develop irrational passions
- differences in judging performance
- the interdependent nature of relationships between sporting organizations
- anti-competitive behaviour
- sport product (a game or contest) is of variable quality
- it enjoys a high degree of product or brand loyalty
- it engenders vicarious identification
- sport fans exhibit a high degree of optimism
- sport organizations are relatively reluctant to adopt new technology; and
- sport often has a limited supply.

Several environmental factors influence the way sport organizations operate, namely globalization, government policy, professionalization and technological developments.

The sport industry can be defined as comprising three distinct but interrelated industries: the State or public sector, the non-profit or voluntary sector and the professional or commercial sector. These sectors do not operate in isolation and often engage in a range of collaborative projects, funding arrangements, joint commercial ventures and other business relationships.

There are some aspects of strategic management, organizational structure, human resource management, leadership, organizational culture, financial management, marketing, governance and performance management that are unique to the management of sport organizations. The remainder of the book explores the three sectors of the sport industry and examines each of these core management issues in more detail.

REVIEW QUESTIONS

1. Define sport management.

2. What are the unique features of sport?

3. Describe the main elements of the environment that affect sport organizations.

4. What sort of relationships might develop between sport organizations in the public and non-profit sectors?

5. What sort of relationships might develop between sport organizations in the public and professional sport sectors?

6. What sort of relationships might develop between sport organizations in the professional and non-profit sectors?

7. Explain the major differences between managing a sport organization and a commercial manufacturing firm.

8. Why does the sport industry need specialist managers with tertiary sport management qualifications?

9. Identify one organization from each of the public, non-profit and professional sport sectors. Compare how the environmental factors discussed in this chapter can affect their operation.

10. Discuss whether the special features of sport discussed in this chapter apply to all levels of sport by comparing the operation of professional sports league, an elite government sport institute and a community sport club.

FURTHER READING

Downard, P. and Dawson, A. (2000). *The economics of professional team sports*. Routledge, London.

Hoye, R., Nicholson, M. and Smith, A. (2008). Unique aspects of managing sport organizations. In C. Wankel (ed.), *21st Century management: a reference handbook*. Sage, Thousands Oaks, pp. 499–507.

Jarvie, G. (2006). *Sport culture and society*. Routledge, London.

Masteralexis, L.P., Barr, C.A. and Hums, M.A. (1998). *Principles and practice of sport management*. Aspen, Maryland.

Nicholson, M. (2007). *Sport and the media: managing the nexus*. Butterworth-Heinemann, Oxford.

Parkhouse, B.L. (2005). *The management of sport: its foundation and application*, 4th edn. McGraw-Hill, New York.

Parks, J.B. and Quarterman, J. (2003). *Contemporary sport management*, 2nd edn. Human Kinetics, Champaign.

Quirk, J. and Fort, R. (1999). *Hard ball: the abuse of power in pro-team sports*. University Press, Princeton.

Sandy, R., Sloane, P. and Rosentraub, M. (2004). *Economics of sport: an International Perspective*. Palgrave Macmillan, New York.

Slack, T. (ed.) (2004). *The commercialization of sport*. Routledge, London.

Slack, T. and Parent, M. (2006). *Understanding sport organizations: the application of organization theory*, 2nd edn. Human Kinetics, Champaign.

RELEVANT WEBSITES

The following websites are useful starting points for general information on the management of sport:

European Association for Sport Management at http://www.easm.net

North American Society for Sport Management at http://www.nassm.com

Sport Management Association of Australia and New Zealand at http://www.smaanz.org

CHAPTER 2

The Role of the State in Sport Development

OVERVIEW

This chapter examines the different ways in which the State can influence the development of sport systems and practices. Particular attention is paid to the reasons why the State should want to intervene in the building of sport infrastructure and its operation and the different forms the intervention can take, specifically interventions that assist and promote sport, in contrast to those that control and regulate sport. A distinction will also be made between State initiatives that increase levels of participation and State initiatives that improve levels of elite athlete performance. Throughout the chapter, examples, incidents and cases will be used to illustrate both the concepts and theories that underpin State intervention in sport and the outcomes that arise from this intervention.

After completing this chapter the reader should be able to:

- Explain the role and purpose of the State

- Explain how and why the State intervenes in nation's economic, social and cultural landscape

- Identify the different forms the intervention can take, paying particular attention to assistance and support on one hand and regulation and intervention on the other

- List the different ways the State can influence the development of sport structures and practices

- Distinguish between socialist, reformist, neo-liberal and conservative ideologies and how they influence the way the State goes about assisting and regulating sport

- Explain how each of the above ideologies shapes the values, structure and operation of sport.

15

DEFINING THE STATE

The State, by which we mean the structures that govern and rule societies, has always played an important role in the provision of sport experiences to people. The ancient Olympic Games and other sport festivals were funded and organized by the various city states that made up ancient Greece and ruling monarchs in Europe during the Middle Ages organized an array of tournaments and combat games to hone the skills of their warrior classes (Mechikoff and Estes, 1993). As the world became industrialized and modernized, the State expanded its provision of sport activities. In the USA for example, many government funded schools and colleges established sport facilities ranging from manicured playing fields and small indoor arenas to large stadiums seating anywhere from 10 000 to 70 000 spectators.

Today, the State, through its government institutions, provides a complex array of sport facilities and services. Many sport stadiums throughout the world were initially financed by government funds and, while subsequently controlled and operated by independent operators, are subject to government legislation and policy guidelines (John and Sheard, 1997). In most western nations, the central government has funded both the establishment of training centres for elite athletes and their ongoing operation. As a result many thousands of coaches, sport scientists and sport facility managers are now on the government payroll.

In Practice 2.1 The Role of the State in Establishing Elite Sport Training Institutes

Over the last two decades the world has changed dramatically. Large slabs of the Communist world fell apart with the fragmentation of the Soviet Union, the USA asserted both its economic and cultural power over the rest of the world and international trade expanded in response to the dismantling of many trade barriers. This was also accompanied by a revolution in the telecommunication industry, culminating in the mass consumption of mobile phone and Internet services. In short, the world has become globalized. Globalization has not only had significant impact on the structure and operation of major resource and manufacturing industries like oil, iron ore, coal, motor vehicles, electronics, telecommunications and pharmaceutical supplies, but also on less tangible industries like international finance, tourism, the arts and sport. In fact, sport is an exemplar of how the forces of globalization create an international market in which global brands are traded around the world and customers regularly shift between the parochial and the international. As a result, local leagues and competitions thrive while mega-sport events like the Olympic Games, the World Soccer Cup, the World Cricket Cup and the Tour de France saturate the global sports landscape.

The globalization of sport has also created a hyper-competitive international environment where hundreds of nations seek their moment of glory on the world sport stage (Miller et al., 2001). In reality, only a few nations share the limelight and most of them got there by being wealthy or powerful enough to allocate significant resources to sport development. During the last 30 years of international sport competition, a number of nations have decided that investing in elite sport is an effective means of gaining international credibility and respectability. The old Soviet Union (USSR) and German Democratic Republic (GDR) mobilized the State apparatus in the 1970s and 1980s to establish a successful sport factory system that regularly produced world champions in a wide array of sport activities (Riordan, 1977). Their success, and those of other communist countries like Cuba, demonstrated that a State-managed system of Olympic sport development produced superior elite athlete outcomes to a system that depended upon an energetic but relatively uncoordinated combination of the commercial and volunteer sectors. During the1970s and early 1980s, the GDR, with a population of less than 20 million, amazed the world sporting community as it accumulated a swag of Olympic Games medals. At the 1976 Montreal Games, it came third on the medal count with ninety, which was only bettered by the USSR and the USA. In fact, its gold medal haul of forty exceeded the USA count of thirty-four. While it was later established that a significant number of medals were won with the aid of performance enhancing drugs, there was no doubt that the GDR had put in place a very effective system for developing talented athletes in a variety of sports (Brohm, 1978).

More recently, China, another communist nation, has mobilized its State apparatus to achieve impressive performances on the international sporting stage. Since 1949, when the Peoples Republic of China was founded, sport has played a significant role in shaping Chinese society. Not only was sport seen to be a means of making its citizens physically and mentally tough, it was also used to demonstrate the superiority of communism over the various forms of western style capitalism (Riordan, 1978). One of the key features of Chinese communism is its bureaucratic structure with power and funds flowing from the Communist Party Central Committee to tightly controlled administrative bodies in the cities and provinces. Sport was slotted into this model and, as a result, the Chinese sport development system has for the most part been centrally planned and managed by the Chinese Sport Ministry. Notwithstanding the economic reforms that occurred during the rule of Deng Xiaoping in the 1980s, the State still controls most sport programmes, although there is now more authority in the hands of city and provincial councils (Fan Hong, 1997). This centralized sport development system has enabled the Chinese to identify talented young athletes at an early age and provide them with specialist training and coaching. The Chinese sport bureaucracy has also been effective in targeting sports in which it already has a competitive advantage, like table tennis, gymnastics, diving and women's weight-lifting, and allocated the resources to ensure a smooth pathway to international success. China's haul of 32 gold, 17 silver and 14 bronze medals at the 2004 Athens Olympic Games (which gave it second place behind the USA) was testament to the effectiveness of its elite sport system. Its medal tally at the 2008 Beijing Games was even more impressive which, in this instance, was not only the result of its State sponsored elite

Continued

In Practice 2.1 The Role of the State in Establishing Elite Sport Training Institutes—cont'd

sport programme, but also the result of its massive pool of potential elite athletes and its home-ground advantage.

So what is it that gives the State-sponsored systems of sport development such a competitive edge in international sporting competitions? The fundamental advantage that centrally planned and coordinated systems have over systems entrusted to the voluntary sector (with varying degrees of State support) is their capacity to target young athletes with potential and provide them with a highly structured pathway to elite competition. While this approach is seen by critics to be mechanistic and taking the fun out of sport, it is efficient in that it does not waste resources on athletes who do not have the potential to succeed. A State-controlled system of sport development also enables athletes to train and compete on a full-time basis, which allows them to hone their skills and improve performance. In contrast, a voluntary sector system is frequently underpinned by a romanticized notion of amateurism, which means that not only are athletes not allowed to obtain material benefits from their international success, but are also expected to earn a living in an occupation outside of sport. This clearly disadvantages athletes from many non-communist nations, which was clearly in evidence throughout the 1970s and 1980s (Bloomfield, 2003).

This centralized and highly rationalized model of sport development has been copied by many western nations that would have normally left sport development to the commercial and volunteer sectors. France was an early adopter of the Communist model of sport development when it designed a Sport Charter in 1975, which included provision for State support of elite training institutes, sport facility construction and funding of amateur athletes (Chalip et al., 1996). This was followed by the establishment of a National Sport Development Fund in 1979, which increased the funding to elite athletes. The funding base was further expanded in 1985 when a Sports Lottery was set up. Canada followed a similar path and, in the mid-1970s, began to fund national sporting bodies so they could improve their levels in international sport performance. In 1979, an Athletic Assistance Programme was introduced in which athletes (who were nominally amateur) were handsomely rewarded for doing well in international sport competitions. During the 1980s and 1990s, countries as disparate as Australia, Brazil, Britain and Japan adopted the Communist sport development model and set up training institutes, elite coach education programmes, sport science support systems and generally increased the level of financial support to elite athletes (Henry and Uchium, 2001). For the most part, there was a subsequent improvement in their international sports standing. More recently, Great Britain has established elite sport training institutes. Using Australia as a template, Great Britain has jettisoned the old amateur/volunteer/club-centred sport development model and embraced the sport academy/talent nurturing model in a variety of sports including highly traditional ones like rowing and cricket and less culturally important like cycling (Houlihan and White, 2002).

REASONS FOR STATE INTERVENTION

The State has always intervened in the affairs of its society for the fundamental reason that it enables it to set the nation's economic and political direction. More specifically, the State believes that by its various interventions it can improve the well-being of society. For example, by providing rail and road infrastructure it can improve transport systems and thereby increase the levels of overall efficiency in industry and commerce. Similarly, by funding the establishment of schools, universities and hospitals it can go a long way not only to improve the educational abilities of its citizens, but also enhance their capacity to work more productively and more vigorously participate in the cultural and commercial affairs of the nation. The same sort of logic underpins the State's goal of having a fit and healthy people that can defend the nation's sovereignty in times of war and generate international kudos and prestige through the success of its elite athletes.

At the same time, the State may wish more directly to control the behaviour if its citizens by establishing laws that prohibit things like anti-competitive behaviour by businesses and various forms of discrimination and anti-social behaviour of individuals. In this context, the State has a history of regulating sport to ensure the safety of it participants. One of the best examples is boxing, where the risk of injury is very high and rules are essential to ensure a lower chance of sustaining acute injury and long-term brain damage.

Because of sport's potential to deliver significant social benefits, there are a number of sound reasons for the State wanting to invest in it. However, government resources and taxpayer funds are always scarce and sport is one of many institutions that want to claim part of the government budget. As a result, sport assistance cannot always be guaranteed and it must compete with defence, health, policing, social welfare and education. And, in capitalist economies at least, sport has also traditionally been seen as outside the scope of government responsibility on the grounds that it is far removed from commerce and more in the territory of volunteer amateurs. However, it is not that difficult to mount a case for State intervention in sport. For example, a case can be made to support the view that not only will society be better off with more sport facilities and services, but that without State support, the resources invested in sport will be far less than optimal.

Market failure and the supply of sport services

In capitalist nations like Australia, Canada, Great Britain, New Zealand and the USA, resources are, in the main, allocated in markets through the interaction of demand, supply and prices. However, there are often cases where markets do not operate in the best interests of the community or nation. This is known as market failure. Market failure can occur when the full benefits of markets are not realized because of an under-supply of socially desirable products, or alternatively, an over-supply of less desirable products. Market failure and under-supply arise in situations where there are significant external or social benefits in addition to private benefits. Private benefits are the value consumers obtain from the immediate purchase of a good or service and are measured by the prices people are prepared to pay for the experience. In sport, private benefits arise from a number of activities and practices. They include attending a major sport event, working out at a gymnasium, playing indoor cricket or spending time at a snow resort. Social benefits, on the other hand, comprise the additional value communities obtain from the production of a good or service. These social benefits are over and above the private benefits. In those cases where social benefits can be identified, society would be better served by allocating additional resources into those activities. However, private investors will not usually do this because of a lack of profit incentive. Consequently, it will be left to government to fill the breach and use taxpayers' money to fund additional sporting infrastructure and services.

In other words, since sport provides significant social benefits, it deserves State support to ensure that the welfare of the whole community is maximized. According to the proponents of sport assistance, social benefits can arise from both active participation and spectator sport. In the case of active participation, the benefits include improved community health, a fall in medical costs, a reduction in the crime rate, the inculcation of discipline and character, the development of ethical standards through the emulation of sporting heroes, greater civic engagement and the building of social capital. Research into social capital building suggests that sport not only expands social networks, but also produces safer neighbourhoods and stronger communities (Productivity Commission, 2003). Moreover, the social benefits linked to social capital are extended when sport groups and clubs look outward and encompass people across diverse social cleavages. This bridging or inclusive social capital can be contrasted with bonding social capital, which characterizes sport groups and clubs with a narrow ethnic, social, or occupational base (Putnam, 2000). Either way, sport is seen to be a great builder of social capital.

In the case of elite and spectator sports, the social benefits include tribal identification with a team or club, social cohesion, a sense of civic and national pride, international recognition and prestige, economic development and the attraction of out-of-town visitors and tourist dollars (Gratton

Table 2.1	Social Benefits of Sport Development	
Arising from Active Participation		**Arising from Elite Athlete Successes**
Improvement in community health and productivity		Tribal identification and belonging
Fall in medical costs		Social cohesion
Reduction in juvenile crime rate		Civic and national pride
Development of character and sense of 'fair play'		International recognition and prestige
Building of social capital, social cohesion and civic engagement		Economic development and tourism

Adapted from Stewart et al. (2004)

and Taylor, 1991). When these social benefits are aggregated, the results are quite extensive, as can be seen in Table 2.1. At the same time, they are often difficult to quantify and, in some cases, the evidence to support the claimed benefit is soft and flimsy.

Sport as a public good

A case can also be made for the State's involvement in sport on the grounds that sport is often a public or collective good (Li et al., 2001). Public goods are those goods where one person's consumption does not prevent another person's consumption of the same good. For example, a decision to visit a beach or identify with a winning team or athlete, will not prevent others from doing the same. Indeed, the experience may be enhanced by others being in proximity. This is the non-rival feature of the good. Public goods are also goods where, in their purest form, no one can be prevented from consuming the good. Again, a visit to the beach and identifying with a winning team meet this criterion. This is the non-excludable feature of the good. Public goods can provide substantial benefits throughout the whole of society and are usually not rationed through high prices. However, they are not attractive to private investors since there is no assurance that all users will pay the cost of providing the benefit. As the number of so-called free-riders increases, there is a shrinking incentive for private operators to enter the public good market. In this instance, it is argued that the State should provide for this higher demand by increasing its funding to ensure an appropriate infrastructure and level of service.

Sport equity and inclusiveness

Finally, it can be argued that the State should be funding sport on equity grounds. For example, it might be argued that the whole community benefits from being fit and healthy and therefore no one should be excluded because of low income or lack of facilities. In these cases, the optimal community benefit can only be realized if everyone has access to appropriate sport and recreation services help them to improve their health and fitness, enhance their self-image and build the community's social capital. In order to improve accessibility and ensure equality of opportunity, the State can establish its own low-cost sport facilities, subsidize existing sport activity providers and design targeted programmes for disadvantaged groups.

REGULATION AND CONTROL

There are also many situations where the State may want to regulate and control the provision of sport activities and limit the resources devoted to some activities (Baldwin and Cave, 1999). For example, it may be necessary to enact laws and rules that safeguard public order when a large number of people are spectators of, or are playing in a sport event. In most countries there are laws that clearly define the parameters within which sport grounds are to be constructed. These laws will cover things like design specifications, the provision for seating, the number of entry and exits points and fire prevention facilities (Frosdick and Walley, 1997). There may also be rules that govern the behaviour of spectators. Most commonly, these laws will relate to the consumption of alcohol and disorderly and violent behaviour.

One of the most highly regulated activities is horse-racing. It is not just a case of ensuring the animals are treated humanely, but of also making sure the gaming and gambling practices that surround the sport are tightly controlled so that corrupt practices are minimized. There are many cases around the world where horses have not been allowed to run on their merits. This can involve doping activities where stimulants will be given to horses to make them run quicker and depressants administered to make them go slower. In both instances, the aim is to undermine the betting market and, through the use of inside information, to back the horse that has been advantaged and avoid the horse that has been slowed.

Another form of regulation involves the media in general and TV in particular. In both Australia and England, there are anti-siphoning rules that effectively give free-to-air television stations privileged access to major sport events at the expense of pay and cable television providers. This means that a major sport event like the Australian Football League (AFL) Grand Final must initially be offered to free-to-air stations before being offered to pay TV stations. This is done on the grounds that a sport of national significance should be made as widely available as possible. In Australia, the pay TV subscriptions cover less than 50% of all households and it would therefore be inequitable to give rights to a pay TV station only.

In Practice 2.2 State Regulation Over Sport: Boxing and the Martial Arts

In some sports, there are very few rules that govern the conduct of its activities. The relatively gentle sport of lawn bowls is a case in point. Apart from having to abide by the laws of the land, lawn bowlers are not externally regulated in any additional ways by the State. At the same time, it has to be said that players in lawn bowls clubs are sometimes highly regulated internally, particularly when it comes to dress codes for the playing rink.

At the other extreme are the more combative sports of boxing and the martial arts, including judo and karate. As mentioned above, one of the most highly regulated sports is boxing, particularly at the professional level. Many countries have legislation which effectively sets up government-controlled agencies that both issue licences to promoters and participants and monitors the conduct of the sport.

Take the case of the state of New South Wales in Australia. Boxing and kickboxing are the largest professional combat sports in New South Wales and the industry is regulated under the *Boxing and Wrestling Control Act of 1986*. The Act provides for the establishment of the Boxing Authority of NSW (BANSW) to control and regulate the conduct of professional boxing events in this State. According to BANSW, professional boxing is an inherently dangerous sport and, as a result, it is essential that some type of boxing control authority is established to regulate the industry and safeguard its participants.

The Act sets out the requirements for registration of professional boxers and industry participants, which includes promoters, matchmakers, managers, trainers, seconds, referees, judges and timekeepers. It further determines the conditions under which competitors can compete and events can be staged. It effectively restricts free entry into the industry and makes participation conditional upon meeting certain safety and registration requirements. The Act also controls wrestling, amateur boxing and kickboxing through a permit system administered by NSW Sport and Recreation under Ministerial delegation.

Registration of all boxers and industry participants together with permits to conduct promotions are required under the Act and can be obtained through the NSW Department of Sport and Recreation on behalf of the Boxing Authority. The Department of Sport and Recreation maintains a register of all professional boxers and industry participants and provides general assistance to the industry. Permits are also required for the conduct of amateur boxing, kickboxing, amateur and professional wrestling and the Department of Sport and Recreation sets out conditions for permits to conduct such events.

A similar model operates in the USA, where there is a national Boxing Commission that regulates the professional boxing industry and ensure minimum acceptable standards of operation. Its rules are enforceable under the *Professional Boxing Safety Act of 1996*. The Act begins by identifying the key stakeholders involved in the planning and conduct of a boxing match, which include the following:

1. 'boxer' meaning an individual who fights in a professional boxing match

2. 'licensee' which means an individual who serves as a trainer or second

3. 'manager' which means a person who receives compensation for service as an agent or representative of a boxer

Continued

In Practice 2.2 State Regulation Over Sport: Boxing and the Martial Arts—cont'd

4. 'matchmaker' meaning a person that proposes, selects and arranges the boxers to participate in a professional boxing match

5. 'physician' which means a doctor of medicine legally authorized to practice medicine by the State in which the physician performs such function or action

6. 'promoter' meaning the person primarily responsible for organizing, promoting and producing a professional boxing match.

Under the above 1996 Act, the Commission also has a responsibility to register all boxers. It requires that boxers register with the boxing commission of the State in which the boxer resides. In those instances where boxers are residents of a foreign country, or reside in a USA state where there is no boxing commission, they must register with the boxing commission of any other state. In short, all boxers who want to fight professionally must be registered somewhere in the USA.

The other crucial thing the Boxing Commission does is to uphold basic safety standards. Under its current standards, no person may arrange, promote, organize, produce or fight in a professional boxing match without meeting each of the following requirements as a means of protecting the health and safety of boxers:

1. A physical examination of each boxer must be conducted by a physician. The physician must then certify whether or not the boxer is physically fit to compete safely in the boxing match. Copies of the certification must be subsequently submitted to the Boxing Commission

2. Other than in exceptional circumstances, an ambulance or medical personnel with appropriate resuscitation equipment must be continuously present on the site of the boxing match

3. A physician must be continuously present at ringside

4. Health insurance must be provided for each boxer in order to ensure medical coverage for any injuries sustained in the match.

While the degree of control varies from country to country, the most severe controls are in Norway, where professional boxing is banned. Any Norwegian boxer who wants to enter the professional ranks must relocate to another country.

The basic reason why boxing and the martial arts have such problematic status is because they provide not only community benefits, but also community costs. The community benefits include an opportunity to engage in a vigorous sport that requires both extreme physical fitness and mental toughness. There is also some evidence that boxing and the martial arts are a very effective means of channelling the energies of disadvantaged youth into socially constructive activities and subjecting them to a valuable form of personal discipline. On the other hand, boxing and the martial arts are highly combative and have high injury rates. In the case of boxing, there is a high risk of brain damage, which brings with it enormous personal and social costs. Therefore, in order to minimize the risk of physical damage to the participants, a high degree of regulation is required. More generally, boxing is seen as a brutal sport that has little relevance to a civilized society where there are rules against physical assault in everyday life. There are a number of medical associations and groups whose aim is to ban competitive boxing on the grounds that it has a net social cost to the community and that as a result we would all be better of without it. However, most national governments do not agree. At the amateur level in particular, it is supported and funded and, in addition, is still an integral part of the Olympic Games schedule.

EXTENT AND FORM OF STATE INTERVENTION

As indicated above, the State can intervene in sport in all sorts of ways. The extent of the intervention and the form it takes is strongly influenced by the ideology, values and overall philosophy of the State and its governing institutions.

The first ideology is *conservatism*. A conservative ideology values tradition and customary ways of doing things. Conservative governments have a tendency to regulate the social lives of people and therefore want to censor works of art and literature they find offensive. They also want to control the distribution of legal drugs like alcohol and generally act to protect people from themselves. On the other hand, they believe that business should be left to its own devices, where the combination of individual self-interest, the profit motive and market forces, will ensure a favourable outcome. However, because conservative governments believe a strong private sector is the key to progress, they are prepared to assist and protect industry when the need arises. While on one hand they recognize sport as an integral part of the social life of most people, they do not want to assist or protect it since it is not part of the world of business. Indeed, for many conservatives, it is another world altogether that should be best kept at a distance from business. This sport world is underpinned by the belief that sport fulfils its function best when it is done for its own sake, played by amateurs, managed by volunteers and generally left to look after its own affairs.

The second ideology is *reformism*, or as it is also known, welfare statism, or social democracy. Reformism is primarily concerned with social justice and equity. While reformists recognize the necessity of a strong private sector, they believe it cannot be trusted to deliver fair and equitable outcomes. It therefore needs to be strictly managed. This could take the form of additional state-owned enterprises or tight regulations on business behaviour. Reformists share the conservative view that assistance and protection may be necessary in the public interest. Unlike conservatives, though, reformists believe primarily in social development, which not only means legislating for social freedom, but also for social justice. Income redistribution to disadvantaged groups is important and is done by ensuring that wealthy individuals and corporations are taxed most heavily. State spending is also crucial to reformists, since it is used to stimulate the economy when demand and spending is low. Reformist governments tend to be more centralist and aim to use this centralized power to engineer positive social outcomes. Reformists consequently see sport as a tool for social development and aim to make sport more accessible to the whole community. In these cases, programmes are established to cater for the needs of minority groups like the disabled, migrants who speak another language and women. In short, reformist government policy focuses more on community and less on elite sport development.

The third ideology is *neo-liberalism*. Neo-liberals believe that society is at its most healthy when people can run their daily lives without the chronic intrusion of the State. The rule of law is important, but beyond that, people should be free to choose how they organize their social lives and businesses should be free to organize their commercial lives as they see fit. Neo-liberals see little value in State-owned enterprises and argue that the privatization of government services produces greater efficiency and higher quality outcomes. Moreover, deregulated industries are seen to run better than tightly controlled ones. In short, neo-liberals believe Government should not engage directly in most economic activity, but rather provide only base level infrastructure and legislative guidelines within which private business can thrive. Sport is valued as an important social institution, but should not be strictly controlled. However, neo-liberals also believe sport can be used as a vehicle for nation building and economic development and should be supported in these instances. This produces a sport policy that tends to focus on elite sport at the expense of community sport.

The final ideology is *socialism*. Socialists believe that a combination of privately owned and unregulated markets will produce severe levels of inequality and alienation. As a result, capitalist modes of production and distribution need to be replaced by a strong State where resource allocation is centrally controlled. Like neo-liberals, socialists agree that sport is an important social institution, but unlike neo-liberals, go on to assert that sport should be controlled from the centre to ensure a fair spread of clubs and facilities throughout society. To this end, a socialist system of sport development will be driven by a central bureaucracy that sets the sport agenda. The State also provides most of the funds and resources by which to develop sport at both the community and elite levels.

Each ideology not only contains quite different assumptions about the proper role of the State, but also different ideas about what sport can do to improve the welfare of society. As a result, each ideology will produce different sport development outcomes and the ideology often overrides the claims of interest groups like sport scientists, coaches and officials. The four ideologies described provide a simplified typology and, in practice, the State will often take bits and pieces of each ideology when forming its position on a particular sport issue or problem. At the same time, most States will be characterized by more of one, and less of another ideology. Table 2.2 outlines the different ideologies and indicates how they can shape the State's views on sport development.

As a result there are a broad array of arrangements by which the State can fund, develop and deliver sport facilities and programmes. At one extreme, the State can distance itself from sport development by claiming that sport is a private matter for individuals and communities and is therefore best left to the market and voluntary sectors to run. This arrangement was the primary feature of Australian sport until the 1970s when the national government resolved to fund sport facilities and programmes (Stewart et al., 2004). In the USA, the national government has also adopted an arms-length approach to sport and has left the funding and development of sport to the market and the school and university sectors (Chalip et al., 1996). At the other extreme, the State sets the sport agenda by both establishing sport facilities across the nation and funding the management of their operations. This approach was exemplified in the sport development programmes of most communist nations during the 1970s and 1980s. In the Soviet Union (USSR) and the German Democratic Republic (GDR), a national sport programme was

Table 2.2   Links between Political Ideology and Sport Development

Ideological Type	Features	Implications for Sport Development
Conservatism	Private ownership of business Regulation of social practices	Arms-length association with sport. Sport is seen as a private activity that grows out of the community and is managed by the volunteer sector
Reformism	Mixed economy Regulation of both social and economic affairs	Direct involvement in sport facility construction and community sport participation
Neo-liberalism	Emphasis on the market De-regulation of industry	Most resources go to the elite end of sport development and its commercial outcomes
Socialism	Limited scope for the market Central planning Bureaucratic control over resource allocation	Direct involvement in all aspects of sport development. Often tightly regulated. Both community and elite sport are resourced

integrated into the school curricula and sport schools were used to identify and nurture talented young athletes. In addition, sports that had a strong civil defence and para-military flavour were conducted in factory and trade union facilities. Cuba had a similar sport development model in which the State, through its government bureaucracy, managed the whole sport experience for both the sport-for-all participant and the Olympic athlete. While Cuba banned professionalism in sport, it handsomely rewarded its national sporting heroes by giving them government jobs or enrolling them in college and university courses that they could complete at their convenience. In Cuba, like the USSR and GDR, sport success was not just a sporting victory but a 'psychological, patriotic and revolutionary' one as well (Riordan, 1978).

In Practice 2.3 State Assistance to Sport: The Australian Experience

Australia has always seen itself as a sports-loving nation and has used sport a means of generating civic pride, national identity and international recognition (Stewart et al., 2004). Between 1945 (the end of the second world war) and 1972 (the election of a Labour reformist government for the first time in 23 years) Australians were very successful on the world sporting stage, producing a proliferation of world champions in swimming, tennis, cricket, rugby league and cycling (Cashman, 1995). However, this was achieved with a minimum of government support. While local government provided many excellent playing fields and indoor sport facilities, the national government provided nothing to most national sport governing bodies and neither did it fund the construction of many sport venues. All it did was contribute to Olympic and Commonwealth Games teams every two years, provide small annual grants to help life saving clubs to patrol beaches and provide financial assistance to State government run fitness councils. In short, sport was left to run its own affairs.

However, this all changed in the 1970s in response to two significant forces. First, a reformist Labour national government was elected which had a mandate to change the social conditions in Australia. It replaced the stable but conservative Menzies Government that had increased the nation's prosperity, but had done next to nothing for sport. One of the first things the Whitlam Government did was to establish a Ministry of Sport and start funding a programme that both increased the number of community leisure centres around Australia and assisted national sporting bodies to improve their operations. Second, the failure of the Olympic Games team to win a gold medal at Montreal in 1976 traumatized the nation to such an extent that the national government resolved to intervene directly in the sport development process. Although the Fraser Liberal Government (which replaced the Whitlam Government in 1975) was for the most part highly conservative, it decided to establish a training academy for talented young athletes in response to growing community agitation that Australia was no longer a world leader in sport. The Australian Institute Sport (AIS) was opened for business in 1981 and quickly became internationally recognized as a successful training centre for elite athletes (Bloomfield, 2003). In 1984, the Australian Sports Commission was established in order better to manage the national Government's sport funding initiatives and generally implement government sport policy in a systematic and orderly manner. The rest, as they say, is history and, in the space of 25 years, the national government's annual sports budget increased from around $A5million to just over $A150 million (Stewart et al., 2004). These funds have been used both to increase Australia's sporting infrastructure and expand the operations of the national governing bodies for sport. At the same time, there has been a change in the values and culture of Australian sport as sport became more commercialized in response to a growing involvement from the market sector. When combined with the ever-increasing national government support for sport, the whole sport system became more professionalized and created many career opportunities for players, administrators and coaches.

Current Government sport assistance is multidimensional, but it fundamentally wants to strike the elusive balance between elite sport development and community sport participation (Stewart et al., 2004). It can be conveniently divided into four strategic, but interconnected outcomes. First, it aims to develop an effective national sports infrastructure by enhancing the management capabilities of national sporting bodies. Programmes are directed at improving coaching standards, the management skills of officials, the day-to-day operation of national sporting bodies and the capacity of Australian sport to export its expertise. Second, it aims to improve participation in sport activities by encouraging more people to engage in club-based sport through its junior sport activities and assisting marginalized groups in securing places in sport clubs and associations. These groups include aboriginals, people with disabilities, women, children and older adults. Third, it aims to provide for continuous improvement in the performances of Australians in international sport. In this case, programmes are directed at assisting national sporting bodies to nurture talented athletes, enhancing the Australian Institute of Sport scholarship programme, providing sport science support and assisting athletes in managing their future careers. Finally, it aims to provide a climate and culture of fair play. The focus here is on not only drug control, but also eliminating discrimination and harassment, assisting indigenous communities and dismantling barriers to disabled athlete participation. The breadth of the current government sport-assistance arrangements is revealed in Table 2.3.

All of these programmes beg the question as to whether or not Australia's sport system has been improved by State intervention or whether Australia's sport development should have been left in the hands of the commercial and voluntary sectors. If Olympic and Commonwealth Games medal tallies are any indication, then State intervention is the best thing that has ever happened to Australian sport. Whereas Australian athletes won only nine medals at the 1980 Moscow Olympic Games, the tally increased to 14 at the 1988 Seoul Games, 27 at Barcelona in 1992 and 41 at Atlanta in 1996. Even better results were achieved at Sydney in 2000 when 58 medals were snared, while in Athens in 2004, Australia (with a population of only 21 million) placed fourth in the medal tally when its athletes collected 49 medals. These successes provided the national government with

Continued

In Practice 2.3 State Assistance to Sport: The Australian Experience—cont'd

further evidence that its elite sport policy was working and, as a result, it substantially increased its funding arrangements to support the team for the 2008 Beijing Olympic Games.

However, sport development is about much more than just winning medals at international sport events. The State also has a responsibility to provide the community with rewarding sport experiences and to make sure disadvantaged groups have open and easy access to facilities (Houlihan, 1997). In the past decade, the Australian government has made some good progress to increase the general level of participation but, at the moment, it has plateaued. Australia is now one of the most obese nations in the world, second only to the USA. This is another challenge the Australian government will be facing over the next few years. It will be interesting to see if more State funding of sport participation will solve this serious public health problem.

Table 2.3 Australian National Government Interventions in Sport: 1980–2008

Focus of Intervention	Examples
High performance	Australian Institute of Sport (AIS), athlete scholarships grants, elite coach education
Management improvement	Australian Sports Commission (ASC) training programmmes, grants for management improvement and staff training
Economic benefit	Government agencies to secure significant sport festivals and championships. Subsidies to ensure viability of mega- sport events
Drug education and enforcement	Australian Sports Anti-Doping Authority (ASADA), Drug education programmes, testing and sanctions
Community participation	Programmes and funding to encourage greater participation at grass-roots level. Working with national sport bodies to develop modified games and implement junior development programmes
Social capital	Volunteer training programmes and grants to local sport bodies to improve sport facilities and administrative systems
Diversity and equity	Women's sport programmes, anti-harassment and anti-discrimination programmes including design of member protection policies (MPP), funding to assist indigenous and disabled sport

Adapted from Stewart et al. (2004)

SUMMARY

The State is just one of three social orders or supports that underpin the operation of society. The other two social orders are the market and civil society. The State has the capacity significantly to shape the structure and scope of sport through a number of mechanisms. First, it can construct sport facilities; second, it can fund the day-to-day operations of sporting associations and clubs; third, it can deliver sport programmes to the community directly; fourth, it can establish training facilities for elite athletes to assist their ongoing development; and, finally, it can control the operation of sport by introducing various laws, regulations and rules (Hylton et al., 2001). However, the scale of State support and the form it takes will vary between nations depending on the dominant political ideology and the overall cultural importance of sport to society. In some cases, the State will directly control and manage sport, while at the other end of the political spectrum the State will step back from the sport system and encourage the commercial and volunteer sectors to take up the slack. At this point in time, the evidence suggests that governments have a pivotal role to play in supporting both the community participation and elite-sport ends of the sport development continuum. Through the establishment of sports infrastructure and facilities and the funding of sport programmes, it can create all sorts of health and social benefits, improve international sport performance and enhance a country's international status and prestige.

REVIEW QUESTIONS

1. What is the role of the State?

2. How does the State go about shaping the political and economic landscape of a nation?

3. Apart from the State what other social forces contribute to national development?

4. Explain how the State may contribute to sport development.

5. What can the State do to increase the level of sport participation and sport club membership?

6. What can the State do to increase the level of elite sport performance?

7. Why should the State want to intervene in sport?

8. Would sport development be best left to the voluntary and commercial sectors?

9. Is there any evidence that a centralized model of elite sport development is any more effective than a market-based sport development model?

10. How might the State go about increasing the scale of sport participation at the community or 'grass-roots' level?

FURTHER READING

For a thorough analysis of the ways in which government can go about regulating a nation's economic, social and cultural affairs, see Baldwin and Cave (1999). There are now a number of publications that examine the ways in which the State has intervened in a nation's sport development. To get a detailed picture of the Australian experience you should read Bloomfield (2003) and Stewart, et al. (2004). The British experience is reviewed in Green and Houlihan (2005), Houlihan and White (2002) and Hylton et al. (2001). For some comparative analysis of State involvement in sport the most comprehensive treatment is contained in Chalip et al. (1996). Houlihan (1997) provides an excellent comparative study of Australia, Canada, Ireland and the UK. The most definitive account of sport in socialist Cuba, although now a little dated, is Pattavino and Pye (1994).

RELEVANT WEBSITES

- To find out more about the State and Australian sport go to the Australian Sports Commission site at http://www.ausport.gov.au

- To get more details of the English experience go to the Sport England site at http://www.sportengland.org

- For a comprehensive review of the State's involvement in New Zealand sport go to New Zealand Government Sport and Recreation site at http://www.sparc.org.nz

- To secure a detailed and comprehensive, if politically skewed analysis of Cuba and its recent progress, go to the US Department of State website at www.state.gov/r/pa/ei/bgn/2886.htm

Case Study: The Structure and Organization of Sport in Cuba

Cuba is the largest island of the West Indies group, occupying nearly 111 000 square kilometres. By contrast, Australia takes up 7.7 million square kilometres, while the UK occupies 243 000 square kilometres. Cuba is also the westernmost island, just west of Haiti and the Dominican Republic, around 150 km south of the USA coastline and at the entrance to the Gulf of Mexico. The island is mountainous in the southeast and south-central area, but relatively flat elsewhere. Cuba also includes numerous smaller islands, islets and cays. The population of Cuba is 11.5 million, with Havana, the nation's capital accounting for nearly 2.7 million people. As a point of comparison, Australia has a population of 21 million, while the population of the UK is 61 million. Cuba's GDP per head is just over $4000 which makes it a relatively poor if rapidly developing nation. Its main industries are agricultural, with an emphasis on sugar, tobacco, citrus fruits and coffee. It is also a large exporter of nickel.

Christopher Columbus discovered Cuba in 1492 and by 1511, the Spaniards under Diego Velásquez had established permanent settlements and Havana's superb harbour made it a common transit point to and from Spain. By the early 1800s, Cuba's sugarcane industry was booming and its colonial masters secured massive numbers of black slaves to work the fields. A simmering independence movement turned into open warfare from 1867 to 1878 and slavery was abolished in 1886. In 1895, the poet José Marti led the struggle that finally ended Spanish rule, thanks largely to USA intervention in 1898 after the sinking of the battleship *Maine* in Havana harbour.

An 1899 treaty made Cuba an independent republic under USA protection. The USA occupation, which ended in 1902, suppressed yellow fever and brought large American investments. The 1901 Platt Amendment allowed the US to intervene in Cuba's affairs, which it regularly did during the first thirty years after 1900. Cuba terminated the amendment in 1934 and, in 1956, Fidel Castro launched a revolution from his camp in the Sierra Maestra mountains. Castro's brother Raul and Ernesto (Ché) Guevara, an Argentine physician, were by his side and many landowners supported the rebels. The USA ended military aid to Cuba in 1958 and, in 1959, Castro took over the government.

The USA initially welcomed what looked like a democratic Cuba, but a rude awakening came within a few months when Castro established military tribunals for political opponents and jailed hundreds of dissidents. Castro disavowed Cuba's 1952 military pact with the USA, confiscated US assets, established Soviet-style collective farms and, in the early 1960s, formalized Cuba's alliance with the Soviet Union. Thousands of Cubans fled the country and Cuba consolidated itself as a socialist nation where the State not only took over the ownership of land and businesses, but also assumed control most aspect of people's lives. This included not only core industry sectors like agriculture and but also sport.

Today, Cuba sees itself as a centrally-planned and government-controlled democracy where the key resources are owned by the State. In practice, it is more of a communist dictatorship ruled by the Castro family. Like many communist States before it, Cuba has a strong health care system and runs a comprehensive education programme for all its residents. As a result, its citizens are healthy and well educated. On the other hand, it is a one-party State and tightly regulates the social behaviour of its citizens, a case in point being its rigid control over Internet use over recent years.

Sport in Cuba

Cuba punches above its weight in international sport. That is to say it does better than its material level of welfare and population would suggest. Cuba does well in sport for three reasons. First, it has a strong history of participation; second, sport is central to Cuban identity; and, finally, it has a strong, well resourced and centrally managed sport system. Take baseball for example, which is the national sport of Cuba. It was first played on the island around 1865. According to local historians, the first baseball Championship in Cuba was held in 1878, with the first two teams established in 1874. By the beginning of the 20th century, other countries

Continued

in the American continent began to play baseball. The first amateur baseball championships were held in Havana in 1905, while a national amateur league was founded in 1914. Since that time Cuba has been an international force in baseball, particularly at the Olympics and has supplied many elite players to the professional leagues in the USA.

Boxing is another sport with a long history in Cuba and a sport that, like baseball, has produced many champions. Nearly 40 medals have been won at Olympics events. Cuban boxers are classified as amateurs and as a result do not challenge for the professional 'world titles'. Three of the best known boxers are Teófilo Stevenson, Félix Savón and Maikro Romero, who have built international reputations for their strength, skill and finesse.

Systems for Developing Athletic Talent

Cuba has also made its mark in track and field. One of the best known athletes is Yipsi Moreno Gonzalez who became a world champion hammer-thrower in the early 2000s. Yipsi, like all other elite athletes in Cuba, followed a clearly identifiable sport development pathway. They move through what is called the 'pyramid of high athletic performance'. The initial phase takes place in primary schools, where teachers help identify the best performing students. They are then sent to specialized centres such as the Schools of Sport Initiation (EIDE) located in each of the 14 province capital towns. The next step in their development is the Superior Schools for Athlete improvement (ESPA). The athlete selection is refined even further when the best are invited to Superior Centres that cater only for high performance athletes.

This very well structured sport development pathway is supported by ongoing government funding that provides the financial backing to ensure that the best athletes are able to develop their athletic prowess without having continually to search for work to help pay their fees. In this context, it should be remembered that Cuban sport is run along amateur lines only. In addition, there is a well organized system of competitions and tournaments that culminate in the National Games which involves the participation of around 7000 students in nearly 30 sport events. These events, held every year, have been the source of more than 90% of the Olympic, Pan-American, and Central American Games participants.

International Successes

As a result of this sport development plan, Cuban athletes have performed at a very high level in international competitions. For example, at the 2000 Sydney Olympic Games, Cuban athletes secured 29 medals comprising 11 gold, 11 silver and 7 bronze. This made it the ninth highest medal winning nation. In contrast, the UK, which is vastly more wealthy and has 45 million more people, could only win 28 medals. At the 2004 Athens Games, the UK managed to just squeeze ahead of Cuba by winning 30 medals, but only won the same number of gold medals, which was nine.

The Cuban sporting experience shows that sporting success does not come naturally. But neither is it just about being a nation that values sport and having a high sport participation rate where all strata of the community engage in some sort of organized physical activity and where winning is important for national self-esteem. The Cuban situation shows that without the ongoing financial support of the State and, in particular, the central government's commitment to elite sport and large-scale infrastructure development, international sporting success will always be difficult to realize.

Case Study Questions

1. How would you describe the political and economic structure of Cuba?

2. How does it differ from a capitalist type society like Great Britain or Australia?

3. Describe the role played by the Cuban central government in developing and managing its sport systems and practices.

4. Identify the strengths and weaknesses of this type of sporting structure.

5. To what extent can Cuba's strong international sporting performances over recent years be explained by its sport development structures?

6. Are there any other factors that might explain its successes?

7. Is there anything that capitalist type societies and their sport associations and leagues learn from the sport development system in Cuba?

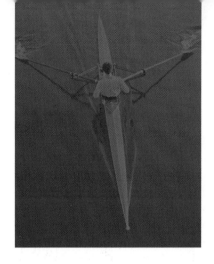

CHAPTER 3

Non-Profit Sport

OVERVIEW

This chapter examines the role of the non-profit sector in sport development. The reasons why the non-profit sector plays such a large part in the provision of sport participation opportunities and the various ways the non-profit sector is involved in sport are reviewed. The scope of the non-profit sector's involvement in sport around the world is examined, with a particular emphasis on the role of volunteers in administration, officiating and coaching and the role of non-profit sport organizations. The chapter also provides a summary of the relationship between non-profit sport organizations and the State.

After completing this chapter the reader should be able to:

- Describe the scope of the non-profit sector's involvement in sport

- Understand the differences in the roles performed by the State and non-profit sport organizations

- Understand the ways in which non-profit sport organizations foster sport development around the world

- Understand some of the challenges facing the non-profit sector in delivering sporting opportunities.

INTRODUCTION

The model presented in Chapter 1 presents the sport industry as comprising three distinct but overlapping sectors: the State or public sector, the commercial or professional sport sector and the non-profit or voluntary sector. This chapter focuses on the non-profit or voluntary sector of the model; the various sport organizations that would be classified as non-profit. Many terms have been used to refer to non-profit organizations that operate in a variety of industry sectors and countries around the world. These terms

35

include voluntary, not for profit, non-government, community, club based, associations, cooperatives, friendly societies, civil society and the third sector. For the purposes of this book we have chosen to use the term non-profit organizations to describe those organizations that are institutionally separate from the State, do not return profits to owners, are self-governing, have a significant element of voluntary contribution and are formally incorporated.

The non-profit sector comprises organizations that are markedly different from State organizations discussed in the previous chapter and also profit seeking organizations that are discussed in the next chapter. Non-profit organizations vary in size, focus and capability and include groups as diverse as community associations, chambers of commerce, private schools, charitable trusts and foundations, welfare agencies and sporting organizations. Non-profit organizations are a major part of many industries in health services, education, housing, welfare, culture and sport.

NON-PROFIT SECTOR AND SOCIETY

Non-profit organizations exist to develop communities, meet the needs of identifiable and discrete groups in those communities and work for the benefit of public good rather than wealth creation for individuals. Non-profit organizations have evolved to fill gaps in the provision of services such as welfare assistance that are not provided by the State or market sector and are driven largely by the efforts of volunteers with the occasional support of paid staff.

A review of non-profit organizations in Canada highlighted a number of unique aspects of non-profit organizations and the contribution they make to Canadian life (Statistics Canada, 2004). Foremost was the recognition that these organizations are vehicles for citizen engagement – they enable individuals to contribute their talent, energy and time to engaging in group activities and causes that are not otherwise provided by the public or private sectors. Non-profit organizations are, in general, governed by volunteers, run on the time and money contributed by volunteers and enable volunteers to contribute to enhancing their local, regional, national and global communities.

To understand the scale of the non-profit sector in one part of the world, let us examine some of the most recent Canadian statistics. In 2003, there were more than 161 000 non-profit organizations in Canada that collectively utilized 2 billion volunteer hours and received more than $CAN 8 billion in donations to deliver their services. At the same time, Canadians took out 139 million memberships in these organizations, an average of four per person

(Statistics Canada, 2004). Clearly, the non-profit sector represents a major part of the economic activity of many nations and plays a pivotal role in encouraging people to engage in social, religious, charitable, philanthropic and sport-related activities.

Non-profit organizations usually focus on delivering services to very specific population groups or within defined geographic areas. Many of them provide services to targeted groups and only a few focus solely on providing services to members. The variety of activities carried out by non-profit organizations is very broad, ranging from providing sporting opportunities to funding hospital and medical services. As a result, the revenue sources, cost base, numbers of paid staff and volunteers and the sophistication of management systems also vary.

The non-profit sector is not without its problems. The larger organizations such as independent schools, colleges and hospitals receive the majority of funding and almost half the funding for most non-profit organizations comes from government. The resourcing of non-profit organizations in some sectors continues to be inadequate as they struggle to keep up with demand, particularly in the welfare, housing and charitable sectors. By far the biggest problem facing non-profit organizations is the inability to fulfil their missions due to problems securing adequate numbers of volunteers, finding board members and attracting enough sustainable funding (Cuskelly, 2004). As governments around the world seek to decrease their costs and devolve responsibility for service delivery to the private and non-profit sectors without adequately funding such delivery, non-profit organizations will find it increasingly difficult to operate.

NON-PROFIT SECTOR AND SPORT

The International Classification of Non-profit Organizations (ICNPO) has a designated category for sports and recreation organizations. This category includes three broad groups:

1. sports including amateur sport, training, fitness and sport facilities and sport competition and events

2. recreation and social clubs such as country clubs, playground associations, touring clubs and leisure clubs

3. service clubs such as Lions, Rotary, Kiwanis and Apex clubs.

Of particular interest are those organizations that operate on a non-profit basis in sport including professional service organizations, industry lobby groups, sport event organizations and sport governing bodies.

Non-profit professional service organizations operate in sport in similar ways to professional associations like accrediting medical boards or associations for lawyers and accountants. These organizations assist in setting standards of practice in their respective industries, provide professional accreditation for qualified members and offer professional development opportunities through conferences, seminars or training programmes. They operate in a business-like fashion but the aim is to return surpluses to members through improved service delivery rather than create wealth for owners.

In Australia, the Australian Council for Health, Physical Education and Recreation (ACHPER) is a national professional association representing people who work in the areas of health education, physical education, recreation, sport, dance, community fitness or movement sciences. The roles of ACHPER include advocating for the promotion and provision of sport opportunities, providing professional development programmes for teachers and accrediting and training people wanting to become community fitness instructors. Similar groups operate in Canada (Canadian Association for Health, Physical Education, Recreation and Dance), the USA (American Alliance for Health, Physical Education and Dance), the UK (British Institute of Sports Administration) and New Zealand (Physical Education New Zealand).

A number of industry lobby groups representing the interests of non-profit sport organizations also operate throughout the world. A leading example is the Central Council of Physical Recreation (CCPR) in the UK, the representative body for National Sports Organizations. They act as the independent umbrella organization for national governing and representative bodies of sport and recreation in the UK to promote their interests to government and other players in the sport industry. This role is undertaken by Sport Industry Australia, a similar non-profit organization in Australia.

Some of the largest and most influential sport event organizations in the world operate on a non-profit basis, including the International Olympic Committee (IOC) and the Commonwealth Games Federation (CGF). The IOC was founded in 1894 by Baron Pierre de Coubertin and is an independent non-profit organization that serves as the umbrella organization of the Olympic Movement. The IOC's primary role is to supervise the organization of the summer and winter Olympic Games.

Similar to the IOC, the role of the CGF is to facilitate a major games event every 4 years, but it also provides education assistance for sports development throughout the 53 Commonwealth countries. There are more Commonwealth Games Associations (CGA) (71) than countries (53) because some countries like the UK have seven CGAs (Scotland, England, Northern Ireland, Wales, Isle of Man, Jersey and Guernsey) that all compete in the

Games as separate nations (www.commonwealthgames.com). Both the IOC and CGF fund their operations through contributions from governments that host the games and the sale of international broadcasting rights, corporate sponsorship, ticket sales, licensing and merchandising sales.

There is also a range of specialist non-profit organizations that focus on discrete community groups. Foremost among these is the International Paralympic Committee (IPC) which is the international representative organization of elite sports for athletes with disabilities. The IPC organizes, supervises and coordinates the Paralympic Games and other multidisability sports competitions at elite level (www.paralympic.org). Other similar non-profit organizations include the Cerebral Palsy International Sports and Recreation Association and the International Blind Sport Federation which facilitate major events for athletes.

Our focus for the remainder of the chapter is on those non-profit sport organizations that provide sporting competition or event participation opportunities for their members and other members of the public – sport governing bodies and sports clubs. In countries such as Australia, the UK, Canada, New Zealand, Hong Kong and other others with club-based sporting systems, almost all sporting teams and competitions are organized by non-profit sport organizations (Lyons, 2001). These organizations take many forms. They include small local clubs that may field a few teams in a local football competition; regional associations that coordinate competitions between clubs; and state or provincial organizations that not only facilitate competitions, but also manage coach development, talent identification, volunteer training, marketing and sponsorship. They also comprise national sporting organizations that regulate the rules of competition in a country, coordinate national championships between state or provincial teams, manage elite athlete programmes, employ development officers to conduct clinics and undertake many other tasks that facilitate participation in sport. Finally, there are international sports federations that coordinate the development of sport across the globe and facilitate rule changes and liaison between countries on issues like international competitions.

The common element among all these sport organizations is their non-profit focus – they exist to facilitate sporting opportunities for their members who may be individual athletes, coaches, officials or administrators, clubs, associations or other sport organizations. They are also interdependent, relying on each other to provide playing talent, information to access competitions, resources for coach, official and player development and funding to support their activities. It is important to note that volunteers are at the heart of these organizations, playing significant roles in service delivery and decision-making at all levels of non-profit sport organizations. At the same time though, many of the larger non-profit sport organizations contain a significant number of paid staff who support their ongoing administration and service delivery to member associations and clubs. In Practice 3.1 highlights the scale and scope of the Canadian non-profit sport sector.

In Practice 3.1 Canadian Non-Profit Sport Sector

In 2003, there were 33 649 non-profit sport and recreation organizations in Canada, or 20.9% of all non-profit organizations, making it the largest portion of organizations of this type. There are more non-profit sport and recreation organizations in Canada than religious organizations (19%) and social service organizations (11.8%). In 2005, 18% of all Canadians (aged 15 and older) reported belonging to a club, a local community league or other local or regional amateur sport organization (Statistics Canada, 2008).

The majority of non-profit sport organizations deliver services in a relatively small geographic area such as a suburb, town or city. Eighty-six percent of them deliver services to members rather than the general public. In other words, people who are involved in non-profits sport organizations tend to be registered members who not only sustain the organization but consume the services the organization offers. In addition, the majority (79%) of non-profit sport organizations tend to have individuals rather than organizations as members, which is not surprising given the fact that the majority of them service a relatively small geographic area.

Non-profit sport organizations are also well entrenched in Canadian society with the majority of them having been in existence for more than 30 years. However, while sport and recreation organizations are the largest portion of non-profit organizations (20.9%), they only account for 5.4% of all revenues. They also are relatively self-sufficient with only 12% of their income being provided from government sources and rely on membership dues and direct user pay charges to sustain their operations.

Sport and recreation organizations rely more on volunteers than other non-profit organizations as they account for 28% of all volunteers and 23% of all volunteer hours in Canada. Most concerning is the fact that, between 2000 and 2003, sport and recreation organizations were the ones most likely to report a decline in volunteer numbers compared to all other types of non-profit organizations. The majority of sport organizations do not employ any paid staff (73.5%), while only 11% employed greater than five paid staff. Of these paid staff, the majority of them tend to be in temporary positions (69%).

Given these statistics, it is not surprising that sport and recreation organizations are also more likely to report problems associated with financial difficulties and problems in engaging appropriately skilled volunteers and board members. In summary, Canadian non-profit sport organizations, while making up the largest portion of non-profit organizations, face significant problems in sustaining their operations.

Sources: Statistics Canada (2004). *Cornerstones of community: highlights of the national survey of non-profit and voluntary organizations.* Statistics Canada, Ottawa; Statistics Canada (2008). *Sports participation in Canada, 2005.* Statistics Canada, Ottawa.

GOVERNING BODIES OF SPORT

Sport clubs compete against other clubs in competition structures provided by regional or state/provincial sporting organizations. State based teams compete in competitions facilitated by national sporting organizations and nations compete in leagues or events provided by international federations of sport, such as the Fédération Internationale de Football Association (FIFA), or major competition organizations such as the International Olympic Committee or the Commonwealth Games Association. These organizations are known as governing bodies for sport, that have the responsibility for the management, administration and development for a sport on a global, national, state/provincial level or regional level.

The structure of the International Netball Federation Limited (IFNA) typifies the relationships between these various governing bodies of sport. The members of IFNA comprise 39 national associations from five regions: Africa, Asia, Americas, Europe and Oceania. Each region elects two members to direct the activities of the world governing organization who are responsible for setting the rules for netball, running international competitions, promoting good management in the regions, striving to seek Olympic accreditation for netball and increasing participation levels around the globe.

Netball Australia, one of the 39 members of IFNA, has more than 350 000 registered players who participate through eight state/provincial associations. They in turn have a total of 541 affiliated associations. Each of the state/provincial associations has a delegate to the national board who, along with the staff of Netball Australia, are responsible for communicating rule changes from IFNA to their members, managing a national competition, promoting good management in the state/provincial organizations, increasing participation nationally and bidding to host world events.

One of the largest members of Netball Australia, Netball Victoria, has 110 000 registered players who compete in 250 affiliated associations, organized into 21 regions and six zones across the state. Netball Victoria's role differs markedly from Netball Australia and IFNA, with responsibility for coach, official and player development, managing state competitions, promoting good management in the clubs, providing insurance coverage for players, assisting in facility development, trying to increase participation in the state, bidding to host national events and managing two teams in the national competition. Finally, netball clubs field teams, find coaches and players, manage volunteers, conduct fundraising and may own and operate a facility.

It is important to remember that these sport governing organizations are volunteer based, with volunteers involved in decisions at every level from clubs to international federations. As discussed in Chapter 12, non-profit sport organizations do not operate as top down power hierarchies, with clubs always abiding by regional directives, or national governing bodies agreeing with international policy initiatives. Communication and agreement can be difficult between these organizations that may have competing priorities and localized issues. A spirit of cooperation and negotiation is required to make the non-profit sport system operate effectively. The simple exerting of authority in a traditional organizational hierarchy is not appropriate for most non-profit sport organizations.

THE SPORTS CLUB ENVIRONMENT

At the centre of sport development in countries such as Canada, New Zealand, Australia and the UK is the local or community sports club. It is worth taking some time to reflect on the role of the sports club, how volunteers and staff work in the club environment and how clubs contribute to sport development.

A background report initially prepared in 2001 and updated in 2002 for Sport Scotland provides a snapshot of sport clubs in Scotland (Allison, 2002). The most striking thing about local sport clubs is their diversity. Sport clubs have many functions, structures, resources, values and ideologies and they provide an enormous range of participation opportunities for people to be involved in sport. Most clubs provide activity in a single sport and have as their focus enjoyment in sport, rather than competitive success. Sport clubs in Scotland come in various sizes, with an average membership size of 133, and most tend to cater for both junior and adult participants. They operate with minimum staffing, structures, income and expenditure and often rely on a small group of paid or unpaid individuals to organize and administrate club activities. The majority of club income comes from membership payments, so they tend to operate fairly autonomously. The management of local sport clubs in Scotland is regarded as an 'organic and intuitive process based on trust and experience rather than formal contracts and codes of practice' (Allison, 2002).

The characteristics of local sport clubs in other countries are similar. The vast majority of sport clubs rely almost exclusively on volunteers to govern, administer and manage their organizations and to provide coaching, offici-ating and general assistance with training, match day functions and fundraising.

Administrators

Administrators who fill roles as elected or appointed committee members have the responsibility for the overall guidance, direction and supervision of the organization. According to the Australian Sports Commission (2000), the responsibility of the management committee of a sports club extends to:

- Conducting long-term planning for the future of the club

- Developing policy and procedures for club activities

- Managing external relations with other sport organizations, local governments or sponsors

- Managing financial resources and legal issues on behalf of the club

- Carrying out recommendations put forward by members

- Communicating to members on current issues or developments

- Evaluating the performance of officials, employees (if any) and other service providers

- Ensuring adequate records are kept for future transfer of responsibilities to new committee members

- Acting as role models for other club members.

While governance is covered in detail in Chapter 12, it is important to note here that the ability of clubs to carry out these tasks effectively will vary according to their resources, culture and quality of people willing to be involved. The important administrative roles within local sports club are the chairperson or president, secretary, treasurer and volunteer coordinator. Other committee roles might involve responsibility for coaching, officiating, representative teams, match day arrangements, fundraising or marketing.

The chairperson or president should be the one to set the agenda for how a committee operates, work to develop the strategic direction of the club, chair committee meetings and coordinate the work of other members of the committee. Club secretaries are the administrative link between members, the committee and other organizations and have responsibility for managing correspondence, records and information about club activities. The treasurer has responsibility for preparing the annual budget, monitoring expenditure and revenue, planning for future financial needs and managing operational issues such as petty cash, payments and banking. The position of volunteer coordinator involves the development of systems and procedures to manage volunteers such as planning, recruitment, training and recognition.

Coaches

Coaches working in the sport club system may be unpaid or paid, depending on the nature of the sport and the resources of individual clubs. The role of the coach is central to developing athletes' skills and knowledge, in helping them learn tactics for success and to enjoy their sport. Coaches also act as important role models for players and athletes.

Most sports provide a structured training and accreditation scheme for coaches to develop their skills and experience to coach at local, state/provincial, national or international levels. In Australia, for example, the National Coaching Council established a three tier National Coaching Accreditation Scheme (NCAS) in 1978. Coaches can undertake a Level 1 introductory course, Level 2 intermediate course and Level 3 advanced courses in coaching. NCAS training programmes comprise three elements:

1. coaching principles that cover fundamentals of coaching and athletic performance

2. sport-specific coaching that covers the skills, techniques, strategies and scientific approaches to a particular sport

3. coaching practice where coaches engage in practical coaching and application of coaching principles.

Officials

Sports officials include those people who act as referees, umpires, judges, scorers or timekeepers to officiate over games or events. The majority of officials are unpaid but, some sports, such as Australian Rules Football, basketball and some other football codes pay officials at all levels, enabling some to earn a substantial salary from full time officiating. Other sports such as netball, softball or tennis rarely pay officials unless they are at state or national championship level. Sports officials are critical to facilitating people's involvement in sport but are the hardest positions to fill within the non-profit sport system since they absorb a lot of time and often have low status.

All sports provide a structured training and accreditation scheme for officials in much the same way as coaches to develop their skills and experience at local, state/provincial, national or international levels. The Australian National Officiating Accreditation Scheme (NOAS) was established in 1994, modelled on the NCAS, but does not prescribe formal levels of officiating as these vary greatly between sporting codes. The NOAS aims to develop and implement programmes that improve the quality, quantity, leadership and status of sports officiating in Australia through training programmes that comprise three elements:

1. general principles of officiating and event management

2. sport-specific technical rules, interpretations, reporting and specific roles

3. practice at officiating and applying the officiating principles.

General volunteers

Sports clubs also depend on people to perform roles in fundraising, managing representative teams, helping with match day arrangements such as car parking or stewarding, or helping to market the club. The majority of general volunteers have an existing link to a sports club through being a parent of a child who plays at the club, having some other family connection, or through friends and work colleagues involved in the club.

The Volunteering Australia 2004 publication, *Snapshot 2004: Volunteering Report Card*, provided a detailed picture of volunteer involvement in a range of activities. In the 12 months prior to April 2004, an estimated 4.3 million persons over the age of 15 in Australia were involved in organized sport and physical activity – 27% of the total population. Of those, 1.5 million persons were involved in non-playing roles such as coach, official, administrator, scorer, medical support or other role and about one third of them had more than one non-playing role. Only about 12% of these people received payment for their role, which means that 88% of these 1.5 million people involved in non-playing roles were volunteers. Of these 1.5 million people, 60% also played sport. The majority of non-playing involvement was associated with junior sport. While making comparisons between data sets is difficult due to differences in sampling methods and instruments, the data between 1993 and 2004 indicated that while the numbers of people coaching remains constant, the numbers of people involved in officiating and administration has declined. The majority of these would be volunteers, highlighting the potential fragility of a sport system dependent on volunteers to facilitate involvement.

Figures on voluntary participation in New Zealand show that just under 20% of the adult population was involved as a volunteer in the physical leisure sector in 1998 (Hillary Commission, 1998). These roles included

11.1% as coaches, 8.7% as officials and 8.8% as administrators, with people donating an average of 2.7 hours per week volunteering. This voluntary contribution was estimated to be more than 77% of the equivalent full-time workforce and worth nearly $NZ1900 million a year. These figures clearly illustrate the enormous contribution volunteers make in roles such as coaches, officials and administrators in order to facilitate people's involvement in sport. However, there are some worrying signs that such voluntary involvement may be on the wane and that, in order to sustain current levels of involvement in sport, the management of sport volunteers needs to improve.

GOVERNMENT INTERVENTION

The substantial funds allocated to non-profit sport organizations by governments to support their activities in areas of mass participation or elite performance has meant that governments are increasingly trying to influence the way in which the non-profit sector of sport operates. Examples of these attempts include the Australian Sports Commission Volunteer Management Programme and the policy of Sport England to have national organizations develop 'whole of sport' plans. These are briefly reviewed below to highlight the increasingly interdependent nature of government and sport organizations in seeking improvements in non-profit sport.

The Australian Sports Commission (ASC) developed the Volunteer Involvement Programme in 1994 in partnership with the Australian Society of Sports Administrators, the Confederation of Australian Sport and state departments of sport and recreation. The programme aimed to improve the operation of non-profit sport clubs and associations by providing a series of publications on sport club administration. In 2000, the Volunteer Management Programme (VMP) and the Club and Association Management Programme (CAMP) resources were published and the ASC encouraged all clubs to join a Club Development Network and engage in strategic planning and other management techniques.

Another example is the policy developed by Sport England to require national sport organizations to develop 'whole of sport plans'. In 2003, Sport England identified 30 priority sports, based on their capability to contribute to Sport England's vision of an active and successful sporting nation and is now working with the national sport organizations to develop and implement these plans. The plans are designed to outline how a sport from grass roots right to the elite level will attract and keep participants and improve their sporting experiences. The plans will drive decisions by Sport England to provide funding to national organizations based on clearly articulated ideas of the resources they need to drive their sport. The plans will also provide for measurable performance results and assist Sport England evaluate the benefits that accrue from funding non-profit sport organizations.

The Clubmark programme developed by Sport England is indicative of the approach many governments have taken toward trying to enhance the capacity of the non-profit sport sector at the community club level. In Practice 3.2 explores how this programme operates.

In Practice 3.2 Sport England Clubmark Programme

Approximately 60% of young people in England belong to a sports club outside of school. In order to improve the standard of service delivery that young people receive from community sport clubs, Sport England has invested in 'Clubmark', a cross-sport quality accreditation for clubs with junior sections. The main purpose of Clubmark is to encourage sport clubs to seek accreditation as a Clubmark club. National governing bodies of sport (NGBs) and county sport partnerships (CSPs) award Clubmark to proven high quality clubs. The national scheme has been in place since 2002 and, in 2008, there were more than 2000 accredited clubs across over 20 sports.

Clubmark accreditation is awarded to clubs that comply with minimum operating standards in four areas:

1. The playing programme
2. Duty of care and child protection
3. Sports equity and ethics
4. Club management.

Clubs working towards accreditation can receive support and advice from their NGB and other partners such as CSPs. Circumstances vary between clubs and sports but the process of accreditation is the same. The benefits of implementing a single, national standard for sport club operations gives sports clubs of all types structure and direction, specifically in areas such as:

- Club development – the foundation for any club is its youth structure. By encouraging and attracting young members, it is building a strong future.

- Increased membership – addressing issues like equity and child protection gives parents confidence when choosing a club for their children.

- Developing coaches and volunteers – as part of Clubmark, clubs receive help in developing the skills of those involved in their organization.

- Raised profile – once Clubmark accredited, clubs are listed on a national database and in other directories to help them attract new members and grow.

Continued

In Practice 3.2 Sport England Clubmark Programme—cont'd

The Clubmark programme provides sports clubs with a framework for volunteer management as well as a series of templates that they can adapt for their specific circumstances. These templates cover the following areas of sport club operation:

- Code of practice for club officials and volunteers
- Guidelines for dealing with an incident/accident
- Incident/accident report form
- Attendance register
- Junior membership form
- Task description: Head Junior Coach
- Task description: Assistant Junior Coach
- Risk assessment form
- Equity policy statement
- Constitution
- Code of practice for parents/carers
- Code of practice for junior members
- Introductory letter to parents/carers
- Club partnership agreement
- Development plan
- Volunteer agreement form
- School – Club Links Agreement

Clubmark is managed by Knight, Kavanagh and Page (KKP) on behalf of Sport England. It is responsible for validation of NGBs and CSPs, for moderation of its impact on clubs and for the marketing and promotion of the programme throughout England.

Sources: Sport England, (2007). *Clubmark factsheet*. Sport England, London: and the Clubmark website at <http://www.clubmark.org.uk/about/about-clubmark>.

ISSUES FOR THE NON-PROFIT SPORT SECTOR

A range of challenges exists for the non-profit sport sector around the globe. Foremost among these is the dependence on volunteers to sustain the sports system in areas such as coaching, administrating and officiating. As highlighted earlier in this chapter, there is evidence to suggest that the rate of volunteerism is declining for roles such as officiating and administration in sport. Governments and non-profit sport organizations will need to address this issue if their mutually dependent goals of increasing participation in organized sport are to be achieved.

The increasingly litigious nature of society and the associated increase in costs of insurance for non-profit sport organizations directly affects the cost of participation. In Australia, fewer insurers are providing insurance cover for sporting organizations and insurance premium prices have risen significantly in recent years. For example, the public liability insurance premium for the Australian Parachute Federation increased from $127 000 to $1.1 million in 2 years. Public liability insurance is vital to run sport events and programmes and these costs are passed onto participants for no additional benefits, which raises the question of whether people can afford to keep playing sport in traditional non-profit systems.

A further issue for non-profit sport organizations is the trend away from participating in traditional sports, organized through clubs and associations, to a more informal pattern of participation. Some people are unwilling to commit to a season of sporting involvement and are seeking ways to engage in sport and physical activity on a more casual basis, either through short-term commercial providers or with friends in spontaneous or pick up sports (Stewart et al., 2004). The increase in options available to young people to spend their discretionary leisure dollars, euros or pounds has also presented challenges for non-profit sport organizations to market themselves as an attractive option.

As highlighted earlier, non-profit organizations, including non-profit sport organizations, face significant capacity problems. They are often constrained by the size of their facilities or venues and may struggle to attract enough quality people to manage the operations of their organization. They are also constrained by the interdependent nature of sport – they require other clubs, teams and organizations to provide competition – so they need to work cooperatively with other non-profit sport organizations to expand their 'product'.

The very nature of non-profit sport organizations requires adherence to frequently cumbersome consultative decision-making processes, often across large geographic areas and with widely dispersed and disparate groups of stakeholders. The additional complexity of the governance and management requirements of these organizations present their own set of challenges in terms of making timely decisions, reacting to market trends, being innovative or seeking agreement on significant organizational changes.

Lyons (2001) also suggests that non-profit organizations are unique because they have difficulty in judging performance relative to their commercial counterparts, have to be accountable to a wide range of stakeholders and must deal with tension and possible conflict between paid staff and volunteers. These tensions are due to a lack of clarity about paid staff and volunteer roles and are exacerbated by the lack of clear performance

In Practice 3.3 Challenges for Sports Volunteering in England

A report from the UK based Institute for Volunteering Research (2008) concluded that sport and recreation organizations were most likely to report difficulties with recruiting enough volunteers compared to other categories of non-profit organizations. They also found that these organizations were more likely to say that they experienced difficulties with the retention of volunteers in the last year and that they were most likely to say that they wanted to involve more volunteers. Crucially, the report concluded that organizations in the sports (and arts and culture) fields were less likely to have structured volunteer management practices in place or to have funding to support volunteers. Unsurprisingly, it was also more common for sport and recreation organizations to report difficulties in recruiting sufficient numbers of volunteers compared to other fields of activity. Another report from the same year identified three main problems faced by sports clubs in England: a shortage of volunteers, difficulty in recruiting new volunteers and the fact that work is increasingly left to fewer people.

The reasons why this may be the case can be found in an earlier report commissioned by the peak government agency responsible for sports development in England, Sport England, that (in part) identified the challenges faced by volunteers and volunteer managers in the English sports industry (Leisure Industries Research Centre, 2003). Sport volunteering in England has many of the same problems facing the sports industries of Australia, New Zealand and Canada. The 2003 report concluded that the sport system and its volunteers were subject to a variety of often competing pressures, driven by changes in government policy, technological change and market competition for leisure expenditure. Core sport volunteers, those people who work, have children and participate in sport, were most affected. As national government and sport organizations pursue policies that attempt to increase participation at the grass roots as well as drive improvements in elite performance, volunteers are being asked to deal with an ever increasing complexity and required level of professionalism in organizational procedures and systems. Government funding is increasingly tied to the ability of a sports organization to deliver measurable outcomes and be more accountable for their activities.

Improvements in technology and subsequent demands from end users for sport organizations to use the latest technology have placed increased demands on sport volunteers. An example of this is the shift to artificial playing surfaces for field hockey. These surfaces undoubtedly improve the playing and spectator experience but require volunteers at club level to fundraise continuously to meet significantly increased financial obligations.

The increasingly competitive leisure market has also meant volunteers at the club level have to manage their organizations to meet the demands of diverse 'customers' rather than the traditional member. People who are new to a sport may find it hard to differentiate between community club providers and commercial facilities and expect volunteers to meet their demands without becoming engaged in the life of the club. An example is the parent who treats the non-profit sporting club as a cheap child minding option by dropping off and picking up their child without donating any time, energy or skills to the running of the club.

The capacity of non-profit sport organizations and their volunteers to deal with these pressures varies enormously. Some have well established systems and resources, others flounder from one crisis to the next, continuously playing catch up. The organizations and volunteers at the community level are the ones most affected. The 2003 report recommended the use of a range of flexible and practical solutions to assist non-profit sport organizations deal with these pressures. These included the provision of better education and training resources, simplified government funding requirements, reducing the compliance burden of reporting for sports organizations and talking to non-profit sports organizations in language more attuned to their core values of individual volunteer motivations and commitment than overly sophisticated business and management language.

Sources: Leisure Industries Research Centre (2003). *Sports volunteering in England 2002: A report for Sport England*. Leisure Industries Research Centre, Sheffield; Institute for Volunteering Research (2008). *Management matters: a national survey of volunteer management capacity*. Institute for Volunteering Research, London; and Institute for Volunteering Research and Volunteering England, (2008). *A winning team? The impacts of volunteers in sport*. Institute for Volunteering Research, London.

measures. Non-profit sport organizations are particularly susceptible to these problems, especially where there is a coterie of paid staff in senior administrative positions. In Practice 3.3 explores the challenges facing the non-profit sport sector in the area of recruiting and retaining volunteers.

SUMMARY

Non-profit organizations were defined as those organizations that are institutionally separate from the State, do not return profits to owners, are self-governing, have a significant element of voluntary contribution and are formally incorporated. Non-profit organizations exist to develop communities, meet the needs of identifiable and discrete groups in those communities and work for the benefit of public good rather than wealth creation for individuals. The majority of non-profit organizations are driven largely by the efforts of volunteers rather than paid staff.

Sport organizations that operate on a non-profit basis include professional service organizations, industry lobby groups, sport event organizations and sport governing bodies. By far the greatest number of non-profit sport organizations are those that provide sporting competition or event participation opportunities for their members and other members of the public – sport governing bodies and sports clubs. The common element among all these sport organizations is their non-profit focus – they exist to facilitate sporting opportunities for their members who may be individual athletes, coaches, officials or administrators, clubs, associations or other sport organizations.

They are also interdependent, relying on each other to provide playing talent, information to access competitions, resources for coach, official and player development and funding to support their activities.

Sport governing bodies and clubs rely almost exclusively on volunteers to govern, administer and manage their organizations and to provide coaching, officiating and general assistance with training, events and fundraising. The substantial funds allocated to non-profit sport organizations by governments to support their activities in areas of mass participation or elite performance has meant that governments are increasingly trying to influence the way in which the non-profit sector of sport operates. Finally, a number of challenges exist for the non-profit sport sector including the dependence on volunteers to sustain the sports system, the increasingly litigious nature of society and the associated increase in costs of insurance for non-profit sport organizations, the trend away from participating in traditional sports, significant capacity problems and the additional complexity of the governance and management requirements of these organizations.

REVIEW QUESTIONS

1. What is the role of the non-profit sector?

2. What are the unique aspects of non-profit sport organizations?

3. Describe the role of the Commonwealth Games Federation.

4. Explain how the State and the non-profit sector may contribute to sport development.

5. In what way are volunteers important to the delivery of sport?

6. What are the important management roles in non-profit sporting clubs?

7. Explain the role of a club President.

8. Why does the government attempt to intervene in the management of non-profit sport organizations? Explain how governments do this in your own country.

9. How can non-profit sport organizations reduce the costs to participants?

10. Explain how non-profit sport organizations have to work cooperatively with each other but still compete on the playing field.

FURTHER READING

Cuskelly, G., Hoye, R. and Auld, C. (2006). *Working with volunteers in sport: theory and practice*. Routledge, London.

Green, M. (2006). From 'sport for all' to not about 'sport' at all: Interrogating sport policy interventions in the United Kingdom. *European Sport Management Quarterly*, 6, 217–238.

Houlihan, B. and Green, M. (2007). *Comparative elite sport development. Systems, structures and public policy*. Elsevier, London.

Houlihan, B. and White, A. (2002). *The politics of sports development: development of sport or development through sport?* Routledge, London.

Hylton, K. and Bramham, P. (eds) (2007). *Sports development: policy, process and practice*, 2nd edn. Routledge, London.

Lyons, M. (2001). *Third sector: the contribution of non-profit and cooperative enterprises in Australia*. Allen & Unwin, Crows Nest.

RELEVANT WEBSITES

The following websites are useful starting points for further information on non-profit sport organizations:

Australian Sports Commission at http://www.ausport.gov.au

Sport and Recreation New Zealand at http://www.sparc.org.nz/

Sport Canada at http://www.pch.gc.ca/progs/sc/index_e.cfm

Sport England at http://www.sportengland.org

Sport Scotland at http://www.sportscotland.org.uk

Volunteering Australia at http://www.volunteeringaustralia.org

Case Study: England Netball

This case study explores the difficulties faced by non-profit sport organizations in delivering sport through a network of volunteer-controlled community-based organizations. As the chapter has highlighted, the capacity of non-profit sport organizations varies enormously according to the local environment in which it operates, the degree of support it receives from its local government authority, its asset base, the competitiveness of the local market (i.e. how many other sports can people choose to play) and, crucially, the management system used by its volunteers and their individual abilities, skills and experience in managing a sport organization.

The chapter introduced the approach used by Sport England to try to influence the capacity of sport organizations – the Clubmark system. One sport that has adapted this system for their own purposes has been the All England Netball Association Limited (England Netball), the non-profit governing body for England's biggest female team sport with 61 000 affiliated members. At least one million women and girls play netball every week in England and the sport is the only women's team sport in that country that enjoys weekly television coverage via its partnership with Sky Sports. In 2008, the England Netball head office had 28 full-time and 10 part-time employees working in conjunction with a network of 30 full- and part-time employees in counties and regions throughout England. A Board of voluntary directors comprising the Chairman, Vice Chairman, Treasurer plus a maximum of four Elected Directors and a maximum of three Appointed Directors (appointed by the Board) directs the activities of these staff through a Chief Executive.

The organization of netball competition and participation opportunities in England is divided into nine geographic regions, which in turn comprise 57 counties and three Armed Forces Associations. Within the 57 affiliated counties there are approximately 350 leagues spread across England. England Netball's membership consists of approximately 3000 registered clubs made up from approximately 61 000 individual players. Approximately 2600 schools are also affiliated. The regions and counties are autonomous but are governed by the Constitution and Byelaws of England Netball.

Each county is required to affiliate its playing members, coaches and umpires to England Netball. In addition to funds coming in from affiliation fees, England Netball receives grants from Sport England (the government sport agency) to increase participation and raise standards of performance. Income is also generated through sponsorship and other commercial ventures including the sale of publications and merchandise, event ticket sales and the licensing of products such as netballs and clothing.

England Netball has as its vision to be recognized as the leading women's team sport; to have a thriving network of local communities providing enjoyment and easy access to lifelong netball opportunities; to be successful through the development of strategic partnerships and high quality service delivery; to have a game that is growing and sustainable and self-sufficient in acquisition of our resources; and that its volunteers and professionals are successful by working together to fulfil its ambitions.

In order to achieve that vision, the organization has established four goals:

1. Lifelong participation and competition – develop a coordinated approach to community provision and broaden access to appropriate netball opportunities in quality facilities

2. England leading the world – provide world class programmes and personnel to support and nurture talent and become the best in the world

3. Quality systems and networks – establish effective structures and maximize external opportunities to ensure that the needs of the game and the membership are met

4. Performing as an organization – ensure that the business has the best people, processes, structures and technology to grow and sustain netball.

One of the objectives set by England Netball is to improve the quality and quantity of coaches, umpires, officials and volunteers through the provision of a range of accessible development opportunities. The delivery of netball participation opportunities is dependent on community netball clubs. As noted in the In Practice 3.3 provided in the chapter, a 2008 report from the UK Institute for Volunteering Research concluded that sport and recreation organizations were most likely to report difficulties with recruiting enough volunteers compared to other categories of non-profit organizations, were more likely to experience difficulties with the retention of volunteers and that sport clubs were less likely to have structured volunteer management practices in place or to have funding to support volunteers. In essence, sport clubs, including netball clubs, must deal with three capacity problems associated with volunteers, namely: a shortage of volunteers, difficulty in recruiting new volunteers and the fact that the work of the club is increasingly left to fewer people.

To address these issues, England Netball has developed the Club Action Planning Scheme (CAPS), an accreditation scheme that offers guidelines to help clubs provide the right environment for their members. Once completed, the award provides proof that a club offers a quality environment for all members. CAPS is directly linked to Sport England's Clubmark Scheme and it is about good practice and providing a quality environment for players, coaches and umpires at all levels. CAPS is based on accepted sports development ideas and is flexible enough to fit in the clubs current activities.

In line with the Clubmark award, CAPS focuses on four key areas that impact netball clubs:

- Duty of care and child protection
- Coaching and competition
- Club administration/ management
- Sports equity and ethics.

CAPS offers bronze, silver and gold levels of achievement. Examples of courses clubs will need to attend to achieve CAPS status include:

- Duty of care
- Level 1 & 2 UKCC

- C Award netball umpiring awards
- Club for all
- Equity in your coaching.

At the end of March 2007, approximately 205 out of 3000 clubs had completed CAPS accreditation. The long-term impact of CAPS on improving the capacity of netball clubs and ultimately converting the 1 million players into affiliated members is yet to be determined.

Case Study Questions

1. Access the Sport England website at www. sportengland.org and read about the Clubmark programme. How does this compare to the CAPS run by England Netball?

2. What are the capacity problems in community sport clubs that both Clubmark and CAPS are trying to address?

3. What are the effects on participation levels in sport if community sport clubs continue to experience significant capacity problems?

4. How can the CAPS lead to improvements in both the quantity and quality of opportunities to participate in netball?

5. What are the barriers that might prevent or limit the take up of CAPS by netball clubs in England?

6. What alternative capacity building efforts could England Netball consider in order to improve the delivery of netball in the community? You may wish to explore how other netball governing bodies do this in countries such as Australia or New Zealand.

Sources: England Netball, (2007a). *Student pack*. England Netball, Hertfordshire; England Netball, (2007b). *Annual Report 2006–2007*. England Netball, Hertfordshire; and the England Netball website at www.englandnetball.co.uk.

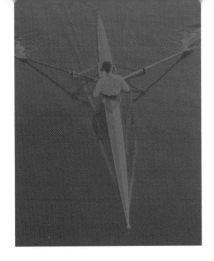

CHAPTER 4

Professional Sport

OVERVIEW

This chapter examines the key features of professional sport organizations and provides examples of the unique features of professional sport leagues and clubs. The chapter does not examine community, state or national sport organizations, but does comment on the relationship between these organizations and professional sport, as well as the impact professional sport has on the sport industry in general.

After completing this chapter the reader should be able to:

- Identify the ways in which professional sport dominates the global sport industry

- Understand and explain the ways in which the media, sponsors and professional sport organizations engage in corporate synergies to market and sell their products and services

- Understand and explain the roles of players, agents, sponsors, leagues, clubs and the media in professional sport.

WHAT IS PROFESSIONAL SPORT?

Professional sport, wherever it is played, is the most expensive, most visible and most watched sporting activity. It captures the lion's share of media coverage, as well as almost all sponsorship revenue and corporate support that is on offer. Professional sport is played in cities all over the world, from Kolkata, India to Rio de Janeiro, Brazil to Melbourne, Australia, in the very best stadiums (Eden Gardens, Maracana Stadium, Melbourne Cricket Ground), by athletes who often earn, depending on the size of the market, millions of dollars. Professional sport, and the industry that surrounds it, dominates world sport and those who play it are cultural celebrities on a global scale. Local, regional, state and national sport organizations are often geared around feeding professional sport leagues by developing player talent or spectator interest. These same organizations are also often forced, somewhat ironically, to compete in vain with professional sport for media coverage, sponsorship and general support (from fans, governments and communities). At its best, professional sport is the peak of the sports industry that supports those organizations below it by generating financial resources and cultural cache. At its worst, it is a rapacious commercial animal with an insatiable appetite for financial, cultural and social resources.

Professional sport leagues, such as the National Football League in the USA, dominate weekly media and social interests within the cities in which they are popular, with fans attracted to plots and sub plots each week in the form of winner and losers, injuries and scandals, sackings, transfers and crisis events (financial, human and organizational). In the late 19th century, American college football games were played on an *ad hoc* basis, largely special events that captured the attention of some football followers and some media outlets. College football only became a part of the national psyche and identity when games were organized around seasons, when media outlets and fans alike could plan their sport production and consumption around a weekly routine. The constancy and consistency of professional sport leagues has been the foundation upon which their popularity has been built. In many cities around the world, professional sport leagues have become an ingrained part of what it means to belong to a cultural or social group. In other words, professional sport leagues and their clubs have become, for many fans, an essential way of understanding and defining who they are.

Professional sport events, such as the Rugby Union or Cricket world cups have also become part of our cultural and commercial consumption. They are held periodically (usually every 4 years) and capture audience attention because they provide out-of-the-ordinary sport action and are typically fuelled by nationalism. At a lower level, we are also exposed to annual events, such as world championships, and to circuits, such as the world rally championship, which hosts rounds in countries such as Japan, Cyprus and New Zealand. Each day of our lives we are bombarded by saturation media coverage of these events through television, radio, magazines, newspapers and the Internet. There is no escaping the reach of professional sport.

Professional sport is now big business. It is not simply about what happens on the field of play, like it once was (in broad terms prior to the commercialisation of sport in the 1970s), but is also about what happens in the boardroom and on the stock exchange. Table 4.1 lists *Forbes* magazine's estimation of the football/soccer teams with the highest value in the world in 2008. It demonstrates that many of these teams are significant corporate

Table 4.1	Highest Value Football/Soccer Teams 2008	
Team	**Country**	**Value (US$)**
Manchester United	England	1 800 000 000
Real Madrid	Spain	1 285 000 000
Arsenal	England	1 200 000 000
Liverpool	England	1 050 000 000
Bayern Munich	Germany	917 000 000
AC Milan	Italy	798 000 000
Barcelona	Spain	784 000 000
Chelsea	England	764 000 000
Juventus	Italy	510 000 000
Schalke 04	Germany	470 000 000

Source: www.forbes.com

entities – seven of the top ten also have annual revenues in excess of US$300 million. In Practice 4.1 examines one of these teams, Liverpool, in order to illustrate how sporting teams have become significant commercial enterprises, which are bought and sold as valuable commodities.

In Practice 4.1 Liverpool FC

Formed in 1892, the Liverpool Football Club has been one of the most successful clubs in the English Premier League (EPL), having won 18 league championships and seven FA cups by 2008. Liverpool's success has not been restricted to its on-field endeavours, however, as it has become one of the highly valued clubs in Europe and, as a result, one of the most prominent professional sporting clubs in the world. For example, in 2006 Liverpool's turnover was £119.5 million, which included £30 million from Premier League television revenues, £25 million in match related turnover, £18 million in sponsorship and £16 million in merchandise sales. In the same year, the club spent £69 million on staff costs, the vast majority of which was allocated to player salaries. As noted in Table 4.1, in 2008, Forbes estimated Liverpool's value to be US$1050 million.

In early 2007, Americans Tom Hicks, who owns the Dallas Stars (a team in America's NHL) and the Texas Rangers (a team in America's MLB) and George Gillett, who owns the Montreal Canadiens (also of the NHL), purchased the Liverpool Football Club for almost £220 million. In many respects the purchase of Liverpool by Hicks and Gillett was not a surprise, but rather was symptomatic of a trend in English football, whereby prominent EPL clubs have been bought by foreign owners. In 2003, Russian billionaire Roman Abramovich purchased EPL club Chelsea; in 2005, American Malcolm Glazer, owner of the Tampa Bay Buccaneers (a team in America's NFL) took over Manchester United and, in 2006, American Randy Lerner, owner of the Cleveland Browns (also of the NFL) purchased English Premier League team Aston Villa. In early 2008, it was announced

Continued

In Practice 4.1 Liverpool FC—cont'd

that Dubai International Capital (DIC), the investment arm of the Dubai government was considering offering Gillett and Hicks between US$400–500 million for the club. In mid 2008, DIC abandoned its takeover plans in the wake of continued infighting between Gillett and Hicks, yet it is clear that DIC's long-term interest in Liverpool is indicative of not only the global appeal and power of English football, but also that professional sport clubs like Liverpool have become commercial property that is able to be bought and sold.

An indication of the financial scale of the English Premier league, as well as the ambition of Liverpool and its American owners, is the construction of a new stadium, due to be opened for the beginning of the 2011–2012 season of the EPL. Designed by architectural firm HKS, which has designed many American sporting stadiums, the stadium at Stanley Park will hold 60 000 with the potential, pending further approvals, to be extended to 73 000. The new stadium, which will replace the existing 45 000 capacity Anfield Stadium, has an estimated cost of £400 million, the vast majority of which will be funded by the club through loans taken by Gillett and Hicks. Financing the stadium via considerable debt might be considered standard business practice outside the sport industry, but within the sport industry it is unusual and has caused concern among Liverpool's traditional supporters. This concern is likely to spread as more clubs in professional sport leagues become privatized and owners are forced to reconcile the dual foci of winning and profit-making.

Source: Liverpool FC Website (http://www.liverpoolfc.tv)

In the first chapter of this book you were introduced to the three sector model of sport: public, non-profit and private. In Chapters 2 and 3 the public and non-profit sectors were examined, while this fourth chapter examines professional sport. It would be a mistake, however, to assume that the terms private and professional are synonymous in the context of sport organizations and their operations. Rather, in this chapter we are examining those sport organizations in which competitive commercial revenue is used to sustain their operations, as opposed to organizations that are funded by the State or almost exclusively through membership fees or subscriptions. It is important to recognize that many of the organizations featured in this chapter are actually non-profit and are not privately owned. Professional sport organizations have two important features that define them. First, they share a scale of operations (particularly commercial and financial) that means they exist at the apex of the sport industry and, second, all the players or athletes are 'professionals' – sport is their job and they are paid to train and play full time. Sports in which the players or athletes are required to find additional employment to supplement their income cannot be considered professional.

The example of the Australian professional football landscape is useful for illustrating and understanding the distinction between private and non-profit organizations within professional sport, as well as the differences that exist between sports. In the Australian Football League (AFL), all the clubs are essentially member-based organizations (in which supporters who buy memberships are entitled to attend games, as well as vote in a Board of Directors). AFL clubs have annual revenues of up to AUS$50 million, but they are non-profit organizations – all the money is used on club operations (e.g. to pay players and staff, maintain facilities or promote the club) and none of the money earned by the clubs is returned to an owner or to share-holders. Although it is essentially a collection of non-profit organizations, the AFL is the wealthiest and most popular professional sport organization in Australia, which captures the greatest share of sponsorship and broadcast rights revenue. Like the AFL, Australia's National Rugby League (NRL) consists of many member-based clubs, but there are also some which are privately owned. In the instances where a club is privately owned, the annual profit or loss is either returned to or borne by the private owner. For example, if the Melbourne Storm, one of the NRL's most successful clubs in the first decade of the 21st century, secures a profit, it is returned to its owner, multinational media conglomerate News Corporation. In contrast to the AFL and NRL, all eight clubs in the Australian A-League (soccer) are privately owned, but the governing body, Football Federation Australia, is a non-profit organization. In this case, the responsibility for ensuring a healthy and viable professional league is shared between private and non-profit organizations. Throughout this chapter and the remaining chapters of the book, it is important to keep in mind that both non-profit and private organizations compete in professional sport leagues.

CIRCUITS OF PROMOTION

In order to describe and explain the interconnections between professional sport, the media, advertisers and business, Whitson (1998) used the concept of 'circuits of promotion'. The key premise that underpins the circuit of promotion concept is that the boundaries between the promotion of sports and the use of sport events and athletes to promote products, which were previously separate, are now being dissolved. In other words, it is becoming increasingly more difficult to see where the sport organization ends and where the sponsor or media or advertiser begins. They are becoming (or have become) one, where one part of the professional sport machine serves to promote the other, for the good of itself and all the other constituent parts.

The relationship between Nike and former Chicago Bulls and Washington Wizards player Michael Jordan is a perfect example of a circuit of promotion at work. The Nike advertising campaigns that featured Jordan contributed to building the profile of both the company and the athlete, while Jordan's success in winning six NBA championships with the Bulls enhanced the corporate synergy between the two 'brands' and helped to increase the return on Nike's investment. Furthermore, the success of Jordan and the global advertising campaigns developed by Nike increased the cultural, social and commercial profile of the National Basketball Association (NBA) in America. In turn, the global promotion and advertising by the NBA, that either did or did not feature Jordan, helped to promote both Jordan, as the League's most visible and recognizable player, and Nike, as a major manufacturer of basketball footwear and apparel, either by direct or indirect association. Lastly, any advertising undertaken by Jordan's other sponsors, such as Gatorade, served to promote Jordan, but also the NBA and Nike through their association with Jordan. At its best, a sporting circuit of promotion is one of continuous commercial benefit and endless leveraging opportunities for the athletes and organizations involved.

SPORT CIRCUITS

Sport circuits involve a league or structured competition. NASCAR has been one of the most popular sports in the USA for over 50 years. It is broadcast on the FOX, SPEED, ABC, ESPN and TNT television networks and stations. Like some other professional sports such as the National Hockey League in America, the Bundesliga in Germany and the National Rugby League in Australia, NASCAR operates to a seasonal calendar, with races in different American cities and towns each week, from February through to November at race tracks such as the Phoenix International Raceway, Daytona International Speedway and the Talladega Superspeedway. Scheduling races at different venues ensures good live attendances, but also enables NASCAR and its competing teams and drivers to capitalize on an array of sponsorship opportunities.

The European Champions League is an example of a global sport circuit that is based around a league model, whereby teams play in different cities depending on who qualifies for the tournament and teams are progressively knocked out until a winner is determined. The men's and women's professional tennis tours are examples of a global circuit in which a series of events represent the structured competition. Each event or tournament on the tour may be entered by ranked players (who may have qualified through a lesser 'satellite circuit'), who compete for prize money, as well as points that go towards an overall ranking to determine the world's best player. In both the above cases, the circuit is managed or overseen by a governing body, although in the case of tennis, the responsibility for managing and running individual tournaments is devolved to the host organization. For example, the Australian Open, the grand slam of the Asia-Pacific region, is managed and run by Tennis Australia, the sport's governing body in Australia.

The locations of events or tournaments that are part of national and global sport circuits are often flexible and cities or countries are able to bid for the right to host the event. In the case of the European Champions League, the teams that qualify for the tournament are entitled to host their home games (a performance based flexibility), while in tennis, the grand slam tournaments of the Australian Open, the US Open, the French Open and Wimbledon are the only marquee events (no flexibility). In Formula One racing, however, cities can compete for the rights to host rounds of the championship. The Formula One season is based around Europe, but events are also held in Asia and North and South America. The races are broadcast to more than 160 countries and cities are often encouraged to bid for rights to host an event by the promise of economic benefits that might accrue as a result of securing a long-term contract. For example, China was added to the circuit in 2004, with racing held at the purpose built Shanghai International Circuit.

The biggest global sport circuits are the Olympic Games and the FIFA World Cup, which are also the biggest events of any type staged in the world. Both events are held every 4 years and have a complex arrangement whereby cities can bid to host the event. For a city to win the right to host the summer or winter Olympic Games, it must go through a stringent two phase selection process. In the first phase – the 'candidature acceptance procedure' – national Olympic committees may nominate a city, which is then evaluated during a 10-month process in which an International Olympic Committee (IOC) administrative committee examines each city based on technical criteria such as venue quality, general city infrastructure, public transport, security and government support. The cities accepted as applicants for the 2012 summer Olympic games were Havana (Cuba), Istanbul (Turkey), Leipzig (Germany), London (Great Britain), Madrid (Spain), Moscow (Russia), New York (USA), Paris (France) and Rio de Janeiro (Brazil). The selected 'candidate' cities move through to the second and final 'candidature phase'. London, Paris, New York, Moscow and Madrid were selected as candidates for the 2012 games. In this phase, the cities must submit a comprehensive candidature file to the IOC and are visited by the IOC's evaluation commission. The evaluation commission's report on the candidate cities is made available to all IOC members, who subsequently elect a host for the games at a full session of the IOC (for the election of the 2012 games the IOC session was held in Singapore in July, 2005, at which it was announced that the London bid had been successful).

There are also global sport circuits in which participation in the event is dependent almost entirely on money, which situates them at the peak of the professional sport apex. Like the Olympic Games, the America's Cup is held every 4 years but, unlike the Olympic Games, a team can only enter if it has enough financial support to mount a challenge. For example, BMW Oracle Racing was one of the challengers to Team Alinghi for the 2007 America's Cup. Oracle is one of the largest software companies, with annual revenues of in excess of US$10 billion, while BMW is one of the world's leading prestige automotive manufacturers. It was estimated that each of the teams that challenged for the 2007 Cup would have allocated in excess of US$100 million to the task, with research and development costing US$20 million, yacht hulls US$1.5 million each and skippers paid in excess of US$500 000 per year.

MEDIA

Media organizations have become essential partners for professional and non-profit sport organizations alike. The breadth and depth of coverage that media organizations provide their professional sporting partners is of such significance that it has the capacity to influence the social and commercial practices of millions, if not billions of people. The scale and scope of the financial relationship they enjoy is also important, so much so that sport and the media are often regarded as interdependent (Bellamy, 1998; Nicholson, 2007). The impact of sport news on the popularity and profitability of new media forms has only been equalled by the transformation that sport has undergone, as a result of its interplay with the media. It might have been possible in the 1890s to think about sport and its social and commercial relevance without reference to the media but, by the 1990s, the task was impossible. It is now as if 'one is literally unthinkable without the other' (Rowe, 1999).

The media are often considered to provide three broad functions in a society: information, education and entertainment. However, in terms of the sport–media relationship, it has become increasingly clear that media organizations and consumers are interested in professional sport because of its entertainment value. The exploits of leagues, teams and athletes are reported throughout the world, across a wide range of print (e.g. newspapers and magazines) and broadcast (e.g. radio, television and the Internet) media. Some of this media coverage is provided as 'news', which essentially means that media organizations report on what is happening in sport in much the same way they report on politics or world events. However, a significant component of broadcast coverage is provided through exclusive arrangements in which media organizations purchase the rights to broadcast an event or season(s). In Practice 4.2 examines the importance of sport broadcast rights to the Walt Disney Company and the revenue secured from media organizations by the NFL.

In Practice 4.2 The Walt Disney Company

Known for creating the most famous mouse in the world, Mickey Mouse, the Walt Disney Company has grown from a small business enterprise founded in 1923 into one of the largest media organizations in the world. The Walt Disney Company is divided into four distinct business segments: 'studio entertainment', which consists of movie studios such as Walt Disney Pictures, Touchstone Pictures, Miramax Films and Pixar, the makers of animated films such as Toy Story; 'parks and resorts', the most notable of which is Disneyland in Anaheim, California; 'consumer products', which includes Disney products and retail stores, as well as Disney Publishing Worldwide; and 'media networks', which includes companies associated with broadcasting, publishing and the Internet, such as the ABC Television Network.

In 2007, the Walt Disney Company's revenue was US$35 510 million of which the 'media networks' segment of the business accounted for US$15 046 million. One of the most significant elements of the 'media networks' segment of the Walt Disney Company business is ESPN, a leading television sport network available via cable, pay or subscription television in America and throughout the world. According to the Walt Disney Company, television viewers in more than 300 million homes in 194 countries receive access to sport events via ESPN's 34 customized television networks.

In order to attract consumers, the ESPN television networks require sport content – the Walt Disney Company and ESPN secure this content by purchasing the broadcast rights to premium American and international sport events and leagues. In 2008, ESPN had the rights to broadcast NFL Monday Night Football, one of the highest rating programmes on American television, Major League Baseball (MLB), the National Basketball Association (NBA), NASCAR, the Women's National Basketball Association, the UEFA Cup, Euro 2008 and the Italian Serie A. The exclusive rights to these leagues and events come at considerable cost to media organizations. In 2007, the Walt Disney Company declared that it had contractual commitments relating to broadcast rights for the NFL, NBA, NASCAR, MLB and college football that amounted to US$19 200 million spread over as much as 8 years (in 2007 ESPN signed a renewed 8-year contract with the NBA).

As in many countries throughout the world, the broadcast rights for football are the most expensive. In 2005, through its parent company the Walt Disney Company, ESPN agreed to an 8-year deal with the NFL to broadcast Monday Night Football from 2006 to 2013 at an annual cost of US$1100 million. The ABC television network, also of the Walt Disney Company, previously owned the rights to NFL Monday Night Football at US$550 million

Continued

Figure 4.1 provides a graphic representation of the relationships that exist between sport organizations, media organizations, advertisers and consumers. Sport organizations supply media organizations with content. In some instances, the sport organization receives a fee, usually from television or radio broadcasters, while in others they provide media outlets, such as newspapers and magazines, with access to games or players. This is done in the hope that the additional promotion and exposure will attract more fans or commercial support. Both the broadcasters and other media represented in Figure 4.1 secure a return on their investment (staff and infrastructure, as well as money) by selling their product to consumers or by selling advertising time and space. The amount of money they are able to charge for selling their product is dependent on its popularity. Professional sport is typically very popular with consumers, particularly football leagues, international sport circuits and major events, which in turn makes it very attractive to media organizations and advertisers.

Whereas sport organizations once relied on ticket sales as their primary source of income, they now rely on the sale of broadcast rights (and to a lesser extent sponsorship revenue). For example, in 1930, 85% of FIFA's income was derived from ticket sales and subscriptions from its member associations, yet by 2002, these revenue sources accounted for only 1%. During the period 1999–2002, the sale of broadcast rights accounted for an average of 61% of FIFA's annual income. The Olympics is also an outstanding example of the growth in broadcast rights fees paid by broadcasting networks across the globe, as well as the actual and perceived popularity of sports. Figure 4.2 illustrates the magnitude of broadcast rights for the Olympics over the previous quarter of a century. Clearly, sport is effective in attracting both audiences and advertisers. Importantly, the relationship between professional sport and the media has reached a point where professional sport would not survive in its current form without the media.

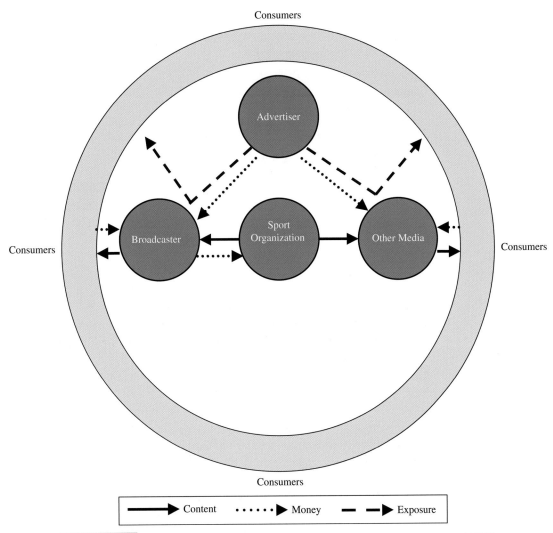

FIGURE 4.1 *Sport and media relationships. Source: adapted from Nicholson (2007).*

SPONSORSHIP

The amount of money available to professional sport organizations through sponsorship arrangements or deals is directly related to the return on investment that the sponsor is able to achieve. In broad terms, the return on investment is dependent on an increase in sales or business, which a sponsor achieves through increased awareness or direct marketing. Sport organizations with large supporter bases, such as Manchester United, are able to

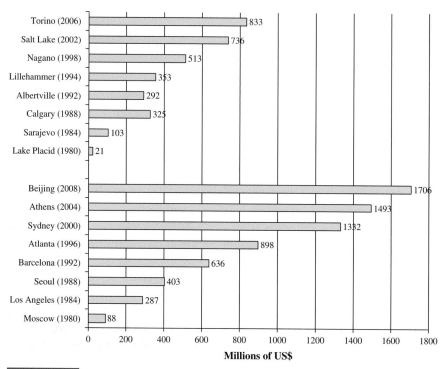

FIGURE 4.2 *Olympic broadcast rights 1980–2008 for summer and winter games. Source: www.olympic.org.*

secure significant sponsorship deals because the sponsor is able to market its product directly to a large number of Manchester United supporters, as well as increase its awareness through media coverage of the club and the English Premier League. Sport organizations with global, regional or strong national profiles have a distinct advantage in the sponsorship market.

Sponsors want to be involved with a club or league that has very good network television coverage, which reaches a broad audience. This is most often achieved through exclusive broadcast rights arrangements. However, the general 'news' media coverage that a club or league receives in a variety of media forms and outlets, including television, radio, newspapers, magazines and the Internet, can also influence its attractiveness to sponsors. This media coverage promotes the club or league and generally encourages fans to consume the sport, either by attending the game live or by accessing a mediated version. The club or league that is able to attract a greater amount of this 'news' media coverage is more likely to be embedded in the commercial consciousness of audiences and consumers. Thus, the amount of media coverage received is a measure of the audiences that can be reached by advertisers (or sponsors) through a commercial association with a professional sporting club or league and is directly proportional to the worth of the sponsorship.

The value of sponsorships differs between sports, between leagues, between clubs and across countries. At the highest level, the IOC created 'The Olympic Partner Program' (TOP) in 1985, in order to provide companies with exclusive worldwide marketing rights to the Games. Coca-cola, McDonalds, Kodak, Omega, Visa and Panasonic are among the IOC's worldwide partners, while Volkswagen, the Bank of China and Adidas were official partners of 2008 Beijing Olympic Games. At other levels of professional sport, the sponsorship or marketing arrangements may go further, as clubs and leagues are willing to enter into sponsorship arrangements whereby commercial organizations are able to acquire naming rights or enter into arrangements that give them either exclusive or increased access to fans. The development of the Internet and online marketing has been particularly instrumental in this respect.

The English Premier League provides an example of the proliferation of sponsors within professional sport leagues and clubs. The competition is known as the Barclays Premiership, sponsored by a UK-based financial services group engaged in banking, investment banking and investment management. The English Premier League also has a range of secondary or associate sponsors. For example, Budweiser is the official beer of the league, while pharmaceutical company GlaxoSmithKline is a sponsor through its Lucozade sport drink. Furthermore, the clubs that play in the Barclays Premiership have significant sponsorship deals. The primary sponsor of each club is entitled to place its brand prominently on the front of the playing strip. Manchester United's primary sponsor is AIG, an international insurance and financial services company, a deal which is worth £56.5 million over 4 years. Arsenal is sponsored by Emirates, one of the world's leading airlines (previous sponsors of Chelsea), Chelsea is sponsored by Samsung, an electronic goods manufacturer, Liverpool is sponsored by Carlsberg, a Danish beer, Everton is sponsored by Chang, a Thai beer (interestingly, both are competitors with the official beer of the league) and Tottenham Hotspur is sponsored by Mansion.com, an online casino.

Like broadcast rights revenue, sponsorship revenue within professional sport has grown exponentially. In the early 1960s, NASCAR driver Fred Lorenzen's sponsorship, from a Ford dealership, was US$6000 for an entire season. By the late 1980s, it was estimated that approximately US$3 million in sponsorship was required for a team to break even over the course of the season. In 2000, UPS announced its sponsorship of the Robert Yates No. 88 team driven by Dale Jarrett, which was estimated to be worth US$15 million per year.

The sponsorship of professional sport goes further than commercial agreements between clubs and leagues. Individual athletes also have sponsorship agreements that provide them with additional income to supplement their playing contracts (for team sports) or prize money (for individuals). In Practice 4.3 explores the case of Tiger Woods as an illustration of the scale and breadth of one athlete's sponsorship portfolio. Well chosen brands with a global profile can enhance an athlete's overall image and, in the case of more popular athletes, a sponsor can establish the athlete as a brand in their own right. Sponsorship of professional athletes is not restricted to superstar athletes like David Beckham of the Los Angeles Galaxy (football/soccer), Tiger Woods (golf) or Yao Ming of the Houston Rockets (basketball). Rather, sponsorship of professional athletes exists wherever there is a market, whether a mass market in the case of global athletes or a niche market in the case of small or cult sports.

In Practice 4.3 Sponsoring a Tiger

Tiger Woods is one of the most recognizable athletes in the world. By 2008, he had won 87 tournaments, including four US Masters, four USPGA Championships, three US Open Championships and three British Open Championships. Woods' on-course successes have been mirrored off-course by his commercial endorsements and media profile. In 2008, he was sponsored by a wide range of companies and products, including the following:

Accenture: a global management consulting, technology services and outsourcing company

Buick: an American car manufacturer

EA Sports: an interactive entertainment software company that produces software for Internet, PC and video game systems, such as 'Tiger Woods PGA TOUR'

Gatorade: the leading brand of sport's drink in America, which has produced a special line of products – 'Gatorade Tiger Thirst Quencher'

Gillette: a company that produces shaving products

Golf Digest: a golf magazine

Nike: one of the world's largest manufacturers and distributors of athletic apparel and equipment

Tag Heuer: A Swiss watch manufacturer.

Many of Woods' sponsorships are sport or golf related, such as EA Sports, Gatorade, Golf Digest and Nike, where there are obvious commercial benefits for Woods and the sponsor. When Nike signed a contract to begin sponsoring Woods in 1996, its golf shoes and apparel were an insignificant part of its overall business, but more than a decade later the Woods led 'Nike Golf' is a major product line. However, many of the sponsors are non-sport and non-golf related, such as Buick, Gillette and Tag Heuer. Woods is one of three 'Gillette Champions', along with tennis player Roger Federer and footballer Thierry Henry, as part of Gillette's global marketing campaign. Car manufacturers have long been associated with sport leagues, teams and athletes, as has Gillette and watch manufacturers such as Tag Heuer. What demonstrates Woods' global appeal within and outside the sport industry is his sponsorship by Accenture, a company that has more than 178 000 employees in 49 countries and recorded net revenues of US$19 700 million in 2007. Accenture's sponsorship is also indicative of golf's audience.

In 2007, *Sports Illustrated* estimated, in its list of the top 50 American athletes (by earnings), that Tiger Woods was the first athlete to earn more than US$100 million in a year. *Sports Illustrated* estimated that Woods' salary was almost US$12 million and that his endorsements and sponsorships were worth US$100 million per year. In 2008, Forbes magazine estimated Woods' annual income had grown to US$115 million and reported that he was second only to Oprah Winfrey in the list of highest earning American celebrities and predicted that Woods would be the first athlete to accumulate US$1000 million (in all likelihood by 2010).

Sources: Tiger Woods Official Website (http://www.tigerwoods.com); Sports Illustrated Website (http://sportsillustrated.cnn.com); Forbes Website (http://www.forbes.com).

PLAYER MANAGEMENT

As sport has become increasingly professional and the amount of money secured through broadcast rights and sponsorship deals has increased, the salaries of players and athletes have also increased. The growth in player and athlete income has been mirrored by a concurrent rise in the expectations of clubs and leagues, an increase in the complexity of contract negotiations and greater off-field commercial opportunities for prominent 'sport stars'. These developments in the world of professional sport have led to the evolution of an industry focused on player and athlete management, which is essentially geared towards providing players and athletes with services in return for a share of their income.

One of the most prominent player and athlete management companies is the International Management Group (IMG), which was formed in the 1960s and employs in excess of 2000 staff in 70 offices in 30 countries. What began exclusively as a player management business has evolved into a complex commercial operation that includes television and publishing divisions. Golfer Arnold Palmer, winner of the US Masters golf tournament in 1958, 1960, 1962 and 1964, the US Open in 1960 and the British Open in 1961 and 1962, was the first athlete in the world to be branded by Mark McCormack, the creator and head of IMG. Back in the 1960s, the 'brand-name' principle by which Palmer and McCormack approached sport was the first attempt to transform the business activities of leading athletes. Sport and business were previously related, but the scale of their operation was unique. The level of vertical and horizontal integration was essential to what became known as 'Sportsbiz' (Boyle and Haynes, 2000). McCormack took the relationship of the agent further than before and began to handle contract negotiations, proactively sought business opportunities and planned the sale of the Palmer brand on a long-term basis, rather than previous attempts that might be characterized as *ad hoc*. McCormack set an important precedent by selling people as marketable commodities.

Octagon is a global sport marketing company and competitor to IMG. It represents and promotes more than 800 athletes in 35 different sports across the world. Its clients include some of the most prominent sportsmen and women, such as tennis players Amelie Mauresmo and Jelena Jankovic. Octagon provides a broad range of services for the athletes it manages, including the following:

- Contract negotiations

- Marketing initiatives and endorsements

- Public relations and charity involvement

- Financial planning

- Media management

- Property development

- Speaking engagements.

Octagon claims that it generates annual marketing revenues of in excess of US$300 000 000, by maximizing its athletes' off-field corporate relationships. The company states that it does this by developing a unique and individual marketing plan for each of its athletes. Octagon represents American swimmer Michael Phelps, winner of the 400 m individual medley and 200 m butterfly at the 2004 Athens Olympic Games. The company claims Phelps is a perfect case study in what successful sport marketing and management can provide for an athlete in the contemporary hyper-commercial sport environment. Octagon suggests that Phelps laid the foundation with his performances in the pool, but that Octagon enhanced the Phelps story with a targeted publicity campaign, which included appearances in *Time*, *People*, the *Wall Street Journal* and *USA Today*. The result was what Octagon claims to be the creation of a connection between Phelps and corporate America, including the largest ever endorsement deal in swimming with Speedo and subsidiary deals with VISA, Omega and AT&T Wireless.

In many respects, athletes competing in individual sports are logical targets for both agents and sponsors, however, athletes in team sports are often as valuable, if not more so. In the USA, the term 'multiples' is used to refer to an athlete that has the ability to attract multiple media and endorsements. The multiples' play on the field is at the highest level, they help to bring fans to the game, help the team to secure broadcast contracts or sponsorships deals, help the team in merchandising and licensing and, in the extreme cases, have the potential to increase the net financial worth of the organization. Thus, the athlete's commercial potential can be calculated in individual earnings (through the team or an agent), but also in terms of the growth of the club or league of which they are a part. In 2002, Yao Ming led the Shanghai Sharks to the championship in the Chinese Basketball Association, averaging 32.4 points, 19.0 rebounds and 4.8 blocked shots. A member of the Chinese national team since he was 18 years old, 229 cm Ming was selected as the first pick in the 2002 NBA draft by the Houston Rockets. In his first season in the NBA, Ming was voted rookie of the year and the Rockets improved their winning percentage from 34% to 52%. The Houston Rockets website is available in English or Chinese, in order to cater for Ming's enormous popularity in China (www.nba.com/rockets). Ming's success with the Rockets means that merchandising and broadcast possibilities are significant, for both the team and the league. 'The Year of the Yao', a movie about Ming's first year in the NBA and his transition from China to America was released in cinemas in 2005, further evidence of Ming's popularity and commercial value.

Professional sport stars are well paid by any measures. Importantly, their salaries are relative to revenue of the clubs, leagues, tournaments and events

Table 4.2	Highest Value Football/Soccer Players 2008	
Player	**Team**	**Annual Earnings (US$)**
David Beckham	Los Angeles Galaxy	48 900 000
Ronaldinho	Barcelona	32 600 000
Thierry Henry	Barcelona	25 100 000
Ronaldo	AC Milan	21 200 000
Cristiano Ronaldo	Manchester United	18 500 000
Kaka	AC Milan	17 700 000
Fabio Cannavaro	Real Madrid	17 500 000
Andriy Shevchenko	Chelsea	17 500 000
Steven Gerrard	Liverpool	17 100 000
John Terry	Chelsea	17 000 000

Source: www.forbes.com

of which they are a part. In fact, in some professional sports with strong player unions, the level of remuneration for players is set as a percentage of league revenue. Table 4.2 lists the highest paid football/soccer players in the world in 2008. Their annual earnings are indicative of their on-field worth and the significant investment made by their respective teams, as well as their commercial worth off the field. That David Beckham is by far the world's highest paid soccer player, but plays in a relatively minor league (in comparison to the major European leagues), is indicative of the importance placed on individual celebrity athletes by teams and leagues. Beckham was recruited by the LA Galaxy for his global profile and marketing appeal as much as his on-field abilities.

OWNERSHIP AND OUTCOMES

Professional sports utilize different ownership and governance models in order to regulate and manage their businesses effectively. Some of the models have strong historical traditions, while others have been selected or adapted for their utility. One of the key distinctions is between professional sport teams and leagues that can be considered 'profit maximizers' and those that are 'win maximizers'. There is some debate as to whether these terms accurately reflect the practice of professional sport teams and franchises, but they are useful for broadly categorizing operational and financial priorities. Profit maximizing teams, such as those in the major American professional sport leagues, are typically owned by individuals or businesses who seek to maximize the financial return on investment. In some sports, however, such as English, Scottish and Australian football and cricket (Quirk and Fort, 1992), the need to win is a greater priority than the need to make a profit. In fact, in some instances win maximizing teams will place the club in financial jeopardy, particularly by purchasing players it cannot afford.

In some cases, the ownership model has adapted to meet specific conditions brought about by commercial change. In the J-League, Japan's professional football (soccer) competition, teams like the Kashiwa Reysol are privately owned. The Reysol is owned by the Hitachi corporation that specializes in the manufacturing of electrical goods and equipment. Originally established as an amateur team of the Hitachi corporation, the Reysol was professionalized in order to participate in the inaugural J-League season in 1993.

Whether teams are win maximizing or profit maximizing, they must cooperate with each other at some level to ensure that fans, sponsors and the media remain interested and involved with the sport. Sport leagues that are dominated by one or two teams are often perceived to be less attractive to fans than leagues in which the result of games is uncertain. There is, however, a long history of leagues in which strong rivalries have maintained interest in the game (Los Angeles Lakers versus Boston Celtics in the NBA and Rangers versus Celtic in the Scottish Premier League for example), although often the teams that are part of the rivalry benefit at the expense of teams that perform poorly. A league that is not dominated by only a couple of teams and in which there is an uncertainty of outcome (of a game or season) is said to have 'competitive balance' (Quirk and Fort, 1992). Leagues across the world have instituted a range of measures to try to achieve competitive balance, which is often elusive. Perhaps the most obvious and publicized measure is the draft system that operates in football leagues such as the National Football League in America or the Australian Football League. The draft allows the league to allocate higher draft preferences (the best athletes on offer) to poorer performed teams, in order to equalize the playing talent across the league and create more competitive games.

SUMMARY

This chapter has presented an overview of professional sport and some of the central relationships that are essential to its ongoing prosperity and survival. The media, sponsors, agents, owners, advertisers, leagues, clubs and athletes are part of a self-sustaining commercial alliance, in which each of the partners promotes and supports the activities and interests of the others. Commercial networks are the binding forces that are holding professional sport together in the 21st century. Since the middle of the 20th century, professional sport leagues and clubs have increasingly become willing partners in the promotion of their activities (sports and events), as well as the promotion of subsidiary products and services and, in the process, have become major players in a multibillion dollar industry.

REVIEW QUESTIONS

1. Use the circuit of promotion concept to explain the role of sponsors and the media in the professional sport industry.

2. Explain the rationale behind a company sponsoring a professional sport club, league or athlete.

3. Are the media important to the survival of professional sport? Why?

4. Identify an international and a domestic professional circuit and examine its operation. What are the special features that attract fans and media?

5. Choose a professional sport league and identify the fees paid by television broadcasters over the previous 20 years for the broadcast rights. Has it increased or decreased over the period? Explain why.

6. Choose a sport in which the location of events or tournaments is not fixed. Imagine that the city you live in is going to bid for the right to host the event and create a list of potential benefits – consider such features as the economy, environment, transportation, public services and housing.

7. Choose a high profile athlete and identify what companies or products sponsor the athlete. Is the athlete represented by an agent or did they secure the sponsorships or endorsements themselves?

8. Choose a sporting league of the world and identify whether it should be classified as 'win maximizing' or 'profit maximizing'. Provide a rationale for your answer that includes a commentary on the ownership of teams in the league.

9. Create a list of the top five paid sportspeople in the world. What does the list tell you about the size of the commercial markets that the sports are played in and the popularity of the sports?

10. Create a fictional international sport circuit. What cities of the world would host your events and why?

FURTHER READING

Bellamy, R. (1998). The evolving television sports marketplace. In L. Wenner (ed.), *MediaSport*. Routledge, London, pp. 73–87.

Boyle, R. and Haynes, R. (2000). *Power play: sport, the media and popular culture*. Longman, London.

Cousens, L. and Slack, T. (2005). Field-level change: the case of North American major league professional sport. *Journal of Sport Management*, 19, 13–42.

Euchner, C. (1993). *Playing the field: why sports teams move and cities fight to keep them*. John Hopkins University Press, Baltimore.

Fielding, L., Miller, L. and Brown, J. (1999). Harlem Globetrotters International, Inc. *Journal of Sport Management*, 13, 45–77.

Nicholson, M. (2007). *Sport and the media: managing the nexus*. Butterworth-Heinemann, London.

O'Brien, D. and Slack, T. (2003) An analysis of change in an organizational field: the professionalization of English Rugby Union. *Journal of Sport Management*, 17, 417–448.

Shropshire, K. (1995). *The sports franchise game*. University of Pennsylvania Press, Philadelphia.

Stewart, B. (ed.) (2007). *The Games are not the same: the political economy of Australian Football*. Melbourne University Press, Melbourne.

RELEVANT WEBSITES

Americas

National Football League – http://www.nfl.com
National Basketball League – http://www.nba.com
Major League Baseball – http://www.mlb.com
National Hockey League – http://www.nhl.com
Nascar – http://www.nascar.com
Professional Golfers' Association – http://www.pga.com
Ladies Professional Golf Association – http://www.lpga.com

Australia and New Zealand

Australian Football League – http://www.afl.com.au
Cricket Australia – http://www.baggygreen.com.au
National Rugby League – http://www.nrl.com
Super 12 Rugby Union – http://www.rugby.com.au
New Zealand Rugby – http://www.nzrugby.com

Great Britain

English Premier League – http://www.premierleague.com
British Rugby League – http://uk.rleague.com/

Asia

J-League – http://www.j-league.or.jp/eng/
Japanese Sumo Association – http://www.sumo.or.jp/eng/index.html
Chinese Professional Baseball League – http://www.cpbl.com.tw/html/english/cpbl.asp

Europe

European Champions League – http://www.uefa.com/
Serie A (Italy) – http://www.lega-calcio.it/
Real Madrid – http://www.realmadrid.com/portada_eng.htm

Bundesliga (Germany) – http://www.bundesliga.de

European Professional Golfers' Association Tour – http://www.europeantour.com

Global

Olympics – http://www.olympic.org

World Cup – http://www.fifa.com

America's Cup – http://www.americascup.com

Tour de France – http://www.letour.fr/indexus.html

Formula One – http://www.formula1.com

Association of Surfing Professionals – http://www.aspworldtour.com

Association of Tennis Professionals (men) – http://www.atptennis.com/en

Women's Tennis Association – http://www.wtatour.com/

World Rally Championship – http://www.wrc.com

Case Study: UEFA Champions League

This case explores the organization and operations of the UEFA Champions League, with specific reference to the nexus between national and global leagues. As the chapter highlighted, the success of professional sport leagues is dependent on their levels of public support, media coverage, media revenue and sponsorship revenue, as well as the ability to retain and promote their players as brand icons. The Champions League is no different, as it has high levels of corporate support and is popular with fans. However, it cannot be regarded as equivalent to national football leagues, because it based on a model which rewards national and regional excellence and is supported by regional and global interest. Its relatively unusual structure means that the Champions League provides an interesting perspective on a range of issues that are pertinent to the study and practice of professional sport.

FIFA is the world governing body for football. It is comprised of six regional football confederations: Africa, Asia, South America, North and Central America and the Caribbean, Europe and Oceania. Although the African football confederation has the largest number of members, the European confederation is by far the most powerful – it contains many of the world's best football nations, as well as being home to the most prominent leagues, including the English Premier League, The Italian Serie A, the Spanish La Liga and German Bundesliga. The Union of European Football Associations (UEFA) is the governing body for football in Europe. UEFA organizes elite club competitions such as the UEFA Champions League and the UEFA Cup, as well as national competitions such as the European Championships at senior and youth level.

In 2006/7, EUFA's income was €1 151 597 000. Broadcast rights revenue of €810 759 000 represented 70% of total revenue, with €269 471 000 in commercial rights (sponsorship) equivalent to 23%. By contrast, ticket revenue (€22 497 000) and hospitality revenue (€37 865 000) were relatively minor contributors to UEFA's overall income. A closer examination of EUFA's finances reveals that its premier competition, the Champions League, accounted for a significant proportion of the confederation's overall revenue. Broadcast revenue from the UEFA Champions League was €625 080 000, or 77% of total broadcast revenue, while commercial rights (sponsorship) was €193 466 000 or 72% of total commercial rights revenue. Advance payments for the 2008 European Championships skew these results and misrepresent the importance of the Champions League. For example, in 2005/6, UEFA Champions League broadcast revenue represented 94% of total UEFA broadcast revenue.

Most national sport leagues are fairly static in that they contain a fixed number of teams from year to year and have well-defined promotion and relegation rules. For example, there are 20 teams in the English Premier League and each year the three lowest teams from the Premier League are relegated to the Football League Championship (the next highest League in England) and three teams from the Football League Championship are promoted based on their performance (the top two teams plus a third as a result of a playoff system). European football leagues such as the Italian Serie A and the German Bundesliga operate on similar principles.

By contrast, the total number of teams that compete in the Champions League is fixed, but the composition of the League is dependent on national league performances, as are the number of teams that are able to compete from a single competition. The number of teams that are able to compete in the Champions League from individual national leagues is dependent on their recent performance (over the previous five seasons), which EUFA uses to calculate a coefficient ranking. In 2008, the top eight ranked nations were: 1. Spain; 2. England; 3. Italy; 4. France; 5. Germany; 6. Portugal; 7. Romania; and 8. Netherlands. The national performance based entitlements are illustrated in Table 4.3.

The European Champions League is conducted from July until May the following year, with three qualifying rounds, a group stage and a knockout stage. Participating clubs

Continued

are allocated to the various rounds and stages in the following way:

First qualifying round – 28 teams

28 champions from associations 25–53 (not including Liechtenstein)

Second qualifying round – 28 teams

14 winners from the first qualifying round

8 champions from associations 17–24

6 runners-up from associations 10–15

Third qualifying round – 32 teams

14 winners from the second qualifying round

7 champions from associations 10–16

3 runners-up from associations 7–9

6 third-place finishers from associations 1–6

2 fourth-place finishers from associations 1–3

Group stage – 32 teams

1 current Champions League holder

16 winners from the third qualifying round

9 champions from associations 1–9

6 runners-up from associations 1–6

Knockout Stage – 16 teams

2 teams in each of 8 groups progress to the knockout stage

Note: the composition of the group stage and the qualifying rounds differs if the Champions League holder qualifies as the Champion of its national league.

Not surprisingly, the clubs that dominate the Champions League come from the most powerful European leagues, particularly those ranked in the top 6 based on UEFA's coefficient system, which have at least two clubs in the group stage. In the five seasons from 2003/4 to 2007/8, a select number of clubs have consistently competed at the group stage of the tournament, including the most prominent and powerful clubs in Europe: Manchester United (England), Chelsea (England), Liverpool (England), Arsenal (England), Real Madrid (Spain), Barcelona (Spain), AC Milan (Italy), Internatzionale (Italy), Juventus (Italy), Roma (Italy), Bayern Munich (Germany), PSV Eindhoven (Netherlands), Ajax (Netherlands), Porto (Portugal) and Lyon (France). As illustrated in Table 4.1, many of these clubs are estimated to be in the top ten most valuable football (soccer) clubs in the world.

Some of the reasons that the same clubs dominate the Champions League from year to year are that the composition of the tournament is based on national league performances and the biggest and most powerful European leagues lack competitive balance. In other words, in these leagues the governing body has not enforced regulations, such as a salary cap or a player draft, which would spread the playing talent evenly and ensure competition. In the main, these types of regulations work well in football leagues in countries such as America or Australia, where global or regional player migration is either severely limited or non-existent. As a result of the organization of the European leagues, the richest, most powerful and most prominent clubs are able to purchase the best players, which enables the team to win national and regional competitions, which ensures they remain highly profitable, which in turn means that they are able to attract the best players. This cycle invariably means it is very difficult for lowly ranked clubs to break the stranglehold of those that occupy the top echelon.

In 2006/7, UEFA distributed €585 000 000 to the 32 clubs that participated in the group stage of the Champions League, compared with €23 500 000 distributed to clubs in 1992/3, the first season of the Champions League. In 2006/7, each club received a participation bonus of €3 000 000 and a further €400 000 per group match (a total of €2 400 000). Each group match victory was worth €600 000 and each draw €300 000. Each of the 16 clubs that made it through to the knockout stage received a participation bonus of €2 200 000, quarter-finalists an additional €2 500 000 and semi-finalists an additional €3 000 000. The winners received €7 000 000 and the runners-up received €4 000 000. Excluding the final, the home club kept all gate receipts, a significant source of income for clubs with large stadiums and supporter bases. Furthermore, clubs also received a share of Champions League distributions based on the value of the club's national television market. In 2006/7, the winner of the Champions League, AC Milan, received almost €40 000 000, with Chelsea, Barcelona, Internatzionale, Bayern Munich, Liverpool, PSV Eindhoven, Valencia, Roma, Real Madrid, Olympique Lyonnais and Manchester United earning between €20 000 000 and €35 000 000.

Case Study Questions

1. As noted in the case, distributions to clubs via the Champions League increased from €23 500 000 to €585 000 000 during the period 1992/3 to 2006/7. What are some possible reasons for the increase in distributions?

2. Is the proportion of media revenue higher within UEFA and the Champions League than it is within European national leagues, or for individual clubs? Why is this so?

3. Do the top European clubs earn more from their participation in their national leagues or from their participation in the UEFA Champions League?

4. Would the top European clubs be better off in a European 'Super League'?

5. Would mechanisms to induce or improve competitive balance, like those used in the National Football League (America) or the Australian Football League, work in Europe's national football leagues?

Sources: UEFA (2007). Financial Report 2006–2007. UEFA, Nyon, Switzerland; and the UEFA Website at <http://www.uefa.com/index.html>.

Table 4.3	National Performance Based Entitlements for Domestic Leagues
Position	**Entitlement**
1–3	Four clubs in the Champions League
	Three clubs in the UEFA Cup
4–6	Three clubs in the Champions League
	Three clubs in the UEFA Cup
7–8	Two clubs in the Champions League
	Four clubs in the UEFA Cup
9–15	Two clubs in the Champions League
	Two clubs in the UEFA Cup
16–21	One club in the Champions League
	Three clubs in the UEFA Cup
22–53	One club in the Champions League
	Two clubs in the UEFA Cup

Sources: UEFA (2007). Financial Report 2006–2007. UEFA, Nyon, Switzerland; and the UEFA Website at <http://www.uefa.com/index.html>.

PART 2

Sport Management Principles

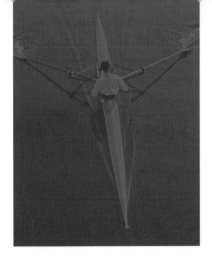

CHAPTER 5

Strategic Sport Management

OVERVIEW

This chapter reveals the processes and techniques of strategic management. Specifically, it focuses on the analysis of an organization's position in the competitive environment, the determination of its direction and goals, the selection of an appropriate strategy, the leveraging of its distinctive assets and the evaluation of its chosen activities. These processes are reviewed within the context of a documented plan.

After completing this chapter the reader should be able to:

- Understand the difference between strategy and planning

- Appreciate why strategic management should be undertaken

- Differentiate the steps of the strategic management process

- Identify the tools and techniques of strategic management

- Specify the steps involved in the documentation of a strategic plan

- Explain how the nature of sport affects the strategic management process.

STRATEGIC MANAGEMENT PRINCIPLES

In the simplest terms possible, strategy is the match or interface between an organization and its external environment. Looking at strategy in this way is a helpful start because it reinforces the importance of both the organization itself and the circumstances in which it operates. At the heart of strategy is the assumption that these two elements are of equal importance. Furthermore, strategy concerns the entirety of the organization and its operations as well as the entirety of the environment. Such a holistic approach differentiates the strategy management process from other dimensions of management.

One troublesome aspect of strategic management is its complex, multi-faceted nature. Johnson and Scholes (2002), for example noted several important features associated with strategic decision-making:

1. Strategy affects the direction and scope of an organization's activities

2. Strategy involves matching an organization's activities with the environment

3. Strategy requires the matching of an organization's activities with its resource capabilities

4. The substance of strategy is influenced by the views and expectations of key stakeholders

5. Strategic decisions influence the long-term direction of the organization.

With Johnson and Scholes' points in mind, it is easily concluded that the management of strategy requires a keen understanding of the organization, the environment, as well as the consequences of decisions. But these points miss one vital outcome in the strategy process. The central purpose of strategy is to become different to the competition. From this viewpoint, strategy should help explain how one football club is different from the next, or why a customer should choose to use a recreation facility over another in the same area. The match between an organization and its environment should result in a clear competitive advantage that no other organization can easily copy.

Before we proceed, it is necessary to make several important distinctions in definition and terminology. The first point to make is that strategy and planning are not the same things. Strategy can be defined as the process of determining the direction and scope of activities of a sport organization in light of its capabilities and the environment in which it operates. Planning is the process of documenting these decisions in a step-by-step manner indicating what has to be done, by whom, with what resources and when. In short, strategy is a combination of analysis and innovation, of science and craft. Planning identifies in a systematic and deductive way the steps and activities that need to be taken toward the implementation of a strategy. Strategic management marries strategy and planning into a process.

The second point to make about terminology is concerned with the use of the word strategy. The term can be legitimately used to explain three levels of decision-making. The first is the identity level where a sport organization is faced with the task of establishing clarity about what business it is actually engaged in. For example, is the core business providing sport competitions, managing facilities, developing players, winning medals, championships and tournaments, selling merchandise, making a profit or improving shareholder wealth? At the second level, the term strategy is commonly used to identify how the organization is going to be competitive against others. Strategy here is an explanation of how competitive advantage is going to be created and sustained. Strategy is also used at an operational level to identify how regular activities are to be undertaken and how resources are to be deployed to support them. For example, a broader strategy to improve player scouting methods might be supported by an operational strategy specifying the purchase of some computer software. The lesson is that strategic management is a process and way of thinking that can be applied to multiple levels of a sport organization.

WHY UNDERTAKE STRATEGIC MANAGEMENT?

Surprisingly, the need for management of the strategy process is not always considered necessary. Some managers believe that the fast-paced nature of the sport industry precludes the use of a systematic strategic management process. Strategy for these managers is developed 'on the run' and in response to emerging circumstances and events. However, this approach is fundamentally contradictory to the principles of strategic management, which emphasize the importance of actively shaping the future of one's own sport organization rather than waiting for circumstances to prompt action. Proactivity is at the heart of good strategy because it helps to reduce the uncertainty that accompanies chaotic and changeable industries like sport, where on-field performance can have such a radical effect on an organization's success.

Those versed in the concepts of strategic management would argue that with more uncertainty comes the need for greater strategic activity. Thus, a sport club that can generate a sizable surplus with a performance at the top of the ladder but a dangerous deficit with a performance at the bottom of the ladder should engage in the strategy process in order to seek new ways of managing its financial balance. In addition, those who favour reactive approaches to strategy assume that opportunities are always overt and transparent. This is seldom true. Identifying new opportunities that have not already been leveraged by competition is rarely easy and requires thorough analysis and innovative thinking. Neither of these can be achieved easily without the investment of time and energy on strategy development.

Allied to the notion of proactivity is the importance of coordination. Without a broad approach to the strategy process, different parts of the organization are likely to pursue their own agendas. It is therefore essential that scarce resources are deployed in a coordinated and integrated manner that is consistent with an overarching strategy. Such a coordinated approach to strategy ensures that new strategy represents change. For many sport organizations for which change is a necessary condition for survival, strategy represents the intellectual part of management that can be planned. The result of this process should be a coordinated attempt to achieve goals that have been agreed upon by organizational stakeholders that takes into account a balance between the achievement of goals and the resources required to do so. This is another way of saying efficiency is an important benefit of sound strategic management.

STRATEGIC SPORT MANAGEMENT

One of the biggest issues in sport strategy comes in finding the balance between two or more divergent obligations. For example, it is common in sport organizations to seek both elite success as well as improved participation levels. Deploying resources to both of these commitments is troublesome from a strategic viewpoint because they are not necessarily as compatible as popular assumptions would suggest (Stewart et al., 2004). It is commonly assumed that international success for a particular sport serves as a motivator for people to participate. The success of a team or athlete in a particular sport at the Olympics might be the trigger for some people to become involved in that sport. However, the retention of new participants in sport tends to be poor in the medium term and negligible in the longer term.

Assumption is a dangerous activity in strategic decision-making. To make matters more complex, the choices of direction inherent in sport can be distracting, from the necessity to develop players or increase participation, to the pressure to make more money or win at all costs.

In Practice 5.1 Strategic Opportunities and the NBA China

Early in 2008, the United States National Basketball Association announced that it had finally secured the formation of the NBA China which will oversee the league's business activities in the country. The NBA China promises to be the realization of a tremendous strategic opportunity marrying one of the most prominent and established sporting brands in the world with a vast new marketplace in love with basketball and its NBA hero, Yao Ming, who plays for the Houston Rockets. The opportunity of taking the NBA to China is not lost on the commercial world either, with five strategic partners investing US$253m to obtain 11% of the new entity. The interest of one of the five companies, ESPN, the sport broadcasting division of the Walt Disney Company, is indicative of the media profile and content that NBA China could generate.

From a strategic viewpoint, the NBA must be acknowledged for both its prescience and patience in making the NBA China possible. It has not been quick in coming. As early as 1985, the NBA was involved in Chinese basketball, hosting the national team, providing coaching clinics, exhibition games and establishing political goodwill between the respective administrations. In 1992, the NBA opened an office in Hong Kong, which has expanded to accommodate over 100 employees across four locations in Greater China.

It is difficult to underestimate the potential opportunity the NBA China has at its fingertips. NBA.com/China is the most popular sport-related website in the country and, according to the senior director of NBA China, Wendy Yu, the phrase 'NBA China' is among the five most frequently searched terms in Chinese search engines. The website has over two million daily hits. At least some of the interest in the NBA can be attributed to the Chinese and Houston Rockets superstar Yao Ming. In addition, the localized production of NBA games is also pivotal, where local commentators call the games. The 20-year relationship the NBA has enjoyed with Chinese national broadcaster CCTV has evidently been pivotal in popularizing the league. Now more than 500 NBA products are available at Chinese Wal-Marts, Adidas outlets and other retail locations. The league also played numerous preseason games in China during 2007.

As a combination, the NBA brand and the Chinese marketplace appear to make an obvious strategic alliance. The NBA is broadcast in 215 countries, but none have the potential audience of China, where basketball is played in almost every school and the national squad is among the best in the world. There are more than 250 million basketball players in China. They will look towards the NBA China for their entertainment and inspiration.

THE STRATEGIC MANAGEMENT PROCESS

Strategic management is the process designed to find the intersection of preparation and opportunity. This way of thinking has emerged from the first uses of the strategy concept, which came from the military. On the battlefield, the importance of imposing conditions that disadvantage the enemy in combat is paramount. For example, one of the key principles of military strategy is to manoeuvre your adversary into a position where they are outnumbered at the point of conflict. Variables like terrain and the opportunity to outflank or attack the enemy from both the front and side simultaneously, make strategic decisions more complicated. These principles are also applied in the strategic sport management process, which is illustrated in Figure 5.1.

Like a general, the sport manager must first make an assessment of the 'battle' conditions. They do this by studying the capacities and deficiencies of

FIGURE 5.1

The strategic management process.

| Strategy Analysis | *Internal Analysis* *(capabilities, deficiencies & stakeholders)* | Strengths Weaknesses |
| | *External Analysis* *(environment, competitors & customers)* | Opportunities Threats |

| Strategy Direction | *Mission* *Vision* *Objectives* | Performance Measures |

| Strategy Formulation | *Strategic Options* | Generic Strategies *Cost Leadership* *Differentiation* *Focus* |

| Strategy Implementation | *Deployment of Strategy* | Products Services Systems Structure Culture |

| Strategy Evaluation | *Performance Measurement* | Corrective Action |

their own organization, competing organizations, stakeholder groups and the business environment or 'battlefield'. This first stage in the strategic management process is known as *Strategy Analysis*.

Next, and in light of the information obtained from the first stage, the sport manager must make some decisions about the future. These are typically concentrated into a 'mission' statement recording the purpose of the organization, a 'vision' statement of the organization's long-term ambitions and a set of objectives with measures to identify the essential achievements along the way to the vision. This second stage of the strategic management process is called *Strategy Direction*.

Setting a direction only determines what an organization wants to achieve. In the next step, the sport manager must consider how the direction can be realized. This is the most creative part of the strategic management process. Here, the sport manager, and his or her team, must work together to imagine the best methods or strategies for the organization. At this time, the key challenge is to match the unique circumstances of the organization to its unique environmental conditions. When this is undertaken well, opportunities to exploit are found. This stage is called *Strategy Development*.

With a clear direction and a sharp idea of how that direction can be achieved, the task of the sport manager becomes one of implementation. It is at this point that the range of products, services and activities that the organization is engaged with and the systems that support them, are adjusted in line with the overarching strategy that was developed in the previous step. This is known as the *Strategy Implementation* stage.

Finally, it is important to note that strategy is rarely perfect the first time around. Modifications are always essential. Mostly, this means a minor adjustment to the way in which the strategy has been implemented. However, sometimes it does require a rethink about the suitability of the strategy itself. Neither of these can be successfully undertaken without some feedback in the first place about the success of what has been done. That is why the final stage in the strategic management process, *Strategy Evaluation*, is necessary. In this stage, the organization reviews whether objectives have been achieved. Most of the time, some corrective action will need to be taken. It is not unusual that the catalysts for these changes are unexpected events that affect the environment in which the sport organization operates. This necessitates a return to strategy analysis. In this sense, the strategic management process never stops. In fact, it is also quite normal to move back and forth between the stages in order to develop the best outcomes. The strategy process works best when management takes the view that it is not linear or discrete but rather a circular and continuous activity.

STAGE 1: STRATEGIC ANALYSIS

One of the biggest challenges facing sport managers is in combating the desire to set strategy immediately and to take action without delay. While a call to action is a natural inclination for motivated managers, many strategies can fail because the preliminary work has not been done properly. This preliminary work entails a comprehensive review of the internal and external environments. The tools for doing this include:

1. SWOT analysis

2. stakeholder and customer needs analysis

3. competitor analysis

4. the five forces analysis.

SWOT analysis

One of the basic tools in the environmental analysis is called the SWOT analysis. This form of analysis is used to examine an organization's strategic position, from the inside to the outside. The SWOT technique considers the strengths, weaknesses, opportunities and threats that an organization possesses or faces.

There are two parts to the SWOT analysis. The first part represents the internal analysis of an organization, which can be summarized by its *strengths* and *weaknesses*. This analysis covers everything that an organization has control over, some of which are performed well, and can be viewed as capabilities (strengths), while others are more difficult to do well and can be seen as deficiencies (weaknesses). The second part of the SWOT technique is concerned with external factors; those which the organization has no direct control over. These are divided into *opportunities* and *threats*. In other words, issues and environmental circumstances arise that can either be exploited or need to be neutralized.

The purpose of the SWOT technique is to find the major factors that are likely to play a role in the appropriateness of the organization's direction or the success of its strategy. With this in mind, the sport manager should be looking for overarching issues. A good rule of thumb is to look for no more than five factors under each of the four headings. This way the more important issues are given higher priority.

Given that the strengths and weaknesses part of the analysis is a consideration of what is inside the organization, it has a time-orientation in the present; what the organization does right now. Strengths can be defined as resources or capabilities that the organization can use to achieve its strategic direction. Common strengths may include committed coaching staff, a sound membership base or a good junior development programme. Weaknesses should be seen as limitations or inadequacies that will prevent or hinder the strategic direction from being achieved. Common weaknesses may include poor training facilities, inadequate sponsorship or a diminishing volunteer workforce.

In contrast, the opportunity and threats analysis also has a future-thinking dimension, because of the need to consider what is about to happen. Opportunities are favourable situations or events that can be exploited by the organization to enhance its circumstances or capabilities. Common opportunities tend to include new government grants, the identification of a new market or potential product, or the chance to appoint a new staff member with unique skills. Threats are unfavourable situations which could make it more difficult for the organization to achieve its strategic direction. Common threats include inflating player salaries, new competitors or unfavourable trends in the consumption of leisure such as the increased popularity of gaming consoles with young people over playing traditional sports.

Stakeholder and customer needs analysis

Before an analysis of the environment is complete, an assessment of the organization's stakeholders and customers is essential. Stakeholders are all the people and groups that have an interest in an organization, including its employees, players, members, league or affiliated governing body, government, community, facility-owners, sponsors, broadcasters and fans. The constant question that a sport manager has to answer is concerned with whom they are trying to make happy. Either deliberately or inadvertently serving the interests of some stakeholders in preference to others has serious implications for the setting of strategic direction and the distribution of limited resources. For example, some professional sport clubs tend to focus on winning to the exclusion of all other priorities, including sensible financial management. While this may make members and fans happy in the short term, it does not reflect the interests of governing bodies, leagues and employees, for whom a sustainable enterprise is fundamental.

Sponsors and government sport funding departments are prepared to withdraw funding if their needs are not met. A careful analysis of the intentions and objectives of each stakeholder in their affiliation with the sport organization must therefore be completed before a strategic direction can be set. The substance of strategy is influenced by the beliefs, values and expectations of the most powerful stakeholders.

Competitor analysis

Opportunities and threats can encompass anything in the external environment, including the presence and activities of competitors. Because the actions of competitors can greatly affect the success of a strategic approach, *competitor analysis* is used to ensure that an investigation is done systematically.

There are many forms of competitor analysis and they can range in detail considerably. However, most competitor analyses consider the dimensions as summarized in Table 5.1. For each competitor, these eight dimensions should be considered. Time and care should be taken in assessing competitors' strategies, their strengths, vulnerabilities and resources, as well as their next likely actions.

Table 5.1	Competitor Analysis Dimensions
Dimension	**Description**
Geographic scope	Location and overlap
Vision and intent	Ranges from survival to attempts at dominance
Objective	Short- to medium-term intentions
Market share and position	From small player to virtual monopolist
Strategy	Methods of gaining a competitive advantage
Resources	Volume and availability
Target market	To whom the products and services are directed
Marketing approach	The products, services and the promotions, pricing and distribution behind them

Five forces analysis

An extension of the competitive environment analysis is the *five forces analysis,* which was developed by Michael Porter. It is the most commonly used tool for describing the competitive environment. The technique does this by focusing upon five competitive forces (Porter, 1980) (Figure 5.2).

The threat of new entrants

Every organization is faced with the possibility that new competitors could enter their industry at any time. In some forms of professional sport, this is unlikely as the barriers preventing entry are very high. For example, it would be extremely difficult for a private independent league to enter the market against any of the professional football leagues in Europe. On the other hand,

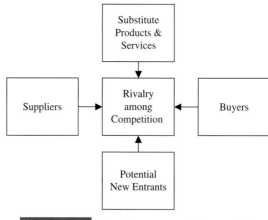

FIGURE 5.2 *Five forces competitive analysis.*

new sport facilities, events, sport apparel companies and new equipment manufacturers are regular entrants in the sport industry.

The bargaining power of buyers

Buyers are those individuals, groups and companies that purchase the products and services that sport organizations offer. The nature of the competitive environment is affected by the strength or what is known as bargaining power of buyers. For example, most football fans in the UK hold little power if the price of football tickets is any indication. When there is buying power, prices are lower. Despite some extravagant sums paid by broadcasters for the media rights of certain sports, the bargaining power of media buyers should be relatively strong. For most sport organizations, however, the chief buyers – fans – do not work together to leverage their power and therefore the bargaining power of buyers is limited.

The bargaining power of suppliers

When suppliers of raw materials essential to sporting organizations threaten to raise prices or withdraw their products or services, they are attempting to improve their bargaining power. This may come from suppliers of the materials necessary in the building of a new facility or from sporting equipment suppliers. The most important supplier issue in sport has come about with the unionization of professional players in an attempt to increase their salaries and the salary caps of clubs. Where player groups have been well organized, their bargaining power has proven significant. A potential strike in 2002 by players in Major League Baseball in the USA was avoided, but the failure to resolve a similar dispute led to the cancellation of the 2004–05 season of the National Hockey League in the USA.

The threat of substitute products and services

Increasingly, the traditional sport industry sectors are expanding and it is more common for different sports to compete against each other. When this threat is high a sport organization is faced with the problem of being out-competed by other kinds of sports, or worse, by other forms of leisure activity.

The intensity of rivalry among competitors in an industry

The more sport organizations offering virtually identical products and services, the higher the intensity of rivalry. For example, in the sport shoe marketplace, the rivalry between Nike and Adidas is extremely intense. Rivalry is more ambiguous between sport clubs in the same league that share a general geographical region. London football clubs, Melbourne Australian football clubs and colleges in the same state in the USA, are examples. In these cases, it is unlikely that one club would be able to 'steal' supporters from another local club. Nor is the alumnus of one college likely to start attending home games of another college team. However, these clubs do intensely compete for media exposure, corporate sponsorship, players, coaches, managers and management staff. Of course, they also compete with the most intense rivalry imaginable for the championship.

STAGE 2: STRATEGIC DIRECTION

Once the strategic analysis has been completed, the strategic direction can be set. There are four conventional tools that are used to clarify and document this direction:

1. mission statement
2. vision statement
3. organizational objectives
4. performance measures.

Mission statements

A *mission statement* identifies the purpose of an organization. While it may seem strange to need to put this in writing, such a statement is important because it reduces the risk of strategic confusion. For example, it is not uncommon for players, members, spectators, staff, coaches, media, sponsors and government representatives to hold different interpretations of the purpose of a sport organization. The mission statement should define why an organization was set up, what services and products it provides and for whom it provides them. When reduced to a single statement, this mission is a powerful statement of intention and responsibility. It usually does not exceed one paragraph.

Vision statements

It goes without saying that behind the idea of setting a strategic direction is the need to be visionary: to look into the future and form a clear mental image of what an organization could be like. Thinking in this manner means being able to interpret the information collected during the analysis stage and find the opportunities they present. A *vision statement* is the culmination of this kind of thinking. It is a statement that declares the medium to long-range ambitions of an organization. The statement is an expression of what the organization wants to have achieved within a period of around three to five years. The statement is normally no longer than a sentence.

Organizational objectives

Given that the vision statement is a reflection of the medium- to long-term ambitions of an organization, *organizational objectives* serve as markers on the way to this destination. Objectives reflect the achievements that must be made in order to realize the vision. For example, if a club is situated at the bottom of the championship ladder, their vision might be to finish in the top three. However, achieving this vision inside a single season is unrealistic, so an objective might be set to indicate the ambition to improve by three places by next season, as a progression toward the overarching vision. Objectives are normally set in each of the major operational areas of an organization, such as on-field performance, youth development, finances, facilities, marketing and human resources. However, it is essential that objectives are measurable.

Performance measures

Key Performance Indicators (KPIs) are used in combination with organizational objectives in order to establish success or failure. KPIs are therefore inseparable from objectives and should be created at the same time. Each time a performance measure is used, care should be taken to ensure that it can indeed be measured in a concrete way. For example, a marketing objective of 'improving the public image' of an organization is meaningless unless it is accompanied by something that is quantifiable. It is worth noting that measures do not have to focus exclusively on outputs like volumes, rankings and trophies. They can also be used to measure efficiency; that is, doing the same with less or doing more with the same.

STAGE 3: STRATEGY FORMULATION

Strategic analysis reveals the competitive position of a sport organization and setting the strategic direction plots a course for the future. The next question is how to get there. In the strategy formulation stage of the strategic management process, the sport manager and his or her team are charged with the task of positioning their organization in the competitive environment. This necessitates a combination of imagination and scenario thinking. In other words, they must consider the implications of each potential strategic approach. To help matters, however, from a strategic positioning viewpoint there are a finite number of strategies available to the sport manager. These are called *generic competitive strategies*.

In Practice 5.2 Sport as Strategy and Dubai Sports City

At the heart of strategic thinking is the ability to think creatively, outside of conventions and the limitations of previous ways of doing things. Dubai Sports City reflects this kind of bold innovation, where strategy is not just about a new sport product or a new venue, but rather is an entirely different way of thinking about the way sport can be delivered and experienced.

Dubai Sports City is intended to be the world's first purpose built sport city, located in the cosmopolitan centre of the United Arab Emirates. The development encompasses 50 million square feet of land which, when completed, will feature four world class sporting venues: a 60 000 seat multipurpose outdoor stadium, a 25 000 capacity cricket stadium, a 10 000 seat multipurpose indoor arena and a field hockey ground for 5000 spectators. In addition, an Ernie Ells designed 18-hole golf course will provide a luxury facility and clubhouse for locals and tourists to enjoy. The city will also house sporting academies, exclusive residential homes, cultural exhibits and shopping precincts. Some of the most prominent include the first purpose-designed Manchester United Soccer School, an International Cricket Council endorsed Global Cricket Academy, a David Lloyd Tennis Academy and a Butch Harmon School of Golf. The academies zones will house a 3000 square metre gymnasium and Olympic swimming pool. The plans for the Dubai Sports City, unveiled in early 2008, revealed substantial urban and hospitality developments including commercial offices, particularly for those connected to the management of international governing bodies of sport, schools, medical facilities, hotels, country clubs, restaurants, as well as numerous shopping plazas and boutiques. The initial construction phase is scheduled for completion in 2010 and will include the golf course, academies and some residential properties.

The overarching strategy behind Dubai Sports City revolves around an attempt to capture a share of the US$50 billion global sports business market, with a heavy emphasis on major events that will attract a proportion of an estimated two billion spectators who live within a four-hour flight of Dubai. Accordingly, the complex is aiming to attract one major event each year in one of six sports: football, rugby, cricket, hockey, golf and tennis. In conjunction with a year round calendar of smaller events, Dubai Sports City is hoping to create a regional hub of sporting activity in the Middle East. Given the vast network of facilities, the strategy also predicts that the area will attract music concerts, festivals and entertainment events, and public gatherings.

With an investment requirement of at least US$4 billion, the success of Dubai Sports City represents a significant gamble, but also one with abundant commercial upside. The world's first city dedicated to sport and built from scratch represents perhaps the most ambitious sport development strategy ever undertaken. In this case, sport is the vehicle for a novel participation, education or entertainment experience.

Generic competitive strategies

Porter (1985) contended that there are only three fundamental or generic strategies that can be applied in any organization, irrespective of their industry, products and services, environmental circumstance and resources. Generic competitive strategies answer the most basic of questions facing a sport manager in forming a strategic choice: What is going to be our source of *competitive advantage*? To put it another way, every sport organization must take a position somewhere in the marketplace. The challenge is to find a position that is both opportune *and* advantageous. As a result, some sport organizations try to out-compete their adversaries because they can provide their products and services cheaper; others compete on the basis of a unique product or service that is hard for others to replicate; others still attempt to position themselves as the exclusive supplier to a small but loyal niche in the marketplace. These three strategic positions are described below.

Cost leadership

To become a cost leader by supplying products and services at the lowest possible cost to as many customers as possible. The logic of this strategic approach is driven by volume and market share where more sales than any other competitors lead to greater profitability. Essential to this generic competitive strategy is efficiency and the ability to keep costs to a minimum. While this approach is common in consumer products like shampoo, it is less common in sport. However, some equipment and sport apparel manufacturers do provide their products at the cheap end of the market in the hope that they can significantly outsell their more expensive competitors. Similarly, many leisure facilities try to attract customers on the basis of their lower prices.

Differentiation

To provide a differentiated set of products and services that is difficult for competitors to replicate. The logic of this strategic approach is underpinned by an assumption that consumers will place a high value on products and service that are unique. Typically, this approach is supported by an attempt to build a strong brand image, incorporate regular innovations and new features, as well as responsive customer service. Many sport organizations are thrown into this position almost by default because of the nature of their offerings. A tennis club, for example, offers a range of services that are by definition differentiated, at least when compared to other sports or leisure activities. However, when two tennis clubs compete in a similar area, it may become necessary for one to take a new strategic position. One option is to further differentiate their services, perhaps by offering something new or innovative like a creche for mid-week players or a gym for conditioning the more seriously competitive players.

Focus

To provide a set of products and services to a niche in the market with the intention of dominating market share. The logic guiding this strategic approach is that being dominant in a small section of a larger market is a way for an organization to have early success, without having to compete with much larger and better resourced organizations. To succeed with this strategic approach it is necessary to choose the market segment very carefully, aware that the products and services provided must fill particular needs for customers. Many sport organizations take this approach as well. Examples include specialist sport equipment and less mainstream sport clubs and associations like rock climbing and table tennis.

The key to making a decision between these alternatives returns to the analysis and direction stages of the strategic management process. A strategy-savvy sport manager is always looking for a way to position the organization in a cluttered market. Part of the choice is in determining what the sport organization is likely to be able to do better than others – their competitive advantage (like keeping costs low or delivering great customer service). The other part is in finding the opportunity in the environment that is worth exploring. Where there is a match between these factors consistent with strategic direction, strategic formulation is born. It is worth remembering that the worst place to be is 'stuck in the middle' between strategies, but that combining strategic options can be advantageous if managed effectively.

STAGE 4: STRATEGY IMPLEMENTATION

Strategy implementation represents the introduction of the organization's choice of competitive strategy. For example, if a differentiation strategy has been selected, the implementation stage considers how it can be brought about across the organization's products, services and activities. There is an important distinction to be made here between the strategic level of decision-making and the implementation level. To return to the military analogy, strategy is concerned with how a whole army is deployed. At the implementation level, tactical and operational decisions are made as well. These are like the choices of what each battalion, unit or platoon does. Always the overarching goal is a reflection of the army's objectives, but each smaller part of the army works towards smaller achievements that will eventually bring about success in the battle.

Once decisions have been finalized concerning the strategy that will be employed to achieve organizational objectives, the task of converting them into action begins. This means that representatives from each major area or department of the organization must become involved in deciding how they can contribute toward the generic strategy. For example, if one objective in a club is concerned with on-field performance, it is likely that the leaders of the developmental programmes will play a role in planning. Equally, an objective associated with financial performance will require marketing staff responsible for sponsorship to become involved. As a result, the strategy implementation process should permeate the organization including junior development, community liaison, coaching, facilities, governance, marketing, finance and human resources, for example. In each of these areas a plan should be developed that illustrates the set of activities that will be performed at the tactical and operational levels to support the generic strategy. Like objectives, each of these actions requires a measure or KPI of some sort. Often the implementation process also requires changes to resource allocation, organizational structure, systems for delivering products and services, organizational culture and leadership. These areas are considered in subsequent chapters.

In Practice 5.3 Strategic Planning and the Special Olympics

The Special Olympics is the world's largest sports movement for people with intellectual disabilities. The organization provides year-round training and competition for athletes with intellectual disabilities via more than 200 programmes in over 180 countries. The following is a summary of their strategic plan from 2006 to 2010.

Mission

To provide year-round sports training and athletic competition in a variety of Olympic-type sports for children and adults with intellectual disabilities, giving them continuing opportunities to develop physical fitness, demonstrate courage, experience joy and participate in a sharing of gifts, skills and friendship with their families, other Special Olympics athletes and the community.

Vision

The Special Olympics is an unprecedented global movement which, through quality sports training and competition, improves the lives of people with intellectual disabilities and, in turn, the lives of everyone they touch. Their strategic plan is outlined in Table 5.2.

Table 5.2 Special Olympics Strategies	
Strategic Goals	**Performance Indicators**
Goal 1: Build a movement wide, diversified and sustainable revenue stream of US $300 million per year by 2010	• Increased funding across the movement Clear and accurate view of revenues by source from all levels of the movement Funding model that promotes raising money for the whole movement Significant shift in resources that are raised for or directed to the local levels Consolidated view and understanding of all donor relationships Efficient cost of fundraising
Goal 2: Expand and engage key audiences with a compelling message to inspire new levels of support and change global attitudes toward people with intellectual disabilities	• Renewed global recognition of the Special Olympics brand Greater perception of Special Olympics as important and essential for people with intellectual disabilities Measurable attitude change toward people with intellectual disabilities Increased involvement of new audiences Advancement of financial resource development goals
Goal 3: Enhance the quality of the local athlete experience, recognizing individual motivations and aspirations for sport performance	• Measurable increases in frequency of training and competitions at the local level Improvement in the athlete-to-participant ratio (as defined in annual athlete participation results) Adoption of minimum training and competition standards by sport Implementation of athlete satisfaction measurements An evaluated pilot of a sport performance programme that enables athletes to achieve their maximum potential
Goal 4: Become a unified and integrated global movement with a common focus on the interests of our core constituents – athletes, families, volunteers and donors Goal 5: Grow to at least 3 million athletes	

STAGE 5: STRATEGIC EVALUATION

One of the more difficult aspects of strategic management is the control or evaluation of what has been done. In sport there are numerous issues that make this process more complicated including the obvious one that on-field performance can have a tendency to overwhelm the other elements of strategy. Chapter 13, Performance Management, considers these important issues in detail.

The *strategic evaluation* stage requires an assessment of two related aspects of the strategy. First, the KPIs associated with each organizational objective need to be compared with actual results and, second, the success of the implementation actions needs to be ascertained.

SUMMARY

This chapter is concerned with the process of strategic management. This process is founded on the principle that opportunity is discovered by analysis rather than luck. Strategic management, we have argued, is therefore at the heart of the success of a sport organization.

Five stages in the strategic management process have been identified. The first stage is strategy analysis, which demands the assessment of both internal organizational capacities as well as external environmental conditions. The second stage is strategy direction, which sets the vision and objectives of an organization. The third stage is strategy formulation, where a definitive strategic position is selected for an organization. The fourth stage is strategy implementation, where the strategy is directed to action across organizational areas. The final stage, strategy evaluation, involves the control and measurement of the process so that improvements can be made.

Strategic management in sport organizations requires preparation, research and analysis, imagination, decision-making and critical thinking. It demands an equal balance of systematization and innovation. This chapter is weighted heavily toward the system side, but that is simply a necessity to convey the principles and techniques of strategic management. It is up to the reader to provide the imagination in their own strategic management activities.

REVIEW QUESTIONS

1. Why is strategic management important in the turbulent world of sport?

2. What is the basic principle that underpins strategic management?

3. Name the five stages of strategic management.

4. What is the relationship between a SWOT analysis and competitor analysis?

5. How do stakeholders influence the setting of strategic direction?

6. Explain the differences between the three generic strategies.

7. What is the relationship between KPIs and strategy evaluation?

8. Select a sport organization that has a strategic plan on its website. Conduct an analysis of this plan and comment on its approach to each of the five steps of strategic management explained in this chapter.

9. Select a sport organization that you know well and that does not have a strategic plan available. Based on your background knowledge, make point form comments under the headings of the five steps in strategic management to illustrate your approach to forming a plan.

FURTHER READING

Chappelet, J.L. and Bayle, E. (2005). *Strategic and performance management of Olympic sport organizations*. Human Kinetics Publishers, Inc, Champaign.

Foster, G., Greyser, A. and Walsh, B. (2006). *The business of sports: text and cases on strategy and management*. Thompson South-Western, Mason.

Parent, M., O'Brien, D. and Slack, T. (2003). Strategic management in the context of sport. In L. Trenberth (ed.), *Managing the business of sport*. Dunmore Press, Palmerston North, pp. 101–122.

RELEVANT WEBSITES

The following websites are useful starting points for further information on sport strategic management:

Australian Sports Commission: http://www.ausport.gov.au

Sport Canada: http://www.pch.gc.ca/progs/sc/index_e.cfm

Sport England: http://www.sportengland.org

Case Study: The Indian Premier League: Bollywood and Business Models

Bollywood came to cricket on the 18th April 2008 when the Indian Premier League (IPL), or more precisely, the DLF Indian Premier League, was launched by the Board of Control for Cricket in India (BCCI) in the format of a Twenty20 competition. The IPL is this generation's version of World Series Cricket; an attempt to take a new and exciting form of cricket to a global audience with a touch of Bollywood, an immense amount of money, astonishing media coverage and a franchise business model duplicating European football. While the strategy behind the IPL is driven by commercial opportunity, its success is contingent upon engaging traditional cricket fans in a new form of the game that is conducted in a frenzy of activity and is all over within three hours. In the world of commercial broadcasting, sport content can be remarkably lucrative. As a result, the IPL has generated enormous medium-term financial commitments from broadcasters, sponsors and team owners in the hopes that this version of the game will capture the imagination of cricket fans eager to see the world's biggest stars in action. Like all bold strategies, the stakes are high. Sport fans can be fickle and the playing stars are not free agents as long as they also want to maintain their domestic and national playing contracts.

The IPL competition is composed of eight teams, each one a franchise representing a city in India. Collectively, the eight franchises were sold for US$700m and were purchased by actors, business entrepreneurs and broadcasters. Most of the world's top cricket playing talent were involved, including the stars of Australia, Sri Lanka, South Africa, New Zealand, the West Indies, Pakistan and, of course, India. The only conspicuous absences were players from England due to a clash with their summer county season. Structured as a tournament, the IPL involved 59 matches in total, concluding in a final on June 1, 2008, with the winning team, the Rajasthan Royals led by Australia's Shane Warne, walking away with US$1.2 million and a gold trophy laden with diamonds, sapphires and rubies.

The IPL model duplicates the UEFA Champions League of European football where the winner and runner-up qualify to play in the Champions League scheduled for October 2008 involving the winners and runners-up of domestic Twenty20 competitions in Australia, South Africa and England, to comprise an eight-team Champions League. The winner of this final competition will receive US$5m.

Strategically, the IPL represents the first serious attempt to globalize cricket in a format that is conducive to media packaging through free to air, pay television, Internet and mobile content. The three-hour Twenty20 format is highly appealing to broadcasters unlike the traditional five-day version of test cricket. Television rights have been sold all around the world including the USA, the Middle East and China as well as in the traditional cricket regions. The amount of money involved is staggering. Television rights for the IPL were sold for US$908m despite the likelihood that the owner, WSG/Sony Entertainment Television, will probably not return a profit on its investment for up to five more years. WSG has committed US$350m for the first five years and around US$550 for another five years. Although risky from a broadcasting perspective, the IPL also represents a tremendous opportunity to reach diverse international markets and to on-sell content in a variety of mobile formats that have really only recently become practical in terms of technological development and cost.

The franchise owners made significant investment commitments without a clear return guaranteed. Each team cost between US$7.5m and US$11m and required almost the same again to build the team infrastructure and secure players. There is also a substantial annual licence fee to pay to the BCCI. On the other side of the ledger, the eight teams share about US$70m (around US$5.5m each) as well as a split of the title sponsorship deal. Add to this

Continued

the revenues from gate receipts and team-specific sponsorships, all of which might amount to around US$4m. Thus, the IPL business model allows each franchise to share media and sponsor revenues but keep gate-receipts and in-venue advertising. Franchises can even be listed on the stock exchange and trade shares as public companies. They can also earn revenue from merchandising, licensing and corporate hospitality, which while initially underdeveloped, are also highly promising. The risk for each franchise is a potential loss of around US$5m a year, but with the upside that most financial projections have estimated that the franchises will recover their investments within three to four years. By then it will be clear whether the IPL will be sustainable with sufficient traction in the international marketplace.

Perhaps the most revealing figure is the IPL's marketing budget of US$108m. Part of the business model involved a player auction where each franchise bid for the best players. Notably, the Chennai franchise paid US$1.5m for India's Mahendra Singh Dhoni, while the Hyderbad franchise paid US$1.3m for Australia's Andrew Symons. Franchises spent a minimum of US$3.3m and a maximum of US$5m per year for players over a three-year contract. The IPL bidding process was a brilliant piece of marketing and attracted enormous media publicity. Some of the IPL marketing has met with mixed responses, however. For example, the NFL's Washington Redskin's cheerleaders were not universally appreciated, although the involvement of Bollywood stars during games was highly successful for local audiences.

The key to understanding the IPL strategy is to appreciate the economic background that allowed it to come about. India's government introduced its first major wave of economic liberalism in the mid-1990s. One of the key moves was the de-regulation of the state-owned telecom monopoly, which suddenly allowed private companies to bid for the rights to deliver specific telecommunication services. As it turned out, telecommunications for the vast Indian marketplace proved lucrative, expanding into broadcasting and entertainment. The limitation with all telecommunications, however, is content. It is this fact which has underwritten the IPL's business model. The BCCI as the owner of the IPL, has effectively duplicated the Indian government's success with commercial de-regulation. Selling off their content in the form of broadcasting rights and franchises, the BCCI has secured nearly US$1.8b. In addition, they have revenues from commissions on the player auctions and sponsorship rights, although two-thirds of the television rights and sponsorship fees are to be shared with the franchisees.

It is clear that the IPL has appropriated dimensions of the strategic models of both European football and professional sport in the USA. The combination has yielded a brand and business model designed for the contemporary sporting environment: media savvy, broadcasting-driven, global, exciting, superstar-oriented, commercial, franchised and new. As a strategic initiative, it is the ideal match of market opportunity and product capability.

As a global, commercial entity, the IPL has a favourable mix of potential global audiences, international talent and a television-friendly playing format packed with entertainment and action. The business model is its most powerful asset, commanding the attention of corporate sponsors and broadcasters. The gambles are mainly associated with a number of key uncertainties. For example, playing talent could be unavailable, there could be clashes with national cricket boards fearful of damage to their traditional test commitments, the probability of escalating player salaries, the extended length of the competition and even the possibility of match-fixing. Success for the IPL is therefore far from assured. There are some significant problems that the IPL must face, especially likely collisions with the International Cricket Council (ICC) and national cricket boards concerned about losing their players during the respective traditional seasons. In the opening IPL season, some players were unavailable to play the whole or part of the IPL season due to clashes with the Australian, West Indian, New Zealand and England national team calendars. Inevitably, the IPL will lead some prominent cricketers to reconsider their playing priorities in the same way that World Series Cricket forced changes in player loyalties. In the end, the outcome could be similar to that seen in European football, where the powerhouse clubs become more influential over players' movements than national teams.

Case Study Questions:

1. Consider the IPL's business model and discuss the strategy that underpins it.

2. Consider the nature of the marketplace in which the IPL is competing. Is there enough room on the competitive sporting map for another team allegiance for fans and another major sporting league?

3. Consider the product itself and how it matches the opportunities in the marketplace for short, fast-paced, television-friendly sport. Purely on the basis of the product, do you think that the league will prosper?

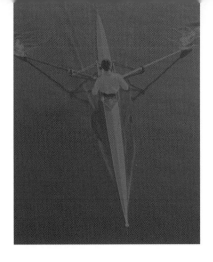

CHAPTER 6

Organizational Structure

OVERVIEW

Organizational structure is a phenomenon that has spawned a large number of textbooks and research articles designed to explain the finer points of organizational structure, as well as its impact on organizational performance, employee behaviour, culture and the drivers of change in relation to organizational structure. Rather than replicate some already excellent existing material on this topic, this chapter highlights the unique aspects of the structure of sports organizations. Consequently, this chapter reviews the key concepts of organizational structure, provides examples of the unique features of sport organization structures and summarizes the key research findings on the structure of sport organizations. The chapter also provides a summary of principles for managing organizational structures within community, state, national and professional sport organizations.

After completing this chapter the reader should be able to:

- Describe the key dimensions of organizational structure
- Understand the unique features of the structure of sport organizations
- Understand the various models of organization structure that can be used for sports organizations
- Identify the factors that influence the structure of sport organizations
- Understand some of the challenges facing managers and volunteers involved in managing the structure of sport organizations.

WHAT IS ORGANIZATIONAL STRUCTURE?

An organizational structure is the framework that outlines how tasks are divided, grouped and coordinated within an organization (Robbins et al.,

2004b). Every sport organization has a structure that outlines the tasks to be performed by individuals and teams. Finding the right structure for an organization involves juggling requirements to formalize procedures while fostering innovation and creativity. The 'right' structure means one in which owners and managers can exert adequate control over employee activities without unduly affecting people's motivation and attitudes to work. It also provides clear reporting and communication lines while trying to reduce unnecessary and costly layers of management.

An organization's structure is important because it defines where staff and volunteers 'fit in' with each other in terms of work tasks, decision-making procedures, the need for collaboration, levels of responsibility and reporting mechanisms. In other words, the structure of an organization provides a roadmap for how positions within an organization are related and what tasks are performed by individuals and work teams within an organization.

DIMENSIONS OF ORGANIZATIONAL STRUCTURE

When designing any organization's structure, managers need to consider six elements: work specialization, departmentalization, chain of command, span of control, centralization and formalization (Robbins et al., 2004b). Netball Victoria (NV), the State Sporting Organization responsible for the management and development of netball across Victoria, one of the major states of Australia, uses a typical non-profit sport organizational structure. Netball is the largest female participation sport in Australia and has more than 110 000 registered participants in Victoria. NV provides a range of programmes and services for netball players, coaches, umpires, administrators, associations and clubs with the aim of increasing and enhancing participation experiences. In addition to facilitating participation opportunities, NV holds the licence for the Melbourne Vixens, the Victorian team that competes in the trans-national netball competition, the ANZ Championships. NV is responsible for the management and marketing of the team and staging the ANZ Championship games in liaison with Netball Australia.

More than 250 associations or groups affiliate with Netball Victoria, which provides access to netball events, programmes and services as well as a pathway to State, National and International representation. These associations are geographically grouped into one of twenty-one (21) regions and then regions are grouped into one of six (6) zones. A team of 30 staff works with a board of management and an extensive network of volunteers to deliver these programmes, services and events across Victoria. The organizational structure for the state office staff developed by NV to enable this to happen is based around the key functional departments of marketing, development, association services, high performance and finances and administration. The structure allows individuals to be appointed to carry out specialized tasks and for the establishment of clear communication between the lower levels of the organization and the Chief Executive (Figure 6.1). The six dimensions of organizational structure help us understand why an organization such as NV is structured a certain way.

Work specialization

Creating roles for individuals that enable them to specialize in performing a limited number of tasks is known as work specialization. This concept can easily be applied in organizations that manufacture things such as sporting goods, or need to process a large volume of resources such as distributing uniforms and information to volunteers for a large sporting event. The advantage of breaking jobs down to a set of routine repetitive tasks is an increase in employee productivity and reduced costs through the use of a lower skilled labour force. This advantage must be balanced against the risks of making work too boring or stressful for individuals which can lead to accidents, poor quality, lower productivity, absenteeism and high job turnover.

The majority of sports organizations employ small numbers of staff who are often required to perform a diverse range of tasks over a day, week or year. In these cases, the structure of the organization will require a low level of work specialization. For example, a sport development officer within a state or provincial sporting organization would be involved in activities such as

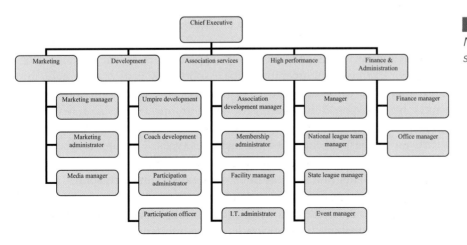

FIGURE 6.1

Netball Victoria structure.

conducting skills clinics with junior athletes, designing coach education courses, managing a database of casual staff or representing the organization to sponsors or funding agencies over the course of a season. These roles require very different skill sets and in such an organization the structure would benefit from a low level of work specialization.

Departmentalization

Departmentalization is the bringing together of individuals into groups so that common or related tasks can be coordinated. In essence, people are assigned to departments in order to achieve organizational goals. Organizations can departmentalize on the basis of functions, products or services, processes, geography or customer type.

The most common form of departmentalizing is based on assigning people or positions to various departments according to the function a person may perform. For example, a state or provincial sporting organization might group their staff according to athlete development, competition management, special events and corporate affairs departments, with each department having a very specific function to perform.

Alternatively, a sport organization that manufactures cricket equipment may group their staff according to the product line they produce, with groups of people handling the manufacturing, sales and service for cricket apparel, cricket bats and training aids. In this case, the functions of marketing, human resource management, financial management and production are all replicated in each department. These criteria can also be applied to service-based sport organizations. For example, an athlete management firm may offer a range of services under financial planning, career development, life skills and public relations training. Again, each department would manage their own marketing, human resource management and financial management systems.

Sport organizations can also design departments on the basis of geography. For example, the operations for a sports law firm may be split into departments for capital city offices or regions. Each of the offices or regions would have responsibility in regard to their operations in a designated geographical region. Finally, sport organizations can arrange their departments on the basis of their various customer types. This approach could be used by an organization like the Australian Institute of Sport, which might create departments that support individual athletes or team sports.

It is important to note that organizations may choose to use more than one criterion to devise departments and their choice will depend on organizational size, capabilities and operational requirements.

Chain of command

The chain of command is the reporting trail that exists between the upper and lower levels of an organization. In essence, it is the line of authority that connects each position within an organization to the Chief Executive. It encompasses the notions of establishing clear authority and responsibility for each position within the organization. Authority refers to the rights managers have to give orders to other members in the organization and the expectation that the orders will be carried out. If managers at certain levels of an organization are provided with the authority to get things done, they are also assigned a corresponding level of responsibility. Having a single person to whom an employee is responsible is known as the unity of command. Having a single 'boss' avoids employees having to deal with potential conflict when juggling the demands of two or more managers and it helps achieve clear decision-making.

Robbins et al. (2004b) argue that the basic tenets of the chain of command are less relevant today due to the increase in the use of information technology and the corresponding ease with which most employees can communicate with each other at all levels of the organization and access information that was previously restricted to top level managers. Nevertheless, managers of sports organizations should be cognizant of the basic principle of the chain of command when designing their organizational structure.

Span of control

Span of control refers to the number of staff which any manager can directly supervise without becoming inefficient or ineffective. The exact number which any manager can effectively control is determined by the level of expertise or experience of the staff – the logic being that more experienced and skilled staff require less supervision. The complexity of tasks, the location of staff, the reporting mechanisms in place, the degree to which tasks are standardized, the style of managers and the culture of an organization also play a role in determining what the ideal span of control might be for an individual manager in an organization. The span of control impacts on how many levels of management are required in any given organization. The wider the span of control, the more employees can be supervised by one manager which leads to lower management costs. However, this reduced cost is a trade-off with effectiveness, as this single manager must devote more of his or her time to liaison and communication with a large number of staff.

The trend over the past 10 years has been for organizations to introduce wider spans of control and a subsequent flattening of organizational structures. This must be done in conjunction with the provision of more employee training, a commitment to building strong work cultures and assistance to ensure staff are more self-sufficient in their roles.

Centralization and decentralization

Centralization refers to the degree to which decision-making is located at the top of an organization. An organization is deemed to be highly centralized when the majority of decisions are made by senior managers with little input from employees at lower levels. Alternatively, an organization is decentralized when decisions are able to be made by employees and lower level managers who have been empowered to do so. It is important to understand that the concepts of centralization and decentralization are relative, in the sense that an organization is never exclusively one or the other. Organizations could not function if all decisions were made by a small group of top managers or if all decisions were delegated to lower level staff.

Non-profit sport organizations tend to be more centralized than decentralized due to the influence of their traditional structures. Decision-making is often concentrated at the board level, where volunteers make decisions related to strategy for paid staff to implement at an operational level. This can lead to problems (see Chapter 12) of slow decision-making or politics. On the other hand, the nature of non-profit sport organizations that are often made up of disparate groups and spread over a wide geographical area, requires local level decision-making for clubs, events and sporting competitions to operate effectively.

Formalization

Formalization refers to the extent jobs are standardized and the degree to which employee behaviour is guided by rules and procedures. These rules and procedures might cover selection of new staff, training, general policies on how work is done, procedures for routine tasks and the amount of detail that is provided in job descriptions. Formalizing an organization increases the control managers have over staff and the amount of decision-making discretion individual staff may have. An organization such as a local sport club may have very few procedures or rules for how things are done, but the tribunal for a professional sports league will have a very detailed set of procedures and policies in regard to how cases are reported, heard and prosecuted.

In Practice 6.1 Surf Life Saving Australia

Surf Life Saving Australia (SLSA) is a highly federated and geographically dispersed organization. It encompasses several organizational layers, including 305 local surf life saving clubs, 17 regional branches in NSW and Queensland and seven state and territory centres. These state and territory centres are the 'owners' of SLSA.

The peak policy and decision-making body for surf life saving in Australia is the SLSA Australian Council (AC), made up of the national President, the seven Presidents of each state and the Northern Territory, the directors of SLSA's three operational areas – Lifesaving, Surf Sports and Development, and SLSA's CEO. The AC delegates the management of SLSA to the Board of Management (BOM), made up of the CEOs (or General Managers) of each State and the Northern Territory, the CEO of SLSA and four senior managers.

By joining SLSA, an individual also joins a surf life saving club, which in turn, is affiliated with its state centre. Membership of SLSA provides access to comprehensive, nationally-accredited, surf life saving training, the option to compete in surf carnivals at local, branch, state, national and international levels, as well as protection through insurance and other policies. SLSA operates a number of subsidiary companies to provide helicopter rescue services in NSW, with the services in Queensland, Victoria and South Australia being operated by their state centres.

SLSA is a foundation member of the International Life saving Federation (ILS), through which it maintains contacts with other 'life saving nations' and develops life saving expertise around the globe, as part of SLSA's broader international humanitarian efforts as a non-government organization (NGO). As one of the more diverse organizations, with a significant sporting profile through its televised events, SLSA operates within a complex organizational structure. This structure has evolved through a mixture of good planning and historical precedents and is a good example of how complicated organizations can be in the sport industry.

Sources: Surf Life Saving Australia website at http://www.slsa.com.au

STRUCTURAL MODELS

The types of structure adopted by sports organizations can be categorized into four common types: the simple structure, the bureaucracy, the matrix structure and the team structure. Let's examine each of these briefly and explore their relevance for sport organizations.

The *simple structure* has a low degree of departmentalization and formalization, wide spans of control and would most likely have decisions centralized to few people. Such a structure would be used by a small sporting goods retail store that might have 10 casual and full-time staff and an owner/manager. There would be no need for departments, as most decisions and administrative tasks would be performed by the owner/manager and all other staff on the sales floor. The majority of procedures would be executed according to a simple set of rules and the owner/manager would have all staff reporting directly to him or her (Figure 6.2). The advantages of the structure in this case are obvious: decisions can be made quickly, it ensures a flexible workforce to cater for seasonal needs and busy periods and accountability clearly rests with the owner/manager.

If the owner/manager wanted to expand the operation and open other stores in other locations, he or she would require a different structure to cope with the added demands of controlling staff in multiple locations, making decisions across a wider number of operational areas and ensuring quality products and services are provided in each store or location. The owner/manager might consider adopting a *bureaucratic structure* (Figure 6.3).

The bureaucratic structure attempts to standardize the operation of an organization in order to maximize coordination and control of staff and activities. It relies on high levels of formalization, the use of departments to group people into discrete work teams that deal with specific functions or tasks, highly centralized decision-making and a clear chain of command. An organization such as Sport England, the Australian Sports Commission, or a state or provincial government department of sport would be structured along these lines. Obviously, as an organization expands in size, increases the number of locations it delivers services, or diversifies its range of activities, the more likely it is to reflect some elements of bureaucratization.

The *matrix organization structure* (Figure 6.4) reflects the organization of groups of people into departments according to functions and products. For example, an elite institute for sport might group specialists such as sports psychologists, biomechanists, skill acquisition coaches and exercise physiologists into discrete teams. At the same time, individuals in these teams might be involved in providing services to a range of different sporting groups

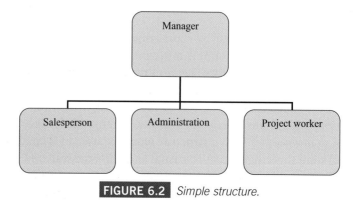

FIGURE 6.2 *Simple structure.*

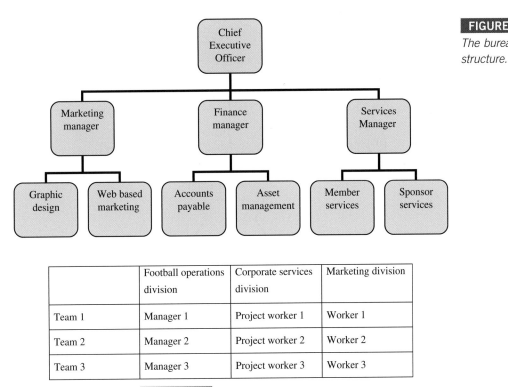

FIGURE 6.3

The bureaucratic structure.

	Football operations division	Corporate services division	Marketing division
Team 1	Manager 1	Project worker 1	Worker 1
Team 2	Manager 2	Project worker 2	Worker 2
Team 3	Manager 3	Project worker 3	Worker 3

FIGURE 6.4 *The matrix structure.*

or athletes, effectively creating two bosses for them. This breaks the unity of command principle, but allows an organization to group specialists together to maximize sharing of expertise while facilitating their involvement in a number of projects or service delivery areas. The argument for this arrangement is that it is better to have the specialists work as a team than to appoint individuals to work in isolation to provide their services. While this allows the organization to provide a range of services, it does increase the potential for confusion in regard to managing the demands from two bosses, which in turn may lead to an increase in stress.

A relatively new structural design option is the *team structure* (Figure 6.5). The team structure requires decision-making to be decentralized to work teams that are made up of people with skills to perform a variety of tasks. A football club franchise might employ such a structure with teams formed for club events or marketing campaigns as it will allow quick decision-making in regard to finance, staffing or impacts on players.

While these generic structures can be applied to all types of organizations, there has been some research that has attempted to categorize the various

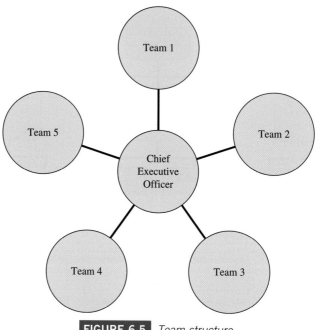

FIGURE 6.5 *Team structure.*

structures that exist within non-profit sport organizations. Kikulis et al. (1989) developed a structural taxonomy for provincial (state) Canadian amateur sport organizations based on the organizational dimensions of specialization, standardization and centralization. The evolution of Canadian sport organizations in the 1980s to a more professional and bureaucratized form prompted the researchers to attempt to establish exactly what form this evolution had taken. Kikulis et al. (1989) identified eight structural designs for voluntary sport organizations, ranging in scale of complexity for the three structural dimensions. Theodoraki and Henry (1994), in a similar study, defined a typology of structures for British sport governing bodies. They too utilized the structural elements of specialization, standardization and centralization to distinguish between various structural designs.

Identifying design types for national level sport organizations was the focus of a study by Kikulis et al. (1992) in which organizational values and organizational structure dimensions were used to identify three distinct designs – kitchen table, boardroom and executive office. Each design represents a distinct mix of organizational values comprising their orientation toward private or public interests; the domain of activities conducted (ranging from broad participation based to a focus on high performance results); the degree of professional involvement in decision-making; and the criteria used to evaluate effectiveness.

Now that we have explored the elements of structure and the various ways they can be used, we can examine the factors that influence the structure adopted by a sport organization.

WHAT INFLUENCES THE STRUCTURE OF A SPORT ORGANIZATION?

There are generally four factors that influence the structure of an organization: strategy, size, technology and environmental uncertainty. Each of these is briefly reviewed.

Strategy

In a perfect world, an organization's structure would be designed purely around the requirement to maximize the chances of an organization's strategic goals being achieved. This is rarely possible, but strategy does play an important part in determining the structure adopted by a sport organization. Whether an organization is pursuing an overall strategy of innovation, cost minimization or imitation will necessitate the design of a specific organizational structure.

An important trend to note in the development of structure for non-profit sport organizations has been the impact of the introduction of paid professional staff, a very deliberate strategy in response to increases in government funding in sport in most club-based sporting systems around the world. The impact of such a strategy on the structure of Canadian provincial VSOs was explored by Thibault et al. (1991). They found that specialization and formalization increased after the introduction of professional staff, but that centralization, after initially increasing, actually decreased over time. It was suggested that centralization increased because volunteer board members sought to retain control over decisions and then decreased as the relationship between board members and staff stabilized. Such resistance to changes in structure were noted by Kikulis et al. (1995), who studied the changes in specialization, standardization and centralization of Canadian NSOs over a 4-year period. They found that incumbent volunteers resisted change across all three elements of organizational structure, highlighting the role of human agents and personal choice in determining organizational change outcomes.

Size

The size of an organization also plays an important part in the determination of what will be its best possible structure. Larger organizations tend to be more formalized, with more specialist roles and departments and more levels of management than smaller organizations. This makes sense, as managers need to implement greater control measures to manage the volume and communication of information in a large organization. Amis and Slack (1996) state that much of the research into the relationship between organizational size and degree of centralization suggests that as 'organizations become larger, decision-making becomes more decentralized'. In terms of non-profit sport organizations they also found that with an increase in size of the organization, control over organizational decision-making remains at the voluntary board level and concluded that a 'central role of decision-making as a means of control and the desire for volunteers to retain this control' (Amis and Slack, 1996) meant that the boards of many sport organizations were reluctant to relinquish control to professional staff.

Technology

Technology does have an impact on organizational structure. Robbins et al. (2004b) argue that if organizations predominantly undertake routine tasks then there is a high degree of departmentalization and a high level of centralized decision-making. This appears logical because non-routine tasks require decisions to be made at the level of organization where they actually happen. In regard to a sport organization such as a professional sport club, the increased use of information and communication technology means that it requires additional specialist staff such as video technicians, statisticians and network programmers who may have replaced staff that used to perform tasks manually. The net effect is a higher level of departmentalization and specialization among the workforce.

Environmental uncertainty

Environmental uncertainty for sport organizations can be influenced by the actions of suppliers, service providers, customers, sponsors, athletes, volunteers, staff, stakeholder groups, government regulatory agencies, as well as general changes in economic or market conditions. For example, if a group of professional athletes behave inappropriately, their actions can affect the ability of their club or team to maintain or develop sponsorships which, in turn, may affect their ability to retain staff and hence require a structural adjustment. Similarly, a downturn in the economy can directly affect sales of sporting merchandise and organizations may have to adjust their structure accordingly to reduce costs or change product lines.

The example of the Singapore Sports Council highlights how the four generic factors of strategy, size, technology and environmental uncertainty can influence the structure of a sports organization.

In Practice 6.2 Singapore Sports Council

The Singapore Sports Council (SSC) is Singapore's lead agency tasked with developing sports in Singapore and performs a similar role to UK Sport or the Australian Sports Commission. It was formed on 1 October 1973 and is a statutory board under the control of the Ministry of Community Development, Youth and Sports. The SSC aims to develop sports champions and create enjoyable sporting experiences for Singapore through the following mechanisms:

1. cultivating a sporting culture
2. achieving sports excellence
3. creating a vibrant sports industry.

The SSC's organizational structure is directly linked to their strategy (Figure 6.6). The SSC sport participation team develops sport outreach programmes for all Singaporeans through lifestyle marketing, collaborative partnerships with the private sector and other government agencies and through improving access to facilities and sport opportunities. The SSC claims that Singapore is one of the most inclusive sport nations in the world today, in terms of public access to sport facilities, services and opportunities. The sport excellence team promotes international sporting excellence in targeted sports. The SSC states that it adopts an athlete-focused, coach-driven approach, while maximizing use of sport science to increase their athlete's competitive edge. The sport industry team is focused on building a sustainable sport industry by supporting a calendar of major events, assisting in the growth of sponsorship and television rights and the creation of new businesses related to the sport industry.

It is clear that each of the four contingency factors noted earlier in the chapter have impacted on the structure of the organization. The SSC has a very clear mandate to deliver professional services and support for elite athletes and to raise the profile of elite athletes in Singapore. Accordingly, the structure reflects these core functions or strategic foci, coordinated through three core teams – High Performance, Sport Facilities and Sport Marketing. In addition, the SSC operates teams for strategic and financial management, knowledge management and organization development that support the efforts of the three core teams. Any increase in the number of elite sports or athletes supported by the SSC would not necessarily lead to a change in structure, rather each of the existing teams would simply expand to cater for the increased service requirements. As a government-owned enterprise, its structure is in part determined by its mandate to deliver services to a discrete group in the sport industry and is unlikely to be unduly affected by environmental uncertainty. The drivers of change in structure would include any significant shifts in strategy or client group, such as a move to focus more on the promotion of mass participation in community sport, which would perhaps require a redesign in organizational structure.

Source: Singapore Sports Council website at http://www.ssc.gov.sg

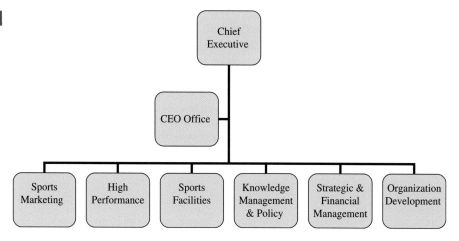

There are some additional drivers of structural change in sport organizations that are worth noting. These include poor on-field performance, changes in personnel due to politics, competition and market forces, government policy changes and forced change via mergers and amalgamations. Poor on-field performance by professional sporting teams or clubs can lead to an end-of-season purge of playing or coaching personnel and may entail a review of how the group of staff involved in coaching, athlete support or allied health services is organized. The political nature of some sport organizations that elect individuals to govern their activities can lead to structural change being implemented due to personal preferences of elected leaders or a mandate for change. Competition and market forces affect all organizations, but the interdependent nature of clubs operating within a league or competition necessitates them sharing information. Consequently, these organizations tend to be structured in similar ways, making structural change difficult. Governments may also change the way they fund high performance programmes or tie funding levels to the performances of international teams or individuals. Poor international performances may consequently reduce funding and, therefore, the capability of an organization to sustain their organizational structure. Finally, structural change may be forced upon sports organizations, either by economic conditions (such as population loss in rural areas forcing clubs to merge) or government policy (such as forcing single gender sport organizations to merge).

CHALLENGES FOR SPORT MANAGERS

An ongoing challenge facing sport managers is the need to strike a balance between lowering costs by using fewer staff and increasing productivity. This can be achieved through a greater use of technology for communication, data management and analysis, the appointment of skilled staff able to use technology and the development of semi-autonomous work teams that are able to make operational decisions quickly. This requires the use of a more flexible organizational structure than perhaps is the norm for the majority of contemporary sport organizations.

A further challenge for sport managers is to ensure that their organizations are flexible enough to react quickly to opportunities in the market or to the demands of their stakeholders, while at the same time, maintaining adequate forms of control and accountability. Sport managers will need to establish clear guidelines for decision-making and acceptable levels of formalization for standard procedures, without unduly constraining the flexibility to modify those guidelines and formal procedures.

An aspect of managing organizational structures that is relatively unique to sport is the presence of both paid staff and volunteers, often with volunteers directing the work of paid staff. Sport managers will need to be cognizant of the need to maintain close links between these two significant parts of their workforce and maintain a suitable structure that allows these groups to communicate effectively and work to achieve organizational outcomes.

Sport managers also need to ensure the structure can enable strategy to be realized. If strategic plans are devised, new markets identified or new product and service offerings developed in the absence of concomitant changes to the organizational structure, then the ability of the organization to deliver such planned changes is questionable. It is imperative that sport managers pay attention to designing their structure to enable specific strategic directions to be achieved.

As illustrated in the previous chapters, organizations that work within the sport industry must work within a myriad of other organizations from the public, private and non-profit sectors. Often, sport organizations have many stakeholders involved in setting the strategic direction of the organization. The organizational structure should therefore facilitate decision-making processes that engage all relevant stakeholders.

Finally, the interdependent relationships that exist between sports organizations that may be involved in a league, a collection of associations, a joint venture or a funding agreement with multiple partners and sponsors, necessitate organizational structures that reflect these connections. This may extend to establishing designated roles for external liaison within the structure or incorporating representation from members of external organizations on internal decision-making committees.

The structure adopted by the British Basketball League represents an attempt to deal with many of these challenges.

In Practice 6.3 British Basketball League

The top men's professional basketball league in the UK is the British Basketball League (BBL). The BBL is an independent company owned by its 12 member clubs, each with an equal shareholding in BBL. Each club has a representative on the BBL Board of Directors who oversee the operation of a central BBL office in Birmingham, which manages administration, marketing and media functions. The interesting aspect of the structure of the BBL is that each club operates as a franchise in designated areas across the UK in order to maximize commercial and media value within their local community.

Unlike other sports where second division champions are promoted to replace the bottom ranked team in the top league, the BBL operates independently of the second tier competition, the English Basketball League (EBL). There is no promotion and relegation between the BBL and the EBL and EBL clubs cannot join the BBL based on their performances in official competition alone. However, EBL clubs and any other organizations can apply for a franchise from the BBL.

The organizational structure or franchise system employed by the BBL is used because of the significant costs of running a team in the BBL compared to running any other team in the UK. The structure attempts to provide financial security and protect investment into clubs by removing the threat that comes with relegation. A salary cap and income distribution policy among BBL clubs also assists with competitive balance and financial management.

Clubs can apply to join the BBL by submitting a detailed business plan to the BBL Franchise Committee that specifies venue details, proof of an acceptable level of financial backing and an explanation of how the club will be sustainable. Because government funding for basketball goes to England Basketball, the BBL receives no government financial support. Instead, it derives its income from sponsorship, media partnerships, merchandising and ticket sales. Commercial and media rights generate the largest portion of income for the league and clubs.

The challenge of organizing a viable professional basketball league in a country dominated by football, rugby and cricket is significant. Competition for sponsorship dollars, access to appropriate venues, securing media rights and maintaining market share in a crowded professional sport market are all challenges for the directors of the BBL and the managers of their member clubs. The organizational structure adopted by the BBL in using the US style franchise system is an attempt to combat these challenges. The structure allows the league and clubs to plan for future expansion, manage income and costs across all elements of the organization and ensure equitable decision-making among the member clubs. The BBL is set for some competition as a rival league, the British Basketball Association (BBA) has plans to create a similar elite competition.

Source: British Basketball League website at http://www.bbl.org.uk

SUMMARY

Organizational structure was defined as the framework that outlines how tasks are divided, grouped and coordinated within an organization. An organization's structure is important because it defines where staff and volunteers 'fit in' with each other in terms of work tasks, decision-making procedures, the need for collaboration, levels of responsibility and reporting mechanisms.

Six key elements of organizational structure were reviewed: work specialization, departmentalization, chain of command, the span of control, centralization and formalization. In addition, four basic models for how an organization may use these six elements to design an appropriate structure were reviewed: the simple structure, the bureaucracy, the matrix structure and the team structure.

The generic contingency factors that influence organizational structure – size, strategy, technology and environmental uncertainty – were reviewed as well as some unique drivers of change to the structure of sport organizations. Finally, a number of unique challenges for sport managers in dealing with structure were presented. Sport managers should be aware of these factors that drive structural change and the specific structural elements they can influence that are likely to deliver improved organizational outcomes and performance.

REVIEW QUESTIONS

1. Define organizational structure in your own words.

2. If you were to manipulate any of the six elements of structure, which do you think could have the most impact on the day-to-day role of the chief executive of a sports organization?

3. Do staff in small sports organizations have a low degree of work specialization? Why or why not?

4. Which structural model would suit a large sports event such as the Commonwealth or Olympic Games? Why?

5. How are organizational strategy and structure related?

6. How does a change in size affect the structure of a sports organization?

7. Compare the organizational structure of a sport manufacturing organization and a local community sports facility? How do each of the six elements of organizational structure differ? Which elements are similar?

8. Explain how environmental uncertainty can force change to the structure of a sports organization.

9. Interview the CEO of a medium-sized sports organization. What is their most significant challenge in managing their organizational structure?

10. Explore the structure of a small community sport club. Are the principles of organizational structure outlined in this chapter directly applicable? Why or why not?

FURTHER READING

The use of organizational theory in the analysis of structures for non-profit sport organizations is well established. Three broad questions have been addressed in these studies. These are: first, investigating the relationship between organizational structure and organizational effectiveness; secondly, attempting to categorize organizational types; and thirdly, exploring the impact of profession-alization on various elements of organizational structure. Students interested in reading further should consult the following journal articles:

Amis, J. and Slack, T. (1996). The size-structure relationship in voluntary sport organizations. *Journal of Sport Management*, 10, 76–86.

Frisby, W. (1986). The organizational structure and effectiveness of voluntary organizations: the case of Canadian national sport governing bodies. *Journal of Park and Recreation Administration*, 4, 61–74.

Kikulis, L.M., Slack, T. and Hinings, B. (1992). Institutionally specific design archetypes: a framework for understanding change in national sport organizations. *International Review for the Sociology of Sport*, 27, 343–367.

Kikulis, L.M., Slack, T. and Hinings, B. (1995). Toward an understanding of the role of agency and choice in the changing structure of Canada's national sport organizations. *Journal of Sport Management*, 9, 135–152.

Kikulis, L.M., Slack, T., Hinings, B. and Zimmermann, A. (1989). A structural taxonomy of amateur sport organizations. *Journal of Sport Management*, 3, 129–150.

Stevens, J. (2006). The Canadian Hockey Association merger and the emergence of the Amateur Sport Enterprise. *Journal of Sport Management*, 20, 74–101.

Theodoraki, E.I. and Henry, I.P. (1994). Organizational structures and contexts in British national governing bodies of sport. *International Review for the Sociology of Sport*, 29, 243–263.

Thibault, L., Slack, T. and Hinings, B. (1991). Professionalism, structures and systems: the impact of professional staff on voluntary sport organizations. *International Review for the Sociology of Sport*, 26, 83–97.

RELEVANT WEBSITES

The following websites are useful starting points for further information on the structure of sport organizations:

University of Calgary Scholarly sport sites web page for sport structures at http://www.ucalgary.ca/library/ssportsite/natorg.html

Australian Sports Commission at http://www.ausport.gov.au

Netball Victoria at www.netballvic.com.au

Sport and Recreation New Zealand at http://www.sparc.org.nz/

Sport Canada at http://www.pch.gc.ca/progs/sc/index_e.cfm

Sport England at http://www.sportengland.org

Sport Scotland at http://www.sportscotland.org.uk

Case study: The Football Association

The Football Association was founded in 1863 as the governing body of football in England and is responsible for all regulatory aspects of the game in England. The FA's primary responsibility is to promote the development of the game among people of all ages, backgrounds and abilities in terms of participation and quality. The FA also regulates the game on and off the field of play through the 'Laws of the Game' and the 'Rules of The Association' and, in so doing, sanctions either directly or indirectly, all matches, leagues and competitions played in England. This regulatory function involves overseeing the administration of the disciplinary system, which is applicable to all participants in the game (each club, player, competition, match official and any other person involved in the game in England is bound by the Rules) and the administration of refereeing throughout the game. In addition, the FA organizes a number of senior men's, youth and women's national competitions (including most notably The FA Challenge Cup) and the participation of England national representative teams in international matches, most notably the men's senior team in the FIFA World Championships and the UEFA European Championships.

The scale of the FA as an organization is incredible. The FA claims football to be the nation's game in more than the spectator sense and cites the following figures to demonstrate its enormous influence in England:

- 7 million participants, plus 5 million in schools
- 500 000 volunteers
- 37 500 clubs, including 9000 youth clubs
- 2000 competitions
- 32 000 schools (17 000 primary)
- 30 000 FA-qualified coaches
- 27 000 FA-qualified referees
- 45 000 pitches (21 000 facilities).

In 2005, the FA commissioned Lord Burns to conduct a review into its structure. Lord Burns produced a report in late 2005 that outlined a number of structural changes designed to modernize the FA and enable it to meet its future challenges. The outcomes of this 2005 review are largely represented in the FA's 2008–2012 vision statement that articulates a new vision, mission and strategy for the FA.

The FA's mission is to:

- During the term of this strategic plan and beyond, working with our professional football partners we aim to put in place measures that will create winning England teams for the future.

- We will work in close cooperation with our clubs, fans, counties, leagues and other key stakeholders to lead the game and foster the growth and the sustained success of English football.

- We will strengthen our relationships with FIFA and UEFA to play a full role in encouraging football, health and education domestically and worldwide.

- We will ensure that English football becomes a major ambassador for fairness, social inclusion, health and education in our society, a role it can play with distinction as the nation's favourite game.

- Based on our values we aim to build The FA into a world-class organization.

In order to deliver the FA's mission, they have identified a strategy of three goals:

Goal 1: Trusted to lead

1.1 Lead and govern with confidence

1.2 Perform as a world-class organization

1.3 Partner the professional game

Goal 2: England teams winning

2.1 Succeed with Club England

2.2 Develop world-class players and coaches

Goal 3: Nation's favourite game

3.1 Grow and improve the National Game

3.2 Bid for the 2018 FIFA World Cup

3.3 Support and develop our great assets

This strategy is to be delivered through a structure made up of discrete departments, each delivering specific measurable services and outcomes which is outlined in the FA's Vision 2008–2012. The FA is one of the few professional sport leagues in the world to own a national stadium and, as such, Wembley Stadium represents a distinct element in its organizational structure.

It is important to remember that the Premier League is but one part of the FA organization that delivers football playing, participation and spectating opportunities. While operating as a separate legal entity with its own CEO and Board, the Premier League comes under the jurisdiction of the FA and must submit its rules each year for approval and sanction. The Premier League is owned by 20 shareholders – the member clubs, whose membership in the league is dependent on the performance of their football team in the Barclays Premier League. Each shareholder is entitled to one vote and all rule changes and major commercial contracts require the support of two thirds of the clubs voting at a general meeting. The FA is also a special shareholder and has the right of veto in certain crucial areas, such as the appointment of Chairman and Chief Executive and promotion and relegation of clubs.

One important point about the FA's structure is that it is an evolving entity. Indeed, one of the key points of the FA's strategy is to 'review our structures and delivery mechanisms which will enable us to perform as a world-class organization'. In order to do this, the FA has set itself the task of reforming their structure to deliver the strategy as set out in 2008–2012 Vision. The FA clearly states that:

> On its own, a new structure is not enough; we will also therefore need to demonstrate commitment throughout The FA structure whether at Executive, Board, Professional Game, National Game or Council level to a unified approach to delivering the strategy – a 'One FA' approach. The organization must be efficient and cost effective, a lean and dynamic organisation driven forward with clear benchmarks (FA, 2008).

Case Study Questions

1. Access the FA website at www.thefa.com and read about the background to the Burns review. What was the major impetus for undertaking the review?

2. What were the core recommendations for structural reform made by Lord Burns? What likely improvements in organizational performance or outcomes were identified to flow from making the recommended changes?

3. Explain how the strategy of the FA for 2008–2012 is aligned to their proposed structure on page 49 of their 2008–2012 vision.

4. What are the barriers or constraints that might prevent or limit the effectiveness of the structure adopted by the FA?

5. What are some of the external market or environmental conditions that the FA needs to be mindful of as they seek continually to review their structure to ensure it is 'dynamic' – in other words moving with the times?

Sources: The Premier leaguer website at http://www. premierleague.com, the FA website at the www.thefa.com, in particular the documents concerning the Burns review at <http://www.thefa.com/TheFA/StructualReview/>, and the FA (2008), *The FA's Vision 2008–2012*, also available on the FA website.

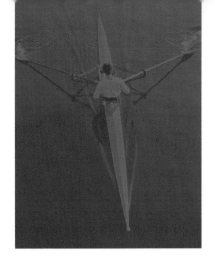

CHAPTER 7

Human Resource Management

OVERVIEW

This chapter reviews the core concepts of human resource management, provides examples of the unique features of human resource management within sport organizations, such as volunteer and paid staff management, and summarizes the key phases in the human resource management process. The chapter examines human resource management within community, state, national and professional sport organizations, in order to illustrate core concepts and principles.

After completing this chapter the reader should be able to:

- Identify the key concepts that underpin human resource management within sport organizations

- Explain why human resource management in sport organizations can be different to non-sport organizations

- Identify each of the phases within the human resource management process

- Explain the ways in which each of the human resource management phases would be implemented in different sport organization contexts.

WHAT IS HUMAN RESOURCE MANAGEMENT?

Human resource management, in business or sport organizations, is essentially about first, finding the right person for the right job at the right time and, second, ensuring an appropriately trained and satisfied workforce. The concepts that underpin effective human resource management are not particularly complex. However, the sheer size of some organizations, as well as the difficulties in managing unusual organizations in the sport industry, make human resource management a complex issue to deal with in practice. Successful sport leagues, clubs, associations, retailers and venues all rely on good human resources, both on and off the field to get their jobs done. Conversely, organizations with staff who lack motivation, are ill suited to their work, under-paid or under-valued will struggle to perform.

Human resource management is a central feature of an organization's planning system. It cannot be divorced from other key management tools, such as strategic planning, financial planning or managing organizational culture and structure. Human resource management can both drive organizational success and is a consequence of good management and planning. Importantly, human resource management is a process of continual planning and evaluation and is best viewed as part of a cycle in which an organization aims to meet its strategic goals. Human resource management, therefore, is an holistic management function in that it can be 'both person-centred and goal-directed' (Smith and Stewart, 1999).

Human resource management can mean different things to different organizations, depending on their context and outlook. For professional sport organizations that are profit driven, such as the American National Basketball Association (NBA), Major League Baseball (MLB) or National Hockey League (NHL), successful human resource management is equated with profitability, long-term growth and success (on and off the court, diamond and rink). This is not to suggest that these things are pursued at the expense of employees, but rather that the success of the employees is measured by dispassionate business indicators and human resource management is a tool for driving the business towards its goals. For example, some player welfare and development programmes within professional sport organizations are designed to produce socially, morally and ethically responsible citizens. This is viewed as a good human resource strategy, not only because of the intrinsic value to the athletes, but for the extrinsic value that results from better public relations and sponsor servicing. In other words, better behaved athletes mean greater profitability and overall success for professional sport teams and franchises.

For non-profit sport organizations, successful human resource management is not always about bottom-line financial performance. Rather, it can encompass a range of strategies and outcomes depending on the organizational context. A local sporting club that has had a problem with alcohol consumption among its junior players may develop a range of programmes to educate its players, coaches and administrators (who may be paid or volunteer staff) in order to encourage a more responsible club culture. This player welfare programme may actually be part of a human resource management strategy, as the inappropriate club culture may have been making it difficult to attract and retain volunteers with expertise and commitment. In the case of the professional team context, the player welfare programme can be used to manage image and maintain brand credibility. In the case of the local community sport club, the player welfare programme can be used to retain volunteers who were being driven away from the club by poor behaviour and a dysfunctional culture. From these two examples, it is clear that human resource management can be both person-centred and goal-directed at the same time.

As illustrated by the above examples, one of the significant challenges of implementing effective human resource management within sport organizations is that not all sport organizations are alike. As Taylor et al. (2008) have illustrated, different types of sport organizations have different staffing profiles. These staffing profiles are dependent on an organization's type, as well as its purpose or reason for being. For example, a professional sport organization, such as a club in the Spanish La Liga, will have an extensive staff of full-time paid professionals engaged in marketing, coaching, sport science and general administration, whereas a voluntary organization, such as local cricket or rugby club, is likely to have no paid staff. Other sport organizations might have a mixture of paid and voluntary staff who work together in the day-to-day operations of the organization or work together in their capacities as staff and members of a committee of management or board of directors. We will investigate the governance of sport organizations later in the book but, at this point, it is sufficient to note that in many sport organizations, paid staff are answerable to a voluntary board of directors. This relationship can be a challenge for the overall management of the organization and the practice of human resource management more specifically.

Many of the functions of professional and voluntary sport organizations are similar, such as event management, promotion, fund raising, membership services and financial management, however, the scale of the organizations is different. While it is true that the scale and type of organization has an impact on the human resource management practices that can and need to be put in place, in many respects, sport organizations are increasingly adopting human resource management practices that are underpinned by the notion of professional and standard practice. Indeed, the implementation of specific human resource management practices has been viewed as an important catalyst in the professionalization of voluntary or community sporting organizations. For example, in the early 1990s, the Australian Sports Commission, in conjunction with the Australian Society of Sports Administrators, the Confederation of Australian Sport and state departments of sport and recreation, developed the 'Volunteer Involvement Program'. The original programme was designed to encourage sport organizations to adopt professional volunteer management practices, which was viewed as essential given the large numbers of volunteers involved in sport organizations and the increasing professionalization of the industry.

The programme has since been revised and improved to provide sporting clubs and associations with resources and training modules for volunteer management ('recruiting volunteers', 'retaining volunteers', 'volunteer management: a guide to good practice', 'managing event volunteers', 'volunteer management policy' and 'the volunteer coordinator'). These modules encourage Australian sporting clubs and associations to develop systematic processes and practices, although it should be acknowledged that the diversity of club-based sporting system, such as that which is in operation in Australia, means that the capacity to professionalize varies considerably.

IS HUMAN RESOURCE MANAGEMENT IN SPORT SPECIAL?

Many of the core concepts that underpin human resource management apply to all organizations, whether they are situated in the world of business, such as soft drink manufacturer Coca-Cola or mining company BHP Billiton, or in the world of sport, such as the South African Rugby Football Union or the Canadian Curling Association. This is not surprising, given that all these organizations employ staff who are expected to execute a range of designated tasks at an appropriate level of performance. These staff will manage finances, undertake strategic planning and produce products like *Fanta*, iron ore, coaching clinics and national championships. There are, however, significant differences between business and sport organizations, which result in modifications to generic human resource management practices.

In particular, professional sport organizations have special features which present a unique human resource management challenge. Sport organizations, such as the Cincinnati Bengals in America's National Football League, revolve around three distinct types of employees. First, the Bengals employ people in what they call 'the front office', such as the business development manager or the director of corporate sales and marketing. Second, the Bengals employ people in what can be referred to as the 'football operations department', such as the coaches, trainers and scouts. Finally, the Bengals employ people that comprise 'the team', the players, who are the most visible people within any professional sport organization. It could be argued that non-sport businesses operate in the same way, with different levels of management, from the chief executive officer all the way through to the employee on the factory floor. The obvious difference in the sporting context is that the human resources at the bottom of the staffing pyramid are the highest paid employees in the entire organization. The difference between sport and non-sport organizations is illustrated in Figure 7.1. It should be noted that sport organizations have employees that could be considered 'the lowest paid', but relative to non-sport organizations they are not equivalent and, as such, a checkered arrow has not been included for the sport organization pyramid (sport organizations are not completely unique in this respect, however, for in many forms of entertainment, such as film or television drama, the actors are the highest paid).

In non-sport organizations, chief executive officers, general managers and other senior executives often receive performance bonuses and have access to share options that allow them to share in the wealth and profitability of the company. The workers producing the product (at the *Fanta* bottling plant or the iron ore mine for example) do not have access to performance schemes and bonuses that might be worth millions of dollars. In professional sport organizations, the situation is reversed and the performance bonuses are typically available to those who produce the product, the players. It is important to keep this special feature of sport in mind when considering the human resource management needs of professional sport organizations specifically and sport organizations more generally.

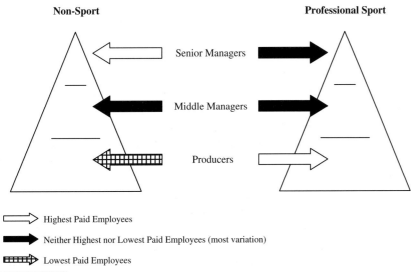

FIGURE 7.1 *Pay and organization levels in professional sport and non-sport organizations.*

Additionally, a significant proportion of staff in semi-professional and non-profit sport organizations are volunteers. The distinction between volunteers and paid staff in the effective management of these groups is a challenge for human resource management in sport organizations. Because sport is often played in a community environment (at a state, regional or local level), it necessarily requires the support of volunteers to maintain services, facilities and events. Some national sport organizations, like the South Africa Rugby Football Union or the Canadian Curling Association mentioned earlier, have paid staff at the national level, whose job it is to coordinate and develop programmes, events, championships and national teams. Equivalent state or regional associations for sports like these might, depending on the size, popularity and government funding afforded the sport, also have paid staff in key management, development and coaching positions. In some instances, these state or regional associations will have more staff than the national body because of the requirement to deliver programmes and services, as well as manage and provide strategic direction for the sport. Local associations, again depending on the size and popularity of the sport, might also have some paid staff, however, at this level, sports are supported by a significant core of volunteers. In Australia, it has been estimated that sporting activities are supported by 1.5 million volunteers who collectively contribute in excess of 150 million volunteer hours per year, while in the UK, it has been estimated that volunteers contribute in excess of 1 billion hours of labour (www.sportengland.org).

A significant proportion of sport is played on a weekly basis within leagues and associations across the world. Depending on whether the sport is played indoor or outdoor, the sport might have a winter season (football or ice hockey), a summer season (baseball) or might be played all year (basketball). The regularity of the season and the competition, whether at the elite or community level, means that the staffing requirements of sport organizations are predictable and remain relatively stable. There are, however, a range of sporting events and championship for which staff planning is difficult and staffing levels fluctuate greatly. These events are either irregular (a city might get to host the Olympics once in 100 years) or big enough that they require a large workforce for an intense period of time (the annual Monaco Grand Prix). The staffing for major annual sport events can be referred to as 'pulsating' (Hanlon and Cuskelly, 2002), as illustrated in Figure 7.2.

In essence, major events need a large workforce, often composed primarily of volunteers or casual workers, for a short period of time prior to the event, during the event and directly following the event, and a small workforce of primarily paid staff for the rest of the year (events such as the Olympic Games or world championships will require a permanent paid staff

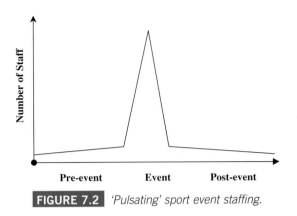

FIGURE 7.2   *'Pulsating' sport event staffing.*

for many years prior to the event, but most staffing appointments will conclude within six months of the event finishing). The rapid increase and decline in staffing within a one- or two-week period is a complex and significant human resource management problem. It requires systematic recruitment, selection and orientation programmes in order to attract the staff and simple yet effective evaluation and reward schemes in order to retain them. In Practice 7.1 examines some of the human resource management practices put in place by a major event with a 'pulsating' paid and volunteer staff.

In Practice 7.1 Vancouver 2010

In the eastern European city of Prague on 2 July 2003, Vancouver, Canada defeated fellow candidate cities of Salzburg, Austria and Pyeongchang, Korea to be elected as host for the 2010 Olympic Winter Games. The challenge for any Olympic Games organizing committee is to secure enough well-qualified and experienced staff and volunteers to ensure that the event is well run and athletes, coaches, administrators, media, spectators and visitors are satisfied with their experience. The Vancouver 2010 organizing committee responded by establishing an online application process to recruit and select a team of 25 000.

Prospective paid staff were encouraged to undertake a self-assessment questionnaire prior to searching for or applying for a job with the Vancouver organizing committee. The self-assessment questionnaire consisted of questions based around the themes of teamwork, trust, excellence, sustainability and creativity, such as 'do you enjoy working as part of a team, or are you a person that likes to work on your own?', 'do you believe there are benefits to working as part of a team and, if yes, what are the benefits?' and 'what would you do if a member of your team was falling behind and needed your help?'. If the prospective staff member elected to proceed after the self-assessment, they were able to search through the job listings and then apply for jobs through an online process.

Continued

In Practice 7.1 Vancouver 2010—cont'd

For example, the job of 'Coordinator, IF and IPSF Services', was needed to support the sport planning and operations manager by acting as the key contact for functional areas in regards to planning for Games-time service levels for International Sport Federations and International Paralympic Sport Federations. The relevant education and experience required for the positions was as follows:

- University graduation or technical diploma from a recognized post secondary institution
- 2–3 years of related work experience
- Knowledge of Olympic and Paralympic winter sports and the International Sport Federations
- Knowledge of IF/IPSF and IOC structure, requirements and rules an asset
- Experience in working with external stakeholders, IOC/IPC, IF/IPSF, NOC/NPC
- Experience in working with high end constituent groups and personnel
- Advanced working experience with the Microsoft Office suite of applications including; Word, Excel, PowerPoint and Outlook
- Previous event experience in planning and executing one or more winter sports an asset
- Previous experience working in a fast-paced, multilevel, project-based environment with emphasis on timelines and delivery an asset.

The Vancouver 2010 organizing committee also attracted Games volunteers through its website. In order to be eligible to apply, applicants needed to be aged 19 years or older on September 1, 2008, as well as be able to complete and pass a Royal Canadian Mounted Police background check. The volunteer functions were segmented in order to provide prospective volunteers with information regarding job descriptions, provide prospective volunteers with a broad choice, as well as ensure that volunteers were allocated to an area of the Games that suited their interests and abilities. Some of the volunteer functions included the following:

- Accreditation: assist in coordinating activities and shifts at accreditation centres, manage accreditation issues and support access control policies
- Anti-doping: verbally notifying athletes of their selection for doping control and escorting them from the field of competition to the doping control station
- Communications: help with communications and incident reporting at all major venues using telephones and two-way radios
- Event services: assist with crowd management, ticket taking, ushering and access monitoring
- Medical services: provide medical services at venue sites and in the Olympic village
- Press operations: provide services to accredited press at the main press centre and all competition venues

- Torch relay: assist with driving and maintaining shuttle services for torch bearers
- Workforce: conduct staff check-in, distribute uniforms, support venue training, manage break areas and meal coupon distribution, assist with staff scheduling, facilitate venue communication, resolve staff issues and ensure proper care and treatment of staff.

Like paid staff, volunteers were able to apply for positions with the Vancouver 2010 Olympic Games via an online application process, which took approximately 30 minutes to complete and involved the applicant providing a range of personal information and choosing a Games function they wanted to be involved with.

Sources: International Olympic Committee Website at <http://www.olympic.org/uk/index_uk.asp>; and Vancouver 2010 Olympic Games Website at <http://www.vancouver2010.com/en>

Large organizations with a large workforce have both the capacity and responsibility to engage in sophisticated human resource management. Often there is a dedicated team or department that manages human resources, led by a senior member of staff. In small to medium-sized organizations, however, there is not always the human or financial capacity to devote to human resource management practices in a formal system. Human resource management in small to medium-sized organizations is often the responsibility of the most senior staff member, such as the chief executive or general manager or is combined with roles performed by another senior manager responsible for finances, planning or marketing, for example.

Sport leagues, clubs, associations and venues rarely have enough staff to warrant employing someone to be responsible solely for human resource management. Often, the other key management roles, such as marketing, events or sponsorship, are considered essential and human resource management is considered either as a luxury or peripheral to the core management functions. Furthermore, human resource management can be confused with personnel management, which encompasses more mechanistic functions such as payroll and record keeping (leave, sick pay, etc.).

Swimming Australia, the national body responsible for managing one of Australia's biggest and most popular sports, has approximately 30 staff, with a chief executive officer and four functional divisions (high performance, sport development, marketing and events and business and stakeholder services). The finance and employee relations division is the smallest, with three employees, supported by the business and stakeholder services manager. Swimming Australia is a good example of a medium-sized organization in which the human resource management responsibilities have been merged with another significant management responsibility, in this case finance.

THE ESSENTIALS OF HUMAN RESOURCE MANAGEMENT

Human resource management in sport organizations aims to provide an effective, productive and satisfied workforce. Human resource management refers to the design, development, implementation, management and evaluation of systems and practices used by employers use to recruit, select, develop, reward, retain and evaluate their workforce. The core elements of the human resource management process are represented in Figure 7.3. The following phases are considered the core functions of human resource management, although it is important to keep in mind that these functions will differ significantly depending on the size, orientation and context of the sport organization in which they are implemented.

Phase 1: Human resource planning

Human resource management planning is essentially about assessing and forecasting the staffing needs of the organization and is often referred to as the most important phase for effective human resource management (Smith and Stewart, 1999). The planning phase of human resource management is short and fairly static for organizations in which the staffing levels remain fairly constant and the types of jobs performed by staff members vary little. For organizations that are dynamic or in a state of flux (as a result of

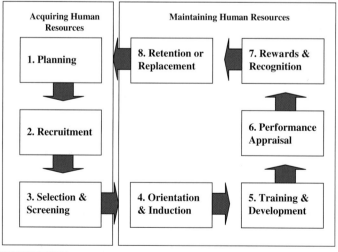

FIGURE 7.3 *The traditional human resource management process.*

economic pressures or opportunities for example), human resource planning is a cycle of ongoing development.

In the planning phase, an organization must assess whether current staffing needs will be adequate to meet future demand (or alternatively, whether fewer staff will be required), whether staff turnover is predictable and can be accommodated, whether the ratios of paid, full-time, part-time, casual and volunteer staff are appropriate or adequate, whether there are annual or cyclical fluctuations in staffing that need to be met and managed and whether specific capabilities will be required in the future that the organization is currently lacking.

Once an organization decides that a new staff member is required or a new position is to be created, the organization must undertake a job analysis, in order to determine the job content (primary and implied tasks), requirements (skills, competencies, qualifications and experience) and context (reporting relationships and job characteristics). Once the job analysis has been completed in as much detail as possible, the organization is ready to develop a job description (a document that covers the job content and context) and a job specification (a document that covers the job requirements, especially skills and knowledge base).

There are four management principles that can be applied to job design. They are most useful for considering how a job might be positioned within an organization, as well as for identifying different types of organizations. These themes are job simplification, job rotation, job enlargement and job enrichment (Chelladurai, 2006). Job simplification refers to the process in which a job (and the organization) is broken down into a series of simplified and specialized tasks. This simplification is intended to increase the specialization of employees, thereby increasing efficiency and productivity. Job simplification can be viewed as a positive management tool, particularly when it comes to evaluating the performance of an individual employee, however, job specialization, depending on the context, can lead to workers becoming bored and subsequently dissatisfied with their work.

The second principle, job rotation, is partly a remedy to the boredom and dissatisfaction that can result from simplification. Job rotation involves workers swapping jobs on a periodic basis, in order to keep fresh and stimulated, although clearly a sport organization will only have a finite range of jobs through which employees can rotate.

Job enlargement refers to a process in which employees are encouraged to enlarge the scope of their work and add tasks, even if they are simplified and specialized. The benefit of this approach is a happier workforce, but the downside is the perception of overwork.

Finally, job enrichment refers to the structuring of the job so that it maximizes employee motivation and involvement. This process relies on being able to design jobs that are flexible and have the capacity for growth and change, as well as the employment of people that can work autonomously. According to Chelladurai (2006), the greater levels of responsibility and challenging work that are available through job enrichment means that it is a superior method of job design.

Phase 2: Recruitment

Recruitment refers to the process by which an organization tries to find the person most suited to the job that has been designed. The greater the pool of applicants, the greater the chance the organization will find a suitable candidate. Generating a pool of applicants is not always simple, however, particularly if the job requires specific skills, knowledge, qualifications or experience that are in demand or short supply. Thus, for the chief executive position in a major professional club with responsibility for a multimillion dollar operation, the search might be extensive and costly. However, recruiting an attendant to check membership tickets at home games of the professional club might only require a small advertisement in a local newspaper. Finally, recruiting 10 000 people to act as volunteers for a major hallmark event might require a nationwide or international advertising campaign across various media forms. Increasingly, recruitment processes are becoming more sophisticated as organizations take advantage of rapidly developing communication technologies. In Practice 7.2 examines the human resource management practices employed at the Wimbledon tennis tournament, in order to illustrate how staff are recruited (as well as selected and inducted).

In Practice 7.2 Wimbledon

The All England Lawn Tennis Club Championships (Wimbledon) is one of the most famous sporting events in the world. In 2007, it was watched live by in excess of 450 000 people, while an estimated global audience of almost 750 million watched the more than 10 000 hours of tennis coverage broadcast throughout 185 countries and territories. It features the best tennis players, including Venus and Serena Williams, Roger Federer and Rafael Nadal, who are famous not only for the quality of their play, but because they have become media and popular culture icons. As well as being an event of significant media and public interest, Wimbledon is also a significant event in financial terms. The players compete for total prize money of almost £12 000 000 and, since the mid-1990s, the surplus generated by Wimbledon for the use of the Lawn Tennis Association within Great Britain has been in excess of £25 000 000.

Wimbledon is a complex event, with staff required across broad areas of expertise. The All England Lawn Tennis Club (AELTC) sources some staff itself, but also uses contractors to manage, operate and staff particular aspects of the tournament. For example, Facilities Management Catering Limited (FMC) operates the catering arm of The Championships and recruits a range of staff including chefs and bar staff, as well as people to work in the Club's silver service areas. FMC employ approximately 1700 staff during Wimbledon, who prepare and serve food within the many restaurants, cafés and food courts that are located at the AELTC for the duration of the tournament, including 190 000 sandwiches, 135 000 ice creams, 28 000 kilos of strawberries and 17 000 bottles of champagne. Once people are selected to work for FMC during The Championships, they undertake an induction during the weekend prior to the tournament, the objectives of which are to:

- Gauge the length of the journey time to work and to find the best route
- Discover how to enter the site
- Register and collect a staff pass for the fortnight
- Find out where the uniform store is and to collect a uniform for the first day
- Find out where the staff rest facilities are
- Find out where the employees' unit is located within the grounds
- Learn what the unit's service standard and menu specifications are
- Meet managers and colleagues
- Have localized health and food safety training
- Have specific service training.

Leisure Support Services provide all the cleaning and court attendance services, while IBM provides all information technology services. IBM employs data collectors, who are required to have excellent tennis knowledge, good communication skills, self-confidence, the ability to work under pressure and must have played the game at a reasonably high level. Security services are also provided by a contractor, G4S Security Services (UK), while the AELTC operates a driver service for players throughout the tournament. The AELTC Championships also require 330 chair and line umpires. Approximately 60 of these are international umpires who travel with the professional tennis circuit, while the remaining 270 are members of the Association of British Tennis Officials. In this respect, the AELTC relies on associated tennis organizations to recruit, train, accredit and provide staff for the duration of the tournament.

Finally, the AELTC Championships also require ball girls and boys on all courts throughout the Championships, to retrieve stray balls and return them to the players when requested. In 2008, ball girls and boys were selected from approximately 20 local schools. The schools were asked to make initial recommendations of appropriate candidates based on a series of criteria. In order to proceed to full training, the boys and girls needed to:

- Pass a written test on the rules and scoring of tennis at Wimbledon
- Be able to carry out instructions and drills
- Be able to complete a circuit and then stand still for 3 minutes

Continued

In Practice 7.2 Wimbledon—cont'd

- Show good speed in shuttle runs
- Pass tests of hand/eye coordination
- Roll three flat, straight balls (one after another arriving in released order)
- Feed, receive and indicate 'no tennis balls' as instructed
- Pivot using correct foot movement
- Adopt the correct stance.

The full training is conducted each year from February to June and is used to select approximately 160 ball girls and boys from the 540 year 9 and 10 candidates and approximately 90 from 150 ball girls and boys of previous years.

Sources: Wimbledon Website at <http://www.wimbledon.org/en_GB/index.html> and Facilities Management Catering Limited Website at <http://www.fmccatering.co.uk/>

Phase 3: Selection

Selection and screening is the process of condensing the candidates that applied for the position during the recruitment phase to a short-list. The selection phase will usually include at least one interview of the short-listed candidates, which will supplement the application form and curriculum vitae submitted by the applicants. These selection tools will be used to determine whether the applicant is appropriate in light of the job analysis and which of the applicants is the best person for the job. Depending on the geographic location of the applicants, the interview might be conducted in person, via telephone, via video conferencing or via the Internet. Industrial relations legislation covers a range of organizational and employment issues in most countries. It is important to comply with these laws and regulations throughout the human resource management processes, such the recruitment and selection phase, so that the organization is not exposed to claims of discrimination or bias (on the basis of race, colour, country of birth, ethnicity, disability, religion, sex, age, marital status, pregnancy or sexual preference). In this respect Smith and Stewart (1999) refer to the types of questions not to ask in an interview:

- How old are you?
- Do you have a problem working with younger people?
- Are you married?
- Do you have any children?
- How will you care for your children when at work?

- How long have you been a single parent?

- Do you intend to have any more children?

- Where do you attend church?

- Do you have a Christian background?

- What are your views on taking prohibited drugs?

- Please send a recent photo with your application form.

- What are you going to do about your weight problem?

- Do you have a communicable disease?

- What clubs do you belong to?

- Do you belong to a trade union or professional association?

- Tell us about your political affiliations?

- Have you undertaken any military service?

An interview is the most common way of determining whether a prospective employee will be best suited to the organization and the position. However, other techniques, such as sophisticated personality and intelligence tests, are increasingly being used to determine whether the applicant has the job requirements identified in the planning phase (skills, competencies, qualifications and experience). For example, the Myers-Briggs Type Indicator (MBTI) is a personality test which, based on questions about psychological processes such as the way people like to interpret information or make decisions, categorizes people into one of 16 personality types. Based on the psychological theories of Carl Jung, the MBTI can be used by sport organizations to determine whether an applicant not only has the appropriate skills and educational qualifications for the job, but also whether their personality, attitudes and values will be a good 'fit' for the organization. In Practice 7.3 highlights the various selection tools used by the Australian Football League, as part of its annual draft camp for prospective players.

In Practice 7.3 AFL Draft Camp

The Australian Football League (AFL) is Australia's most popular national league. It consists of 16 clubs spread throughout Victoria, South Australia, Western Australia, New South Wales and Queensland and is played between April and September each year. In order to make the competition as even and balanced as possible, the AFL has introduced a salary cap, income equalization measures and a player draft. The player draft is the way

Continued

In Practice 7.3 AFL Draft Camp—cont'd

in which the AFL ensures that playing talent is distributed evenly among the clubs. Without the draft and the salary cap, it is likely that only the richest and most successful clubs would get access to the best young players in Australia and overseas.

The AFL draft is held in November each year, at which the 16 AFL clubs choose players based on 'picks' they received depending on the position they finished during the previous season. Prior to the draft, the best young players in Australia are invited to attend the AFL draft camp at the Australian Institute of Sport. Players are selected based on their talent and form in under-age or senior competitions throughout Australia (such as AFL Victoria's TAC Cup Under 18 competition), as well as the national under 18 and under 16 national championships.

Once selected to attend the draft camp, the players are then subjected to a battery of physical, emotional and psychological tests, in order to determine which players are suitable for the AFL competition and in which order they will be drafted by the clubs:

- Physical tests (height, weight, body fat, flexibility, hand span and arm length) to determine whether the players' have the body type suited to AFL

- Medical and eye tests to determine whether the players' have any underlying medical conditions or problems that might prevent them from playing elite sport or might represent a risk for a club

- Psychomotor tests to determine the player's decision-making, reaction time and peripheral awareness

- Shuttle run (otherwise know as a 'beep test') and three kilometre time trial to test the players' endurance

- Vertical jump tests (both from standing and from a running position) to measure the players' leg power

- Sprint tests (time over 20 metres and time over six 30 metre sprints, with 20 second recovery) to assess the players' speed

- Agility tests (running around obstacles) to assess the players' ability to change direction

- Skills sessions to determine the players' football ability (although this is not as important, as club talent scouts are able to determine this by watching players in club games and national championships)

- Psychological tests to determine the players' ability to manage difficult situations and their emotional profile

- Club interviews (individual interviews as well as an individual five-minute taped interview) to determine whether players are suitable for particular clubs.

Many professional leagues, such as the National Football League (NFL) and National Basketball Association in America have similar draft camps at which prospective players are required to perform in a series of physical, medical and psychological tests. For example, in the NFL draft camp, players are required, among other things, to bench press

100 kg as many times as they can in order to test their upper body strength, sit the Wonderlic test, an intelligence type test of 50 questions in 12 minutes, take a urine test for prohibited drugs, have X-rays to determine past and current injuries, as well as have their flexibility and joint movement tested via the Cybex Test.

Sources: Australian Football League Website at http://www.afl.com.au/; National Football League Website at <http://www.nfl.com/> and Top End Sports Website at <http://www.topendsports.com/>

Phase 4: Orientation

Once the employee has successfully navigated the recruitment and selection processes, they are ready to begin work in their new job within the sport organization. Before they start, however, they need to be orientated and inducted. This phase of human resource management is important, as a good quality orientation and induction programme can make an employee feel both welcome and empowered, but a poor programme, or no programme, can make a new employee feel as if they have travelled to a foreign country, in which they can't speak the language, don't know where to go and can't read any of the signs. In short, being in a new organization can be a daunting and frightening experience. The implementation of successful orientation and induction programmes can ameliorate some of the difficulties, concerns and anxieties. Potential problems are compounded if the employee is a volunteer and can be exacerbated further if the volunteer does not have any direct supervision from a paid employee of the organization. This is a recipe for disaster, both for the organization and the employee. Table 7.1 outlines some of the orientation and induction steps that the Australian Sports Commission recommended as part of a series of volunteer management modules.

Once an athlete has been selected to play for a team in a major professional sport league (passed the recruitment and selection processes), they are invariably faced with the completely new world of professional sport and all the demands that accompany it. The National Basketball Association (NBA) in the USA recognized that this was a difficult time for many young athletes and developed a comprehensive orientation and induction programme. Since 1986, the rookie players of the forthcoming season have been required to participate in a week-long training and development camp in the month prior to the season's start. The rookie transition programme is designed so that these young athletes can develop better life skills which, in turn, will hopefully prepare them for the particular and peculiar stresses of a professional athletic career. Through the transition programme, which includes a diverse

Table 7.1	Australian Sports Commission Volunteer Orientation

Orientation Programme Checklist

- ☑ Provide an orientation guidebook or kit
- ☑ Provide copies of current newsletter, annual report and recent marketing/promotional material
- ☑ Provide a copy of the constitution
- ☑ Enter the name, address and contact details of each volunteer into database
- ☑ Gather and file copies of qualifications and accreditation certificates from each volunteer
- ☑ Introduce the organization's culture, history, aims, funding, clients/members and decision-making processes
- ☑ Introduce key volunteers and/or staff (and organization chart)
- ☑ Outline the roles and responsibilities of key volunteers and staff
- ☑ Detail the roles and responsibilities and accountabilities of the volunteer in their new position
- ☑ Familiarize volunteers with facilities, equipment and resources
- ☑ Explain and 'walk through' emergency and evacuation procedures
- ☑ Familiarize volunteers with the organization's day-to-day operations (safety and risk management, telephone, photocopier, keys, filing system, tea/coffee making, office processes and procedures, authorizing expenditure)

Source: Australian Sports Commission website at <www.ausport.gov.au>

range of topics such as sexual health, nutrition and anger management, the NBA hopes that its young players will be able to make better decisions.

Successful orientation and induction programmes revolve around forthright and effective communication of information about the organization and its operations. This information might include a general overview, policies and procedures, occupational health and safety regulations, industrial relations issues, a physical tour of the organization's facilities, an overview of the training and development programmes available to employees or an explanation of the performance appraisal process (Slack, 1997). The focus on orientation and induction is usually magnified when a large number of volunteers is required by the organization, such as at an Olympic Games. A total of 60 422 volunteers participated in running the Atlanta Olympics in 1996, 47 000 volunteers participated in Sydney in 2000, while the 2004 Athens Olympics received in excess of 160 000 volunteer applications from all over the world. At the 2008 Beijing Games, 74 615 volunteers provided services at Games venues, while another 400 000 volunteers provided information, translation services and emergency aid at 550 street stalls throughout the city.

Phase 5: Training and development

Training and development is at the heart of an organization that seeks continual growth and improvement. Sport organizations that do not engage in systematic training and development programmes are destined to operate far below their optimum, not only because they will fall behind in current trends, practices and skills, but because they will not see themselves as learning organizations (Senge, 1990). At its most basic, training and development is a process through which new and existing employees learn the skills required for them to be effective in their jobs. At one end of the spectrum these skills could be associated with learning how to operate automated turnstiles at a professional sport arena (training for the novice employee), or learning how to creatively brand the organizations in order to compete in a hostile marketplace (training for the experienced existing employee). Where training was once a fairly mechanistic activity, it now includes more generic organizational skills that require development and implementation, such as when a major league sport franchise ensures product or service quality, or when a national sport organization develops an organizational culture that encourages compliance from state or regional sport organizations.

Dressler (2003) outlines a five-step training and development process that is useful for sport organizations. Step one is to complete a 'needs analysis', in which the organization identifies the necessary skills for its employees, analyses the current skills base and develops specific training objectives. Step two involves developing the actual training programme, which may be done internally or externally. Most sport organizations, as previously noted, are too small to have sophisticated human resource management departments that have the skill and experience to design, develop and implement comprehensive training programmes. Sport organizations will most often use external training providers, such as universities or consultancy firms, to provide tailored or standard programmes, depending on the needs analysis. Step three, validation, is an optional step in which the organization is able to validate that the training programme that has been developed or contracted satisfies the needs analysis. Step four is the implementation of the programme, during which the staff are trained (this could be anything from a one-day short course, through to a two-year Masters programme). In the fifth and final step, the training programme is evaluated. The successful programme might be expanded to include more employees or more skills, while the unsuccessful programme needs to be discontinued or re-worked, which requires the organization to reassess the needs analysis. Like the entire human resource management process, the training and development process is best viewed as cyclical.

Phase 6: Performance appraisal

This phase of the human resource management process is potentially the most dangerous, as it has the inherent ability to pit 'management' against 'employees' at the macro level and at the micro level cause managers to feel uncomfortable in judging others or cause employees to feel unworthy, as part of a negative appraisal. The performance appraisal process must be approached carefully by sport organizations and human resource managers within an organization must seek to develop a collaborative process in which the employee, as well as the manager, feels empowered. As Chelladurai (2006) has noted, it is useful to think of performance appraisal in terms of its administrative and developmental purposes. The administrative purpose refers to the need within organizations to make judgements about performance that are directly related to rewards and recognition, such as promotions and salary increases. The administrative purpose often requires quantitative measures, so that employees can be appraised based on similar criteria. The developmental purpose refers to developing and enhancing the capabilities of an employee, which often requires a mix of quantitative and qualitative measures, and can be a catalyst for further training and development. The administrative and developmental purposes of performance appraisal demonstrate that the human resource management process is not always a neat cycle. Rather, there is a constant to and fro between the phases.

During the performance appraisal process, managers and leaders need the ability to review performance and suggest improvement, as a way of developing overall organizational capacity. On the other hand, employees need a forum in which they feel comfortable identifying the things they did well and the things they could have done better, as part of a process of ongoing professional and career development. In this respect, the performance appraisal process within any sport organization, whatever its size or type, must be seen within the simple, but effective 'plan, do, review, improve' scheme, which is usually associated with the quality assurance agenda (Deming, 1993).

In professional sports organizations in particular, the performance appraisal process is often very public, if at times convoluted. Athletes and coaches are constantly rated on their performance. In basketball, the number of points, rebounds, assists, turnovers, steals, fouls and blocked shots are recorded meticulously. From year to year, goals are set for athletes and their ability to meet targets in key performance indicators can result in an extended contract with improved conditions. On the other hand, not meeting the targets can mean a player in a sport like baseball has to return to the minor leagues, to return to form or to see out their playing days. For coaches, performance appraisal is often based on one statistic alone, the win–loss record. The fact that the coach is adept at making the players feel good about themselves or has a great working relationship with the administrative staff, will count for very little when it comes to negotiating a new contract if he or she has posted a losing record.

Phases 7 and 8: Rewards and retention

Once a sport organization has planned for, recruited, selected, orientated, trained and appraised its staff, it makes good sense that it would try to retain them. Retaining good quality staff, whether they are in a paid or volunteer capacity, means that the organization will be better off financially and strategically. Organizational knowledge and intellectual property is lost when a sport organization fails to retain its staff. Constantly losing staff will mean that the organization may have the opportunity to encourage and develop new ways of thinking, but the more likely scenario is that it will lead to wasted resources, unnecessarily diverted to rudimentary induction programmes.

The first six phases of the human resource management process all contribute to retaining staff. Poor orientation, training and performance appraisal programmes in particular can all have a negative impact on staff retention. On the other side of the retention equation, rewards and compensation can encourage employees to remain with an organization. At a professional sport organization this may mean, rather than attempting to keep wage costs low, the senior managers will be prepared to pay the 'market rate' (Smith and Stewart, 1999). In a primarily voluntary organization, the reward may take the form of a letter of appreciation for being part of a successful event and an invitation to participate next year. In other words, the reward and retention strategy will depend greatly on the context in which it is being implemented and the existing level of job satisfaction.

SUMMARY

Effective human resource management in sport organizations relies on the implementation of an interdependent set of processes. At one level this can be viewed as quite mechanistic yet, on another more positive level, it can be viewed as a blueprint for the successful management of people through a clearly delineated set of stages. Human resource management planning, recruitment, selection, orientation, training, performance appraisal, rewards and retention strategies are essential for an organization to operate successfully in state, non-profit or commercial sport environments, because good people management is at the core of every successful sport organization, irrespective of the context. Good human resource management allows sport organizations to deal with some of its unique and particular challenges, such as the place of athletes in professional sport organizations, the large casual and semi-permanent workforces required by major events (annual or periodic) and the large volunteer workforce within club-based sporting systems. On the other hand, poor human resource management can result in a workforce that is not only uncommitted, but also subject to low levels of morale and job satisfaction. In short, effective and systematic human resource management should be seen as an important management tool in any sport organization, whatever the size or type.

REVIEW QUESTIONS

1. Which is the most important phase of the human resource management process? Why? Refer in your answer to organizations with primarily paid staff and organizations with primarily volunteer staff.

2. Is human resource management important for the effective management of sport organizations? Why?

3. Examine the human resource management processes of a local sport organization. Are the processes adequate?

4. Examine the staffing levels of a major annual event in your city/province/region. Are the staffing levels stable?

5. Should the human resource management role within sport organizations be combined with another functional division?

6. Should different human resource management strategies be applied to volunteers and paid staff?

7. Does the place of athletes in professional sport organizations make the need for effective human resource management practices more or less important?

8. Compare the orientation and induction processes of a sport organization and a non-sport organization. How and why do they differ?

9. Does the often public appraisal of employees in sport organizations diminish the integrity of the human resource management process?

10. Choose a small to medium-sized organization without a human resource management specialist. Perform a job analysis for a new employee in the role of human resource management.

FURTHER READING

Chelladurai, P. (2006). *Human resource management in sport and recreation*. Human Kinetics, Champaign.

Cuskelly, G., Hoye, R. and Auld, C. (2006). *Working with volunteers in sport*. Routledge, London.

Doherty, A. (1998). Managing our human resources: a review of organizational behaviour in sport. *Journal of Sport Management*, 12, 1–24.

Robinson, L. (2004). Human resource management. In L. Robinson (ed.), *Managing public sport and leisure services*. Routledge, London.

Taylor, T., Doherty, A. and McGraw, P. (2008). *Managing people in sport organizations: a strategic human resource management perspective*. Butterworth-Heinemann, London.

RELEVANT WEBSITES

The following websites are useful starting points for further information on the human resource management of sport organizations:

Australian Sports Commission Resources at http://www.ausport.gov.au/participating/all/volunteers

Sport England's Running Sport Programme at http://www.runningsports.org/

Sport and Recreation New Zealand Resources at http://www.sparc.org.nz/sport/running-your-club/running-your-club

Case Study: Recruiting, Training and Retaining Coaches and Officials

In club-based sporting systems such as those in Australia, the UK, Canada, New Zealand and Hong Kong, the need to attract, recruit, select, train, reward and retain coaches and officials is of utmost importance. Without coaches and officials, the club-based sport system would cease to exist as we know it. Thus, the application of human resource management principles and practices is required not only to maintain the health of club-based sport, but to ensure that it continues to deliver quality experiences for those involved. This case explores the response of the Australian Sports Commission (ASC) to recruiting, training, rewarding and retaining coaches and officials. In particular, it examines research that the ASC has conducted in this area, as well as the programmes it has put in place to effectively manage sport's human resources.

In 2003, the ASC commissioned research into the recruitment and retention issues in sport officiating throughout Australia. Conducted by Griffith University, the research revealed that there was a significant problem in the retention of officials, particularly those classed as inexperienced. The research also revealed that there were significant shortcomings in the training provided for sport officials to deal with abuse and conflict situations and that the skills and abilities of sport officials' coordinators were a major factor in the recruitment, training and retention of sport officials. The recommendations that resulted from the research included that sport organizations needed to improve their recognition of officials, that a more positive image of officiating was required within the broader community and that more training and accreditation opportunities should be provided for officials. Some of the ASC's responses to the problem of recruiting, training and retaining officials and coaches are examined in the remainder of the case.

The ASC's coaching and officiating unit provides leadership in the development of coaching and officiating, with an emphasis on accreditation, training and communication. The coaching and officiating unit manages the 'National Coaching Accreditation Scheme' and the 'National Officiating Accreditation Scheme', has established general principles of coaching and accreditation that guide the practices of more than 70 national sports organizations and provides organizations with help in the recruitment, training and retention of coaches and officials.

The ASC has developed a range of tools to assist clubs in recruiting coaches and officials. First, the ASC suggests that it is important to understand the motivations of people who volunteer for coaching or officiating roles within sport, such as wanting to support a family member, wanting to give something back to the sport, wanting to do something worthwhile for young people within the community or wanting to have fun and make friends within a social environment. An understanding of these motivations can have an impact not only on the ways in which clubs recruit volunteers, but also the ways in which volunteer roles are designed and reward and recognition systems are developed and structured. Second, the ASC recommends that a club's recruiting should start with players, past players, parents and friends, because these people are most likely to have a connection with the club. The ways in which a club might recruit coaches and officials include:

- Personal contacts
- Word of mouth
- University placement/internship
- Media advertising
- Local publicity
- Community agencies
- State associations
- Recruitment agencies.

Table 7.2 is a checklist that the ASC have prepared to assist sport organizations in recruiting and retaining sport coaches and officials. Importantly, the club needs to be prepared to develop a strategy for recruiting coaches and officials if those who participated previously do not return or the demands of the club increase. Furthermore, the club also needs to invest time and resources in the development of job descriptions, which will not only aid in the recruitment of coaches and officials, but will facilitate selection, training and retention. In this respect, it is clear that many of the phases of the human resource management process are interdependent.

Table 7.2 illustrates that appropriate training and development must be engaged if clubs are to retain their largely volunteer workforce of coaches and officials. The ASC has developed training programmes that assist sporting clubs in this arena. In 2008, the ASC launched an online training course aimed at beginner officials, which takes four hours to complete and introduces new or prospective officials to topics such as the ethical responsibilities of officials, safety, effective communication strategies, people management, managing conflict and self-preparation. The course is flexible in its design, so that sport organizations are able to use the course to meet their own needs, such as requiring prospective or new officials to complete the online course prior to completing sport specific training, building the online course into an existing entry-level accreditation programme or requiring new officials to complete the course as part of an orientation or induction process.

The ASC also has an equivalent online training programme available to new or prospective coaches, which contains five training modules and takes approximately six hours to complete. Each of the modules contains an overview, case studies, interactive activities (such as video clips and 360 degree views of coaching scenes), assessment questions and further resources (such as articles and weblinks). In the case studies, the new or prospective coach is confronted with a learning activity that they need to respond to, based on their knowledge and the information provided as part of the training. The trainee is then required to respond to a question that is posed at the end of the case study. Once submitted, the trainee then has the opportunity to view a model answer, which they can use to reflect on their own answer. Each of the online training modules ends with an assessment task, which consists of a series of multiple choice style questions. The trainee must secure a perfect score in each of the modules in order to pass the online training course, although this does not need to be achieved on the first attempt, as the new or prospective coach can attempt the questions as many times as she or he requires.

One of the tools the ASC has developed as part of its programme to retain coaches and officials is the national 'Thanks' programme. The programme aims to: recognize community coaches and officials; educate, assist and encourage sporting clubs and organizations to recognize coaches and officials; educate the community about what is a good coach/official and the importance of saying thanks to coaches and officials; raise the profile of coaches and officials in the community; and raise the awareness of the National Coaching and Officiating Accreditation Schemes. The 'Thanks' programme includes simple strategies such as 'Thanks' certificates that clubs are able to download from the ASC website, as well as award programmes and a series of state based 'Thanks' programmes. For example, Sport and Recreation Tasmania (SRT) provides clubs with information designed to help them recognize volunteers. SRT advises clubs that recognition should be user-orientated in that any programme must be designed to meet the volunteers' needs and, if possible, the volunteers should be involved in the design, in order to facilitate their ownership of the process and the outcomes. The South Australian Office for Recreation and Sport runs 'Thanks Coach, Thanks Official' breakfasts, which provide the opportunity for clubs and sports to recognize the work of individual coaches and officials, and South Australia Volunteers Day, which is celebrated on a public holiday in June each year.

Case Study Questions

1. The Australian Sports Commission's assistance to sport clubs throughout Australia focuses on the recruitment, training and retention/recognition phases of the human resource management process. There is less emphasis on planning, selection, orientation and performance appraisal. What are the likely reasons for this emphasis?

Continued

2. The Australian Sports Commission suggests that understanding a volunteer's motivations will assist in recruitment and retention. Is this only true of non-profit sport organizations and the application of human resource management to volunteers, or does the same apply for sport organizations that are employing paid staff?

3. The case refers to a range of methods that a club might use to recruit coaches and officials. Which is likely to be most effective and why? Would different methods be required for paid positions within a sport organization?

4. Table 7.2 is the checklist the ASC has prepared for community based sporting clubs. Is the work required realistic? Are community sport organizations likely to have the capacity to engage completely with this process?

5. Are the initiatives outlined as part of the 'Thanks' programme likely to be successful in retaining volunteers? What other approaches or strategies are available?

Sources: Sport and Recreation Tasmania (Volunteer Recognition) Website at <http://www.development.tas.gov.au/sportrec/info/volrecognition.html>; Australian Sports Commission Website at <http://www.ausport.gov.au>; Office for Recreation and Sport (Training and Development) at <http://www.recsport.sa.gov.au/training-development/volunteers-thanks.html#1>

Table 7.2	ASC Checklist for Recruitment and Retention of Coaches and Officials

Checklist

Club plan needs to be developed to identify the club requirements for coaches and officials for the approaching season	☐
Appoint a person responsible for the coordination of coaches and officials	☐
Identify the requirements of each team in regards coaches and officials	☐
Find out who is interested and available from last season and existing club members (parents, players)	☐
If additional numbers are still required, develop and implement a recruitment strategy	☐
Develop and write job descriptions for all club coaches and officials	☐
Develop an induction handbook for new coaches and officials	☐
Collect relevant data and personal details about the applicants including information on experience, accreditation, skills and availability	☐
Interview applicants to determine their suitability for the task and to inform them about the club	☐
Determine suitability of applicant by seeking referee checks and/or other working with children checks as specified by state child protection legislation	☐
Finalize selection and appointment of coaches and officials for the club for the season and advise successful applicants	☐
Provide a job description	☐
Discuss various issues related to coaching/officiating philosophy, training and competition schedules, codes of conduct, club support, training and education needs	☐
Conduct orientation sessions and give out induction handbook	☐
Appoint club mentors	☐
Identify training and education needs of new coaches and officials	☐
Source training opportunities	☐
Invest in support resources for coaches and officials (magazines, websites, written resources, courses)	☐
Invite senior coaches and officials to address new people	☐
Monitor performance of coaches and officials – role of coaching/officiating coordinator	☐
Look for opportunities to recognize and reward coaches and officials	☐
Recognize coaches and officials formally	☐
Review and evaluate at end of season, including conducting end of season meetings and performance appraisals with each coach and official	☐
Conduct any necessary exit interviews for coaches or officials not continuing	☐
Make necessary changes for next year as a result of appraisals, exit interviews and reviews	☐
Coaching/officiating coordinator prepares report for management committee	☐
Identify next season's coaching and officiating needs	☐

Source: Australian Sports Commission website at <www.ausport.gov.au>

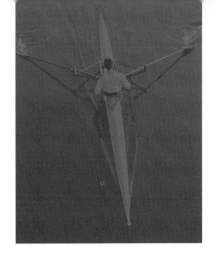

CHAPTER 8

Leadership

OVERVIEW

Leadership is probably the most researched yet least understood topic in the context of management. What we define as excellent leadership and who are great leaders remain points of serious and widespread academic debate. For example, the *Handbook of Leadership: Theory, Research and Managerial Applications* (Bass, 1990) contained over 7500 citations about the concept of leadership. In the USA alone, more than 2000 books on the topic of leadership are published every year. In this chapter we will provide a broad outline of the different approaches that have been used to describe and analyse leadership. We will also use a number of examples and cases to explore leadership. Much of this discussion will take place in reference to the leadership challenges that confront sport organizations.

By the end of this chapter the reader should be able to:

- Describe the need for leaders and for leadership

- Distinguish between leadership and management

- Outline the different levels (in the organization) that leaders can work at and how this impacts their approach to leadership

- Outline the specific challenges that leaders in sport organizations are confronted with

- Provide an overview of your personal leadership development needs.

WHAT IS LEADERSHIP?

It is not easy to find agreement among any group on a definition of leadership. Sometimes leadership is described as 'getting things done through people'. Others argue that leadership is about 'exercising power in order to influence others' or that true leadership is about 'envisioning a bright future and taking others by the hand towards it'. In other words, leadership can be many things to different people. Cotton Fitzsimmons, former coach of the Kansas City Kings argues that 'if you're a positive person, you're an automatic motivator. You can get people to do things you don't think they're capable of' (Westerbeek and Smith, 2005). Vince Lombardi, the famous coach of the Green Bay Packers of the 1950s and 1960s, once said that 'leaders are made, they are not born; and they are made just like anything else has been made in this country – by hard effort. And that's the price that we all have to pay to achieve that goal, or any goal' (Westerbeek and Smith, 2005). According to former US President Theodore Roosevelt, 'the best executive is the one who has sense enough to pick good men to do what he wants done, and self-restraint enough to keep from meddling with them while the do it', and Lou Holts, a former coach of the Notre Dame football team, argued that, 'all winning teams are goal-oriented. Teams like these win consistently because everyone connected with them concentrates on specific objectives. They go about their business with blinders on; nothing will distract them from achieving their aims' (Westerbeek and Smith, 2005). A few things stand out from all these quotes. According to these experienced, but very different leaders, leadership is:

- goal oriented
- about influencing others
- about empowering others
- about seeing the big picture
- about needing others
- about strength of character.

We can use these different components of leadership to construct a leadership definition. For the purposes of this book, we define leadership as 'skilfully influencing and enabling others towards the attainment of aspirational goals'. We do appreciate that we may not do justice to the many aspects one can argue that need to be incorporated in a complete definition of leadership but, as an introduction to the topic in this book, the above definition will serve its purpose. In the next section of this chapter we will further outline the ways that leadership can be viewed.

In Practice 8.1 Li Ning: Olympic Gold Leading to Sporting Goods Dominance

Li Ning is one of China's favourite sons. He won six Olympic medals in gymnastics, three of which were gold, during the 1984 Los Angeles Games. Li Ning has been an important role model for the Chinese people during a time of societal transformation and has been used by the Chinese government as an example of the 'new' Chinese. In 1990, Li Ning set up his own company, appropriately named after himself and, with that, started an exciting journey of building the number one Chinese sporting goods company and possibly the number one sporting goods company in the world in the near future.

As a result of his high visibility in Chinese society and the ubiquitous recognition of his name among Chinese citizens, the company rapidly grew during the first few years of its existence. It seemed that the emerging 'Li Ning' brand could be used to sell anything. However, selling Li Ning perfume, among other things, turned out to be stopping the company in its progress and its ambition to grow quickly. Li Ning realized that his name could be used in the short term to sell lots of different products, but that, in the long term, people would only remember him for his sporting prowess. This made Li Ning and his Board of Directors decide to pursue a focus strategy for the company. Because Li Ning was inextricably related to sport it seemed logical that the company would focus its activities on sport products, in particular sporting goods. This focus on core business has led to Li Ning now being the biggest Chinese sporting goods company in the world and the number three company in China, aggressively pursuing numbers 1 and 2 Nike and Adidas. Li Ning holds 9.6% of the Chinese market, Adidas 12.3% and Nike 13.1%.

Many would argue that it is impossible to overtake sporting goods giants like Nike and Adidas, who have access to enormous economies of scale advantages (due to their market leadership in respectively the USA and EU). However, Li Ning's strategy to grow is surprisingly simple and logical. Their chairman, the visionary Li Ning himself, argues that their primary customers are children in the age category of 12–20. Capture their imagination and they will make sure their parents will buy them a (few) pair(s) of $120 sneakers. Then make sure that you focus on sports that now and in the future will be the ones that Chinese customers favour. These sports are football, basketball, running, tennis and fitness.

Li Ning has a tremendous advantage over Nike and Adidas in China, arguably because they are a Chinese company with a Chinese iconic chairman and are in a better position than Nike and Adidas to understand the Chinese market. If you then realize that the Chinese market for sporting goods is growing four times as fast as the US and EU markets and that the Chinese still spend four times less on footwear than US and UK consumers, it becomes clear that growing home market share over the next decade will greatly contribute to Li Ning also improving its standing globally – home market dominance as a means towards global expansion.

Li Ning has also realized that leadership in the global sporting goods business requires a leadership role in regard to engaging with local communities. This is why the company has developed a programme to educate physical education teachers to work in regional China. To date, the company has provided the resources for 920 teachers to move to

Continued

In Practice 8.1 Li Ning: Olympic Gold Leading to Sporting Goods Dominance—cont'd

regional Chinese communities and assist local schools to develop physical education programmes. It will be interesting to watch Li Ning's progress over the next decade. We may well witness the birth of a global sporting goods giant, built by a Chinese leader in sport, on and off the field of play.

Source: Interview with Frank Zhang, senior Vice President with Li Ning on 16 March 2008, and information at http://www.lining.com

THEORIES OF LEADERSHIP

Personality or trait theories form the basis of the earliest approaches to studying leadership. These theories were underpinned by the assumption that certain traits and skills are essential for leadership effectiveness.

Trait or personality approaches

Although the personality and trait approaches to leadership stem from the earliest of leadership research times, popular leadership literature continues to stress the importance of personality and innate ability in the demonstration of leadership. Locke (1991) argues that trait theories (or great man theories as they are also called) are incomplete theories of leadership, irrespective of traits and/or personality of the leaders being important contributors to, or detractors from excellent leadership. Locke (1991) suggests that the possession of certain traits, such as energy and honesty, appear to be vital for effective leadership. Basketball legend Michael Jordan, for example, has been credited with having an impressive range of innate leadership traits that will put him in good stead of being an excellent leader in many different contexts. Leaders must use their traits to develop skills, formulate a vision and implement this vision into reality. This being the case, it appears that traits only form part of the picture.

Although empirical evidence linking the personality of leaders with their success is weak, it is still valuable examining leadership personalities from a wide range of sources (e.g. popular literature) to provide a better understanding of leadership. In general, the trait theories are based on the assumption that social background, physical features and personality characteristics will distinguish good leaders from poor leaders.

Behavioural approach

When it became clear that good leadership could not simply be explained on the basis of the innate characteristics of the leaders, organizational research began to focus on discovering universal behaviours of effective leaders. Behaviourists argued that anyone could be taught to become a leader by simply learning the behaviours of other effective leaders.

Behavioural strategy takes behaviours as signs of learned responses to contingencies. If research shows that to behave in a certain manner results in success for a leader, then one can learn to discharge those behaviours in particular leadership situations. The behavioural approach to leadership was also a response to early approaches to management as a whole. Frederick Taylor was an early champion of the idea that managers should use science to improve efficiency. This approach became known as Taylorism or Scientific management, a philosophy in which there was limited attention for the human side of the mass production movement. Rather, under Taylorism, humans were simply 'part of the larger machines' and standardization of human labour would lead to great efficiency and higher profits. Managers, according to Taylor, should begin by studying the tasks workers performed, break jobs down by analysing, measuring and timing each separate element of the job in order to determine the most efficient manner of doing the job. The most efficient method for each job became both the standard method that workers were supposed to adopt and a means for measuring worker productivity.

In response to Taylor's ideas, behaviouralists demanded a new 'human relations' approach to management of organizations involving an examination of the interaction between managers and workers. In the Hawthorne experiments, which were originally designed to study the effects of lighting upon factory workers, Elton Mayo discovered that human relations between workers and between workers and supervisors was most important in ensuring efficiency. In other words, to focus on interaction between humans and by studying the best ways of interacting, managers could better lead the people that worked for the organization. Another behavioural approach to the study of leadership is the so-called Theory X and Theory Y, developed by Douglas McGregor. The theories are formulated based on the assumptions that leaders have about individuals. Managers that have Theory X assumptions argue that the typical employee dislikes work and needs direction at all times. They also think that employees need to be coerced to perform their duties. Theory Y managers believe that employees are self-motivated and committed to work and to the company. They naturally seek responsibility for the work they perform. As a result, Theory Y leaders would behave in quite different ways from Theory X leaders.

Another behaviouralist approach was formulated by Blake and Mouton. They developed the managerial grid model along two dimensions, one with a concern for people and one with a concern for production. Blake and Mouton argued that differing levels of concern along those dimensions would lead to different styles of leadership. For example, managers with low levels of concern for people and production will have an impoverished style of leadership, whereas those leaders with high concern for people and production can be typified as having team style leadership qualities. The Blake and Mouton approach has also been used to differentiate person-centred leaders from task-centred leaders. Ultimately, it is important to conclude that the behaviouralist approach to leadership leads to the identification of different styles that can be described as more or less successful.

Contingency approach

It became increasingly clear to those studying leadership that traits and behaviours of leaders were often observed in relation to the situation at hand or, in other words, according to situational contingencies. Isolated behavioural and trait approaches failed to take account of how situational variables, such as task structure, the characteristics of the environment, or subordinate characteristics could impact and moderate the relationship between the behaviour of a leader and the different outcomes.

In contingency theories of leadership, the core argument is that different leadership styles and approaches will apply to a range of possible management situations. This is why, for example, the on-field leadership brilliance of Diego Maradona with the Argentinean team resulted in winning the 1986 World Cup, but when Diego was required to achieve similar results with club teams in different cultures (Napoli in Italy and Barcelona in Spain), he failed dismally, also resulting in the exposure of a number of personal leadership flaws. The centrality of leader behaviour and/or personality needs to be de-emphasized and, in the contingency approach, we turn our attention to the leader in conjunction with circumstances that are specific to the situation at hand, including characteristics of the subordinates and the work setting. In the next section, we will present three situational theories of leadership that have influenced the ways in which leadership is understood and practised. They are:

- Fiedler's Least Preferred Co-worker Approach

- Hersey and Blanchard's Situational Leadership Theory

- Path–Goal Theory.

Fiedler's Least Preferred Co-worker approach

Fiedler's (1967) model is based on the following three axioms:

1. The interaction between the leader's personal characteristics and some aspects of the situation determines the effectiveness of the leader

2. Leaders are either 'task oriented' or 'person oriented'

3. Effectiveness of the leader is determined by the leader's control of the situation.

Fiedler comes to his classification of task or person oriented leadership by the use of a measurement scale called the 'Least Preferred Co-worker' (LPC) scale. The instrument asks leaders to assess co-workers on a series of bi-polar descriptors including pleasant–unpleasant, cold–warm, and supportive–hostile in order to assess to what degree they think they would not work well together with that co-worker. A leader who obtains a low LPC is more motivated by task achievements and will only be concerned about relationships with subordinates if the work unit is deemed to be performing well. A leader who obtains a high LPC score will be more motivated to develop close interpersonal relations with subordinates. Task directed behaviour is of a lesser concern and only becomes important once sound interpersonal relations have been developed. According to Fiedler, if the least preferred co-worker still scores relatively high, it indicates that the leader derives a sense of satisfaction from 'working on good relationships', indicating a person oriented leadership style.

The model further suggests that control is dependent on three combined contingency variables:

1. The relations between the leader and the followers

2. The degree of task structure (or the degree to which the followers' jobs can be specified clearly)

3. The leader's position of power or amount of authority, yielding eight possible conditions presented in Table 8.1.

Hersey and Blanchard's Situational Leadership Theory

A theory claiming that as maturity of the group changes, leader behaviour should change as well, is known as the Situational Theory of Leadership. Hersey and Blanchard (1977) argued that as the technical skill level and psychological maturity of the group moves from low to moderate to high, the leader's behaviour would be most effective when it changes accordingly. When low levels of maturity are enacted in relation to the tasks being performed, a high task behaviour of the leader should be exhibited or, in other words, a 'selling' and 'telling' approach to communicating with the subordinates. At medium levels of maturity, leaders need to be more focused on relationship behaviours and, at the highest levels of subordinate maturity, the leader needs to offer little direction or task behaviour and allow the

Table 8.1	Fiedler's Situational Favourability Factors and Leadership Effectiveness

| | Situational Favourability | | | |
Condition	Leader-Member Relations	Task Structure	Position Power	Effective Leadership
1	Good	High	Strong	Low LPC
2	Good	High	Weak	Low LPC
3	Good	Weak	Strong	Low LPC
4	Good	Weak	Weak	High LPC
5	Poor	High	Strong	High LPC
6	Poor	High	Weak	High LPC
7	Poor	Weak	Strong	High LPC
8	Poor	Weak	Weak	Low LPC

Adapted from Fiedler, F.E. (1967), A theory of leadership effectiveness. McGraw Hill, New York, p. 34.

subordinate to assume responsibilities, or in other words, a 'supportive' and 'delegation' driven style of leadership communication.

According to sport organization theory researcher Trevor Slack (2006), there have been few attempts to test empirically the concepts and relationships that Hersey and Blanchard (1977) have outlined in their work, even in the management and organizational literature. Some attempts have been made to apply the theory directly in sport settings, but results have been inconsistent.

The path–goal theory

The path–goal theory (House, 1971) takes a behavioural and situational approach to leadership. There are many roads that lead to Rome and therefore the path–goal theory suggests that a leader must select a style most appropriate to the particular situation. The theory, in particular, aims to explain how a leader's behaviour affects the motivation and satisfaction of subordinates.

House (1971) is cited in Wexley and Yukl, (1984) arguing that, 'the motivational function of the leaders consists of increasing personal payoffs to subordinates for work–goal attainment, and making the path to these payoffs easier to travel by clarifying it, reducing roadblocks and pitfalls, and increasing the opportunities for personal satisfaction en route'. In other words, characteristics of the subordinates and characteristics of the environment determine both the potential for increased motivation and the manner in which the leader must act to improve motivation. Subordinate preferences for a particular pattern of leadership behaviour may also depend on the actual situation in which they are placed (Wexley and Yukl, 1984). Taking those different perspectives in consideration, the path–goal theory proposes four styles of leadership behaviour that can be utilized to achieve goals (House and Mitchell, 1974). They are:

- Directive leadership (leader gives specific instructions, expectations and guidance)

- Supportive leadership (leader shows concern and support for subordinates)

- Participative leadership (subordinates participate in the decision-making)

- Achievement-oriented leadership (leader sets challenges, emphasizes excellence and shows confidence that subordinates will attain high standards of performance).

The theory is principally aimed at examining how leaders affect subordinate expectations about likely outcomes of different courses of action. Directive leadership is predicted to have a positive effect on subordinates when the task is ambiguous and will have a negative impact when the task is clear. Supportive leadership is predicted to increase job satisfaction, particularly when conditions are adverse. Achievement-oriented leadership is predicted to encourage higher performance standards and increase expectancies that desired outcomes can be achieved. Participative leadership is predicted to promote satisfaction due to involvement (Schermerhorn et al., 1994).

From transactional to transformational leadership

As already noted earlier in this chapter, the scientific approach to management (Taylorism) reduced the individual to performing machine-like functions. The human relations approach to management took into consideration the human part of the labour equation, appreciating that much better results can be achieved if people's individual needs are taken into consideration when leading them towards achieving certain work outputs.

One of the most recent thrusts in leadership research is that of transactional and transformational leadership. Transactional leadership encompasses much of the theories based on rational exchange between leader and subordinate, such as the theories presented above, but transformational leaders, according to Bass (1985), are charismatic and develop followers into leaders through a process that transcends the existing organizational climate and culture. The transactional leader aims to create a cost–benefit economic exchange or, in other words, to meet the needs of followers in return for 'contracted' services that are produced by the follower (Bass, 1985). To influence behaviour, the transactional leader may use the following approaches:

- Contingent reward (the leader uses rewards or incentives to achieve results)

- Active management by exception (the leader actively monitors the work performed and uses corrective methods to ensure the work meets accepted standards)

- Passive management by exception (the leader uses corrective methods as a response to unacceptable performance or deviation from the accepted standards)

- Laissez-faire leadership (the leader is indifferent and has a 'hands-off' approach toward the workers and their performance).

However, leadership theorists have argued that transactional leadership merely seeks to influence others by exchanging work for wages. It fails to build on the worker's need for meaningful work and it does not actively tap into their sources of creativity. A more effective and beneficial leadership behaviour to achieve long-term success and improved performance therefore is transformational leadership. Sir Alex Ferguson, the long-time Manchester United manager, can be described as a transformational leader. He envisioned a future for the club and the Board repaid him with the trust of keeping him at the helm at Manchester United since 1986 for more than 1200 games. Under his guidance and supervision, the club became the most successful team in the new English Premier League and the team has also won multiple Champions League crowns. Sir Alex has prepared the likes of Eric Cantona, Ryan Giggs, Roy Keane, David Beckham, Ruud van Nistelrooy, Wayne Rooney and Cristiano Ronaldo for the world stage of football leadership.

What is transformational leadership?

It has been argued by Bass and Avolio (1994) that transformational leadership is the new leadership that must accompany good management. In contrast to transactional models, transformational leadership goes beyond the exchange process. It not only aligns and elevates the needs and values of followers, but also provides intellectual stimulation and increased follower confidence. Bass and Avolio (1994) identified four 'I's' that transformational leaders employ in order to achieve superior results. These are:

- Idealized influence: transformational leaders behave in ways that result in them being admired, respected and trusted and ultimately becoming a role model. The transformational leader demonstrates high standards of ethical and moral conduct

- Inspirational motivation: by demonstrating enthusiasm and optimism, the transformational leader actively arouses team spirit and motivates and inspires followers to share in and work towards a common goal

- Intellectual stimulation: by being innovative, creative, supportive, reframing problems and questioning old assumptions, the transformational leader creates an intellectually stimulating and encouraging environment

- Individualized consideration: transformational leaders pay special attention to each individual's needs for achievement and growth by acting as a coach or mentor.

Looking closer at the four, it can be argued that charisma (the ability to inspire enthusiasm, interest or affection in others by means of personal charm or influence) is an important component of transformational leadership. Purely charismatic leaders may be limited in their ability to achieve successful outcomes, due to their need to instill their beliefs in others which may inhibit the individual growth of followers. However, transformational leaders are more than charismatic in that they generate awareness of the mission or vision of the team and the organization and then motivate colleagues and followers towards outcomes that benefit the team rather than merely serving the individual interest.

In Practice 8.2 Right to Play: Johan Olav Koss and Bettering the World
The primary objective of *Right To Play*, formerly known as *Olympic Aid*, the legacy project of the Lillehammer Olympic Organizing Committee, is to engage leaders in sport, business and media in the betterment of living conditions and developmental opportunities for children all over the world. In March 2001, *Olympic Aid* became an implementing NGO (non-governmental organization) and, by organizing child development programmes and engaging in research and policy development, it works towards improving the chances that all children are guaranteed their right to play.

Four time Olympic gold medallist Johann Olav Koss, the current CEO and President of the organization, was the driving force behind the transition of *Olympic Aid* into *Right to Play*. Having visited the country of Eritrea during his sporting career, as an athlete ambassador, he was so affected by the living conditions of the local children in particular, that he decided to donate the majority of his Olympic winnings to Olympic Aid. In the process, he challenged other athletes and the public to do the same, leading to the raising of US$18 million. Between 1994 and 2000, Olympic Aid continued to raise funds for children in disadvantaged situations, building on the momentum of subsequent Olympic Games.

Continued

In Practice 8.2 Right to Play: Johan Olav Koss and Bettering the World—cont'd

In early 2003, Olympic Aid evolved into *Right To Play* in order to meet the growing demands of programme implementation and fundraising. Building on the founding legacy of Lillehammer, this transition allowed *Right To Play* to include both Olympic athletes and other high profile sportsmen and women as athlete ambassadors, but also increase relationships with non-Olympic sports, partner with a wider variety of private sector funding agents and to deepen involvement at the grassroots level of sport. In 2005, *Right to Play* was instrumental in setting up the Sport for Development and Peace International Working group (SDP IWG). This initiative emerged from the work of the United Nations Inter-Agency Task Force on Sport for Development and Peace. United in the SDP IWG are delegates from governments, UN agencies and international NGOs that include sport governing bodies and other development agencies. The SDP IWG is run by an Executive Committee and supported by a bureau and secretariat. The Executive Committee has as its members a number of government ministers, deputy ministers and senior UN officials who work together to secure the support of national governments and the UN to use sport for development and peace purposes. The objective of the group is to articulate and promote the adoption of policy recommendations to national governments for the integration of sport and physical activity into their national and international development strategies and programmes. At www.righttoplay.com it can be read that, 'Sport for Development and Peace evolved from a growing body of evidence showing that well-designed sport-based initiatives incorporating the best values of sport can be powerful, practical and cost-effective tools to achieve development and peace objectives. Sport is now recognized by many international experts in the fields of development, education, health, sport, economics and conflict resolution as a simple, low cost, and effective means of achieving a diverse range of development goals'.

The vision of leading athlete Johan Olav Koss has been translated into a highly successful organization that he continues to head up today as an organizational leader, developing and delivering a range of child and community development programmes that use sport and play as vehicles of communication and fund raising. To a large extent, sport leads the way as well.

Source: Experts and information from http://www.righttoplay.com and http://iwg.sportanddev.org/en/index.htm

LEADERSHIP AND MANAGEMENT

At this stage of the chapter, it will be useful to consider briefly the debate about the relationship between leadership and management and how to distinguish between the two. Kotter (1990) has conducted extensive research work in order to find out how to differentiate managers from leaders. He concluded that management effectiveness rests in the ability to plan and budget, organize and staff and control and solve problems. Leadership, however, is principally founded upon the ability to establish direction, align people and to motivate and inspire. According to Kotter, leaders achieve change while managers succeed in maintaining the status quo. Bass (1990), however, states that 'leaders manage and managers lead, but the two activities are not synonymous'. It goes beyond the scope of this book to elaborate further on the distinction between leadership and management. Suffice to say that, in the context of discussing management principles in sport organizations, management without leadership is much less likely to be successful than a capable manager who can also provide excellent leadership. In the next section, we will therefore put forward what can be described as the five key functions of leadership:

- To create a vision
- To set out strategy
- To set objectives and lead towards performance
- To influence and motivate people
- To facilitate change and nurture culture.

To create a vision

A vision can be described as 'a state of the future that lies beyond the directly imaginable by most people'. This view of the future, in the context of an organization, is a positive and bright state of being that only the 'visionary' (one who is characterized by unusually acute foresight and imagination) can see at that time. In other words, the leader is responsible for envisioning a future for the organization that can become reality if the people working in the organization can be aligned towards achieving that 'envisioned state'. It is often said that good leaders distinguish themselves from good managers because they do have a vision, whereas managers do not. How to achieve the vision through strategy is the next function of the leader.

To set out strategy

The process of strategic planning is all about the different ways that a vision can be achieved. It constitutes two principal perspectives: that of the organization and that of the individuals making up the organization. Visionary leaders are not necessarily successful leaders if they are not capable of translating the vision into action strategies. The process of strategic management is therefore concerned with carefully managing the internal organization, including considering the individual needs of workers, and the external environment in which many opportunities and threats impact the ability of the leader to achieve the vision. To be better prepared for action, the leader needs to be involved in setting measurable objectives.

To set objectives and lead towards performance

Setting objectives is the next function of the leader. Once the broad strategies have been set out (and these strategies are never set in concrete, they need constant updating), it is time to link measurable outcomes to these strategies. In other words, what do we want to achieve in the short term, in order to work towards our visionary objectives that lie ahead in the distant future. Stated differently, the leader often is involved in setting objectives at different levels of the organization, ranging from 'visionary' and strategic objectives to mostly delegating the responsibility to set more operational objectives at lower levels of the organization. Only when SMART (specific, measurable, achievable, resources available, time bound) objectives are set, will the leader be in a position to manage the performance of the organization and its employees effectively. An important part of the performance of an organization is achieved through the people management skills of the leader.

To influence and motivate people

In our overview of the different approaches to leadership, we have already commented on the different styles that leaders chose to develop (because they better fit their skill set) in order to influence groups of people and communicate with individuals or teams. Where setting objectives is important in making people aware of the targets of performance, the actual activation and application of people skills is critical when trying to steer people in a certain direction. This is where leaders with charismatic appeal will have an easier job. Their natural ability to inspire enthusiasm, interest or affection in others by means of personal charm or influence will put these leaders in a favourable position in regard to achieving the objectives that were set.

To facilitate change and nurture culture

Finally, it is important to acknowledge that, in this day and age, change is constant. Leaders who are incapable of assisting others to understand why 'change' is needed and how this change can be achieved with minimal disruption and maximum outcomes will have a difficult time surviving in the organizations of the 21st century. Most organizations are required to keep close track of the market conditions that they are working under and the impact changes in market conditions will have on their structures and strategies. Often a rapid response to changing market conditions is needed and this is where the interesting relationship with the organization's culture comes into play. Ironically, a strong and stable organizational culture can contribute to the need constantly to modify direction and changing the systems and structures of the organization. It is the leaders' responsibility to create and nurture a culture in which change is accepted as part of the natural way of organizational life. A strong culture is the backbone of any successful organization and the maintenance of culture is therefore one of the primary areas of leadership responsibility.

In Practice 8.3 Arjan Bos Transforms Professional Speed Skating

Arjan Bos is the Chairman of the Board and CEO of Dutch insurance company TVM. Based in the city of Hoogeveen in the northern part of The Netherlands, TVM has steadily grown from a small player in the international transport insurance industry, to become one of the main specialist insurers in their line of business. Starting their business in the domestic marketplace of the Netherlands, they are now also market leaders in Belgium and Luxembourg and are rapidly gaining market share in countries such as Denmark and some of the new EU members in Eastern Europe. Sport has played a significant role in their rise to dominance.

Arjan Bos was still a law student at Groningen University when his father was heading up TVM as its CEO. TVM is not a family business, it just happened that Arjan was the best candidate for the job when his father decided it was time to retire in 2001. But it was much earlier, in 1988, when Arjan took his first summer job at TVM while finishing his law degree. After 10 years of sponsoring amateur cycling, TVM had become seriously involved as a sport sponsor in 1986 when they decided to start sponsoring a small professional cycling outfit. Arjan travelled with the professional cycling team to the big European summer events such as the Tour de France and the major classic courses, as the hospitality host of the team. TVM had decided to sponsor cycling driven by the company's desire to enter the Belgium marketplace.

Cycling, not football, is the most popular sport in Belgium and without too much further research it was decided that it might be a good idea 'to do something with cycling' in order to gain exposure for TVM products in Belgium. Arjan's working at the coalface of professional cycling taught him many important lessons that were critical in the decisions that he had to take regarding the direction of the company later in life. He learned the importance of building a strong team and what it takes to build a strong team in order to perform at the top level: a good atmosphere, what motivates people, how to inspire individuals and small teams, and last but not least, how one can build his network by entertaining people through sport.

Still a student, Arjan had the private numbers of Ministers and Captains of industry in his notebook. To achieve this he only had to provide them with a great hospitality experience and take them out on a day with the team at the event. TVM liked his work so much that he was promoted to PR manager of the company in 1990, although he was still a student. In 1994, upon graduation, he was offered the position of Head of

Continued

In Practice 8.3 Arjan Bos Transforms Professional Speed Skating—cont'd

Communication and Marketing and he further advanced in the company to become the Director of Sales and Marketing in 1997. His exposure to the cycling team remained intense as the majority of TVM's marketing budget was poured into sport sponsoring.

Throughout the years they had found that sport did offer them a separate place in the mind of the consumer and, if quality is combined with long-term planning, customers will associate the products of the company with similar characteristics. When Arjan Bos was offered the job of Chairman of the Board and CEO of the company, he was the first to acknowledge the importance of his time as public face of the company through the cycling team. As spokesperson, figure head, trouble shooter and networker, he had not only gained the trust of his superiors but also built his reputation as a capable and hardworking colleague among the employees of the organization. In the meantime, TVM had broken its relationship with cycling in 1999 after 13 years of sponsoring a professional team and moved into sponsoring marathon speed skating.

So far the story still looks like a simple sponsor–sponsee relationship – TVM hands over significant resources to a professional skating team to prepare for and participate in competition. However, Arjan's time in professional cycling and his general understanding of 'common' sport sponsorship relations had taught him a few valuable lessons. He found that one of the critical success factors of successful sponsorship was to have unlimited access to the star athletes of the sport, because they are the ones who perform and hence communicate on behalf of the company. Another success factor was to have better control over the publicity and public relations in regard to the sponsored property. Arjan Bos's solution to deal with these issues was surprisingly simple and straightforward. Rather than to sponsor a (skating) team he made them employees of the (insurance) company and integrated them into the company's overall communication strategy. He placed the skating team in a separate structure belonging to the TVM holding company. By turning the athletes into employees, their loyalty first and foremost has to be to their employer, cutting out competition from other potential sponsors. Subsponsor contracts are exclusively entered into by TVM and individual sponsorships for the athletes need to be first approved by TVM.

In regard to preparing for peak performance, the TVM company obtained full control over the appointment of the technical staff and is now in a position to plan for the long-term future (success) of the team. All planning and preparation is geared towards winning multiple gold medals at the Winter Olympic Games of Vancouver (2010) and Sochi (2014). The team now holds multiple world and Olympic champions, including a medal winning top coach. However, it took a visionary sport manager who also turned out to become a highly successful corporate leader, to bring sport and business together as close as they can be, under the wings of one brand and one company.

Source: Interviews with Arjan Bos, Chairman of the Board and CEO of TVM Insurance on 26 May 2008 and 26 June 2008.

LEADERSHIP CHALLENGES IN SPORT ORGANIZATIONS

So far, we have mainly been talking about generic leadership theory and principles, simply, because it applies to sport organizations in the same way as it does to non-sport organizations. We have also discussed the interrelationship between leadership and management and how leadership is largely about establishing visionary direction and then to motivate and align people and structures towards that direction. The In Practice 8.3 has shown that, sometimes, visionary direction needs to be supplied from outside. However, there will also be specific challenges for leaders (and managers) of sport organizations that are based on the unique characteristics of (some) sport organizations. In our discussion of these characteristics, we will take a closer look at the leadership and management challenges sport organizations at the local, national and international levels.

Small community-based sport clubs and regionally-based sport associations

Small community-based sport clubs are traditionally established and managed by the same people; those who share a passion for a particular sport and are interested in participating in some form of organized competition. Regional volunteer associations are similar in their structure and processes in that they largely coordinate the competitions that the community clubs are playing in and, as such, they represent the interests of the individual clubs. Most of these clubs and associations are run by volunteers, leading to relatively low levels of professionalism and standardization of organizational processes. They operate in suburban or regional communities with little desire or incentive to expand and grow beyond their identified community base. The main challenge for the leaders of small clubs and their representatives at the regional level is, first and foremost, to survive in an environment of decreasing levels of volunteer labour and commitment. Increasing competition for the scarce leisure time of members leads to a diminishing supply of free labour. Club and association leaders need to envision how they can transform their ways of operating into more professional and competitive ways of sport service delivery, but they have to do that without abundant volunteer resources. Most of these challenges are of a tactical or operational nature. Typical leadership questions that club and association leaders are faced with today are:

- Can small clubs survive or should they consider merging or relocating?

- How can we retain our younger members and our most valued volunteers?

- How can we attract new resources to the club in order to pay for professional services?

- How can we maintain the culture of the club?

National sporting organizations

Many national sporting organizations (NSOs) have already successfully negotiated and adapted to the changing community landscape of sport and are now in a position to face the next set of challenges. In much the same way as community- and regionally-based sport organizations, national governing bodies are confronted with higher levels of customer expectations in combination with fewer resources to deliver those services. In a better position than community organizations to lobby for resources at the different levels of government, many of the national governing bodies have increased their levels of professionalism and standards of service delivery by employing professionally educated staff in their organizations. Leaders are now facing increased competition for paying customers to become affiliated to the sport's governing bodies. A major dilemma for national governing bodies is the fact that they only have one core product, their sport, which only offers limited strategic scope to expand into existing or new markets. The leaders of national sporting organizations also are confronted by commercial organizations that are only interested in the high performance end of their sport. The TVM example in this chapter shows that the Royal Dutch Skating Association is losing control over its elite skating athletes. NSOs also face the issue of the increasing gap between the 'haves' (i.e. the popular television and Olympic sports) and the 'have nots' (i.e. minority sports). In other words, do leaders want 'all sports for all' or rather, let the market decide about the sports that will stay and grow and those that will fade into insignificance. The answer to this question also impacts where leaders of NSOs will focus much of their attention – on elite or mass participation sport. Most of these challenges are of a strategic nature. Typical leadership questions that the leaders of national sport governing bodies are faced with today are:

- Are we a national or international sport or in other words, what is our marketplace?

- What is best for our sport: a focus on elite, on mass participation, or an equal balance between the two?

- How can we better deliver our sport through the regional and local associations and clubs? (this is a systems question)

- How can we change our systems of governance to be better prepared for radical (short-term) changes in the sport market?

International federations and professional sport

Although there may be quite significant differences in size and structure between the International Federations (IFs) and professional sport organizations (ranging from clubs to the governing bodies), the leaders of these organizations are largely confronted with the same leadership challenges. If NSOs were already concerned with questions about what their marketplace is, then the IFs and professional sport organizations should be able to answer those questions now. As with the lead that NSOs are taking in relation to the community and regional sport organizations below them in the hierarchy, the IFs are leading the way for NSOs in regard to their leadership challenges. Both the IFs and professional sport organizations are required to make genuinely visionary decisions in that competition is forcing them to think outside the square of previous operations. The World Wrestling Federation (now World Wrestling Entertainment – WWE) had to make a decision about operating in the sport or entertainment market, Manchester United and the New York Yankees are working on market expansion beyond football and baseball and the world governing body for football, FIFA, is seriously considering its options beyond simply organizing football competitions (albeit a few very profitable ones). Europe's governing body for football, UEFA, has major headaches about the possibility that the strongest European clubs will create a competition of their own, which will virtually eliminate the highly lucrative Champions League that is owned and operated by the UEFA. The leaders of IFs and professional sport organizations face truly visionary leadership challenges. Typical leadership questions that these leaders are confronted with today are:

- Are we in the business of sport or are we simply competing for people's leisure time?

- How much control do we need to exercise in terms of our chain of distribution? For example, do we need to own our sporting facilities and broadcast centres rather than contracting with other owners?

- How will the market for sport, entertainment and leisure develop over the next decade? Where do we need to be placed in order to become and remain major players in those markets?

- Who will be the leaders for the sport of the future?

SUMMARY

In this chapter we described what it takes to be a leader. We argued that irrespective of leadership type or style, leaders are goal oriented; they influence others; they empower others; they need to remain focused on the big picture; they need others to achieve their goals; and they have strong characters. Based on these components of leadership we discussed a number of theoretical approaches to leadership including the trait/personality, behavioural and contingency approaches, ultimately resulting in a discussion about transactional versus transformational leadership. Prior to looking at the future challenges for leaders in sport at the end of the chapter, we highlighted the differences between managers and leaders by outlining what are the functions of leaders. These functions were the creation of a vision; the setting out of strategy; setting objectives and measuring performance; influencing and motivating people; and finally, to facilitate change and nurture organizational culture.

REVIEW QUESTIONS

1. Are leaders born or can they be made? Justify your answer by comparing the different leadership theories discussed in this chapter.

2. Does sport offer valuable leadership lessons to business? What are the specific characteristics of sport organizations that challenge leaders in sport organizations more than leaders in business and how can this knowledge be transferred to a non-sport context?

3. 'A good manager is also a good leader'. Do you agree or disagree with this statement. Justify your answer.

4. Explain how leadership is important for the performance of a sport organization.

5. Interview the leader of a small sport organization. How would you describe their leadership style?

6. Is their any difference in the leadership skills required to be the CEO of a major professional sport franchise versus the manager of community sports club?

7. What criteria would you use to evaluate the leadership skills of a sport manager?

8. Is it possible to compare the performance of leaders of two different sport organizations? Why or why not?

FURTHER READING

Bass, B.M. (1990). *Bass & Stogdill's handbook of leadership: theory, research, and managerial applications*, 3rd edn. Free Press, New York.

Kotter, J.P. (1990). *A force for change: how leadership differs from management*. The Free Press, New York.

Kouzes, J.M. and Posner, B.Z. (2006). *A leader's legacy*. Jossey-Bass, Hoboken.

Locke, E.A. (1991). *The essence of leadership: the four keys to leading successfully*. Lexington Books, New York.

Slack, T. and Parent, M. (2006). *Understanding sport organizations: the application of organization theory*, 2nd edn. Human Kinetics, Champaign.

Thomas, R.J. (2008). *Crucibles of leadership*. Harvard Business School Publishing Corporation, Boston.

RELEVANT WEBSITES

Right to Play at http://www.righttoplay.com/
Li Ning at at http://www.lining.com/
The Centre for Creative Leadership at http://www.ccl.org/
The Test Café Leadership Test at http://www.testcafe.com/lead/
Leadership directories at http://www.leadershipdirectories.com/
W.K. Kellogg Foundation Leadership Development Websites at http://www.wkkf.org/

Case Study: Leadership within the Royal Dutch Hockey Association

Johan Wakkie has been the CEO of Dutch hockey since 1994. When he took charge of the sport, hockey was in danger of dropping out of the list of Holland's favoured Olympic and participation sports. In June 1999, Wakkie took his vision for hockey to the General Assembly of the Royal Dutch Hockey Association that voted in favour of the proposed Strategic Plan 2010, a plan that was put together in close communication and collaboration with all hockey clubs in The Netherlands. One of the main objectives of the plan is the ambition to grow to 175 000 members in 2010. This ambition is footnoted with the statement that growth should be accompanied with the maintenance of both quality of the hockey experience and of hockey club culture.

During the national hockey congress in 2006, an updated strategic vision was presented which was again agreed to by the General Assembly. This Strategic Plan 2015 became a necessity because hockey as a sport had developed more rapidly then expected and also because ongoing research had put a different light on the societal trends, the association's target marketing and its national policy that were considered the drivers of the previous strategic plan.

Trends 2010

The Stategic Plan 2010 was based on societal trends that were 'translated' to hockey. Three of these trends were specifically applicable to hockey and the fourth trend was important in the wider context of the Dutch consumer society.

Trend 1 – Time, The Most Precious Commodity

People use their time differently compared to the 1980s. Time is a scarce resource and is spread across a range of diverse work and leisure activities. Hockey can capitalize by offering a wider range of facilities and services.

Trend 2 – Growing Competition in the Sport Market

Individualization, growing wealth and globalization have led to growing competition among team sports. Sports aimed at individual players such as skating, climbing and golf offer the opportunity to play at times and places that are convenient for the sport consumer. Hockey will be faced with multiple challenges from these types of sports.

Trend 3 – The Growing Need for Safety and Security

People are increasingly looking for safe and secure environments in which they can find kindred spirits – people they want to play, talk, engage and experience with. The family therefore also becomes more important. Parents want to spend more time with their children and they have a growing concern about exposing them to positive norms and value environments. The hockey club can be such an environment.

Trend 4 – Quality as the Basis for Everything

In this day and age, people are prepared to pay more… as long as this goes with a significant improvement of the quality of the product or service. For example, parents expect that the hockey club provides high quality coaching and facilities. They will quickly take their children to other service providers if hockey does not deliver up to standards expected. Quality should be a common feature of hockey products.

In 1999, when the Strategic Plan 2010 was agreed to, the Royal Dutch Hockey Association had lost members for many years to the point that only 129 000 members remained. If this downward trend had continued they would have ended up with 100 000 members in 2010. Longitudinal research identified that between 1988 and 1999 they especially lost members in the age categories of children aged between 6 and 18 and also in the veterans category. In 1999, the strategic plan was to contribute to a 3% growth per annum till 2010. In 2006, when the strategic plan was revised, growth had occurred at a rate of 4.8% per annum with the result that already 172 000 members were enlisted, just 3000 short of the 2010 target.

In the Strategic Plan 2015 the main objectives were therefore revised to:

- Enlisting 260 000 members in 2015
- Grow the number of hockey clubs by 60 to 370 clubs in the Netherlands
- Establish a balanced member profile (across age and socioeconomic groupings) as a result of excellent target marketing
- Maintain or improve the quality of the hockey product and service offering and the quality of hockey club culture.

Organizational leader Johan Wakkie ensured that throughout the establishment of the revised strategic plan a wide range of stakeholders was consulted. These stakeholders were consistently confronted with three principal lines of thought. First, the attention was always focused on an ambitious but realistic growth target for membership. That the initial target was realistic was evidenced by the fact that higher than expected growth was achieved. The target was therefore adjusted to yet another ambitious but realistic target. Secondly, the stakeholders were invited to consider the question about the quality of hockey being provided by hockey clubs. From multiple perspectives, it was necessary to explore what does 'quality of offering' mean to those different stakeholders? It also had to be considered in light of higher numbers of hockey club members – more members means more teams, the need for more and better coaches, more and better facilities and so on. During the 1999–2003 period, membership of 6–18 year olds grew by 6.8%, whereas older membership (veterans) declined by 0.7%. This shows the importance of balanced growth rather than growth of the absolute number of members. Thirdly, the position of the club and its relation to the Royal Dutch Hockey Association was an important matter of debate with the stakeholders. From the perspective of the hockey club, it was important to know how to deal with more members, who have changing and higher (quality) expectations from the club. This requires not only a vision at the local level, but also the practice of long-term planning by local club boards. However, the Royal Dutch Hockey Association also has to have a clear understanding of what

a contemporary hockey club consists of, what is required of this club to service its membership and what the Association is required to deliver in support structures and activities to assist local clubs in their growth and transformation of service offering.

Johan Wakkie has driven a strategic planning process in which it is noted that growing to 260 000 members is to be achieved by:

- Retaining existing members (longer)
- Achieve market penetration in existing target markets
- Attract new members with new products
- Growth in existing and new clubs.

Ultimately, the Royal Dutch Hockey Association has formulated six strategic choices that can be translated into six questions that need to be solved by both the leadership of the Royal Dutch Hockey Association and the Boards of the clubs at the local level. These questions are:

1. Which focus and differentiation of target markets needs to take place in order better to connect the offering of clubs to the needs and wants of current and future members?

2. Which position do we want to occupy in these different target markets? (image: hockey is a well organized, popular and successful sport, accessible for all who want to play sport in an environment that is conducive to social interaction)

3. Which assortment of products needs to be developed in order to achieve the above? (next to the usual products and introductory formats of hockey there needs to be an 'alternative leisure' offering as well).

4. What will be the core elements of local club strategy? (how to build 'deeper' connections with the club, how to cooperate with other sporting clubs, how to support the new hockey clubs).

5. Which marketing formulas will be used to provide an offering to the market (from differentiation in offering between clubs to a differentiated offering within the clubs?)

Continued

6. How will we approach the marketplace? This can be formulated from three levels:

   • Royal Dutch Hockey Association: general hockey image and Dutch National team

   • From service centres: regional cooperation

   • From clubs: make more use of local connections and of knowledge and experience of members and their networks.

Case Study Questions

1. How can the leaders of Dutch hockey solve these questions and take hockey from strength to strength?

2. Can the current leaders achieve this or is a different kind of leadership required to take the organization to yet another level of success?

3. How important has strong leadership been in regard to what has been achieved?

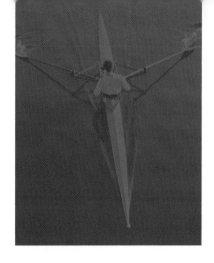

CHAPTER 9

Sport Organizational Culture

OVERVIEW

This chapter explores the influence of organizational culture in sport. It examines why organizational culture is pivotal, highlights its impact and explains how it can be diagnosed. Several cases and numerous examples will be used throughout the chapter to help explain the role of culture in a sport organization's performance.

By the end of this chapter the reader should be able to:

- Define the meaning of organizational culture

- Specify why culture is important to sport organizations

- Explain how different contexts can affect an organizational culture

- Identify how sport organizational cultures can be diagnosed

- Show the dimensions across which sport organizational cultures can be measured

- Discuss how sport organizational culture can be changed.

WHAT IS ORGANIZATIONAL CULTURE?

Culture was originally defined by anthropologists as the values and beliefs common to a group of people. These researchers set themselves the task of investigating, interpreting and translating the behavioural and social patterns of groups of individuals by trying to understand the manner in which they relate to their environment. From an organizational perspective, although people in organizations run the technology and invent the processes, they in turn, as part of the process, have much of their behaviour determined by the system they operate. In other words, there are underlying forces that impact upon behaviour. The concept of culture is a way of putting a name to these forces.

There is no single accepted definition of organizational culture. For example, organizational culture is viewed by some as the 'personality' of an organization while, for others, it represents the things which make an organization unique. Several assumptions about organizational culture are well accepted though. These include:

1. Culture tends to be inflexible and resistant to easy or rapid change

2. Culture is shaped by an organization's circumstances, its history and its members

3. Culture is learned and shared by members of an organization and is reflected in common understandings and beliefs

4. Culture is often covert; the deep values and beliefs causing behaviour can be hidden from organizational members making them difficult to identify

5. Culture is manifested in a variety of ways that affect the performance of an organization and its members.

Although elements of commonality exist in the way in which researchers conceive and define culture in organizations, much inconsistency and controversy can still be found. However, for the purposes of this chapter, we shall discuss organizational culture in a way consistent with the view of Schein (2004), who invokes a more psychodynamic view. This means that he believes culture is, in part, an unconscious phenomenon, driven by deep level assumptions and beliefs and where conscious views are merely artefacts and symbolic representations. For example, most sport clubs members would report that on-field winning is important. Schein's interpretation of organizational culture would lead to questions about *why* winning is important. Does it have to do with a need to belong to a successful group, the pressure of peers or some other more mysterious explanation? While many people involved in sport would think this question easy to answer, it is less easy to specify the underpinning values that drive unusual rituals, ceremonies, myths, legends, stories, beliefs, memorabilia and attitudes. In current and former nations of the British Commonwealth, cricket is played with enormous enthusiasm, but can take up to five days to complete a single match, which often ends in a draw. Similarly, to the uninitiated, American football seems quite strange with each team comprising separate players for offensive and defensive manoeuvres. Off the field can be just as odd. In Australia, many (Australian rules) football clubs have 'sausage-sizzles' (BBQs), 'pie-nights' (involving the traditional meal of a meat-pie) and a host of rituals associated with drinking beer. In addition, many sport organizations are packed with memorabilia and expect their employees to work during evening training sessions and weekend games. Sport organizations are rich with strong, meaningful cultural symbols which, on the surface seem easy to interpret, but sometimes are only superficial symptoms of deeper issues.

What we are searching for is not the superficial, but rather the unconsciously held fundamental concepts of right or wrong; what an organization might perceive as correct or incorrect values. These values, which are the foundation of an organization's culture, do not simply exist or come into being by their own volition. Instead, they are painstakingly built up by members of the organization as they gradually learn to interact and achieve their collective and individual aims. Logically, the originators of the organization, together with the more influential of the organization's past and present members, are usually the most influential in determining the culture. For this reason, we prefer to examine the long-held assumptions and beliefs in an organization, believing that they will more likely explain the organization's culture.

For the purposes of this chapter, we shall define sport organizational culture as follows: *Sport organizational culture is a collection of fundamental values, beliefs and attitudes that are common to members of a sport organization and which subsequently set the behavioural standards or norms for all members*. This definition reflects the view that sport organizations have ways of approaching things that have evolved over time. In many ways, organizational culture holds answers to questions about solving problems. Culture is how 'things are done around here' and how 'we think about things here'.

THE IMPORTANCE OF CULTURE TO SPORT ORGANIZATIONS

In many countries, sport has for some time been regarded as a particularly important social institution. Sporting heroes are often national heroes as well. Examples include Michael Jordan and Vince Lombardi in the USA, Roger Bannister and David Beckham in the UK, Shigeo Nagashima and Hanada Katsuji (Sumo name: Wakanohana) in Japan and Sir Donald Bradman and Ian Thorpe in Australia. Although these names are not necessarily the definitive sporting heroes of the nations identified, their sports and personal profiles are illustrative of the national cultural pressures that influence the sport organizations they host. This quick list, for example, excludes women; a trait common to many sport organizational cultures and one that many are seeking to change. However, the influence of the national culture means that such changes are more likely to occur in some nations than others.

We can expect that different types of sport organizations will possess different kinds of cultures. For example, professional clubs and major national leagues are more likely to emphasize dispassionate business values, while smaller, not-for-profit associations are more likely to value participation and fun. Some sport organizations like Italian and Spanish football clubs are geared almost exclusively to winning and are prepared to go heavily into debt in order to do so. Others, like the company Formula One Holdings, manage the commercial rights to major events and have little other interest than to make money. While the Fédération Internationale de l'Automobile seeks to regulate motor sport, others still, like the International Olympic Committee, are interested in developing sport around the world and, in so doing, acquire vast sums of money and spend it liberally.

Sport organizations are increasingly compelled to join the commercial world and are under great pressure to adopt the operational and structural characteristics of business enterprises. The influence of modern communication has been profound, with sporting results being available from almost anywhere connected to the Internet. Many sporting organizations have realized that in order to remain competitive they must provide similar entertainment value to that provided by other sports on television as well as the wide array of alternative leisure options available. Subsequently, corporate boxes line major sporting venues, sport is blanketed across pay or cable and free to air television, high profile athletes earn extraordinary sums and politicians associate themselves with certain teams. The commercial and competitive pressures placed upon sport organizations from local football clubs, universities and colleges, to professional leagues and teams, have encouraged sport managers to embrace business tools and concepts like organizational culture. Culture is important to sport organizations because a better understanding of it can help to bring about change. Since organizational culture is so influential on the performance of its members, it is critical that cultural traits are both appropriate and strong. In the case of sport, it is common to have strong cultures that have been forged by tradition and a fierce sense of history, but some cultural characteristics like excessive drinking and on-field violence may no longer suit the more professional management approach that needs to be assumed.

Commentaries on organizational culture, while as disparate as the number of researchers pursuing its investigation, generally emphasize its most superficial manifestation. Moreover, organizational business culture is frequently seen as mono-cultural, that is, it is perceived at one level and as one entity. The organization is distinguished as a giant cultural mass, constructed equivalently throughout and with little or no internal variability. However, this way of thinking is difficult to sustain when analysing a sporting organization. Sporting club cultures are inherently multicultural and can be perceived readily at several levels or as several sub-cultures. For example, as an organizational or administrative unit comparable to other business organizations; as a supporter organization, whose aims, objectives and traditions may be different (such as winning matches in preference to making a financial profit); and as a player unit, where motivation may vary from glory to money. While a player may perform for a club because of loyalty or remuneration (or any number of other reasons), the supporters are usually passionately attached to the clubs' colours and traditions, expecting only on-field success in return.

In Practice 9.1 Sport Rage and the Impact of Organizational Culture

An organization's culture has a powerful influence on the behaviour of its members. In some cases, the cultural values embedded in sport organizations encourage positive characteristics such as teamwork, loyalty, sacrifice and belonging. On the other hand, the competitive nature of sport can also introduce less desirable cultural qualities like violence, the desire to win-at-all costs, racism and poor sportsmanship. One example of the last point is the dramatic increase in the number of media reports describing the poor behaviour of disruptive parents at their children's sporting events. There is no shortage of recorded incidents where parents are forced to remove their children from a sport as a direct result of an overly competitive and aggressive atmosphere generated by other parents and coaches. The phenomenon has become known as 'sport rage' and is the consequence of organizational and sporting cultures that tolerate pushy parents and win-at-all cost coaches because of a powerful cultural commitment to high performance.

Sport rage exemplifies the impact of culture on organizational members. For example, clubs which value winning so highly that they encourage parents and coaches to behave inappropriately and exert undue pressure on children, face not only player recruitment problems but also the loss of officials and sponsors as well as an increasing chance of legal action. In addition, clubs which continue to condone or ignore abusive behaviour face the possibility of a future generation of rule intolerant, abusive players who are inclined to emulate the behavioural outbursts they witnessed in their youth.

Combating the problem of sport rage requires the acceptance that it is connected to the cultural priorities of sporting organizations. One approach has involved systematic educational campaigns launched by government and governing associations designed to outline the consequences of antisocial behaviour and how clubs should respond. Another approach has targeted parents as quasi-organizational members who collectively help shape the cultural values of the clubs their children belong to. Through programmes designed to reinforce the importance of fair play, parents are encouraged to commit to a code of ethics specifying what appropriate behaviour comprises. These strategies reflect the assumption that in order to change values, the starting point is to change behaviour.

SUB-CULTURES AND SPORT

In sporting organizational cultures, there is the additional hurdle of translating and adopting a culture directly from traditional business theory. It is dangerously simplistic to assume that a sporting organization should adopt the methods and practices of a traditional business without addressing the cultural variables. While business methods can be transferred to accommodate the organizational strategies of a sporting club, a direct transfer fails to confront the issue of what it is that makes the culture of a sporting organization differ from that of a traditional business enterprise.

Ideal business culture tends to reflect a willingness by an organization's employees to embrace a standard of performance that promotes quality in the production of goods and services in the attempt to generate a financial profit. This cultural ideology, while cognisant of business necessities, is unable to cater for the more diverse structures that exist in a sporting organization. In any business, financial realities must be acknowledged but, in a sporting business, additional behavioural variables require recognition and respect. While different businesses have different cultures, they are less variable than the cultural differences between individual sports. It cannot be assumed, for example, that a single unified culture exists for all sports.

Fighting during a sporting context is an example of the variability of sporting culture. While in just about every ball game it is illegal to punch people, it is acceptable behaviour in some cases. The situation could not be clearer in terms of official rules and regulations. An overt punch in football is an immediate red-card, sending-off offence. In contrast, a punch in ice-hockey is virtually considered an inherent and accepted part of the game, while charging the pitcher, although illegal, is considered to be almost within the batter's moral right should they be struck by a deliberately wayward pitch in baseball. Consider the ramifications of a punch thrown at the Wimbledon Tennis Championships or on the eighteenth green of Augusta? Sport managers must be aware of the cultural nuances of their respective sports and the influence they have upon players, employees, members, fans and the general public.

Culture is not a simple matter within a single sport either. Professional players, for example, have a different cultural attitude from some amateurs and spectators. This variability of attitudes is symptomatic of a wider, more troublesome area: the clash of cultures within sports. This is illustrated best at an international level, where players from different countries have been brought up with profoundly different ideologies of the game and how it should be played. Football – the 'world game' – is indicative of this culture clash, in addition to the immense cultural significance inherent in the game. Like all living cultures, sport is incessantly changing, dynamic in nature and subject to constant reinterpretation by its participants and viewers. The only apparent consistency in sporting culture is the pursuit of competition, the love of winning and the ability to summon strong emotional responses in both victory and defeat.

Clearly, there is a need to study organizational cultures, accounting for the effect of the sport itself. For example, in the same way that we might expect that accounting firms might share some cultural traits, so might we predict that bocce clubs do also. Similarly, the tradition and discipline central to a bocce club might be expected to encourage cultural characteristics different to the youthful and eclectic philosophy found in a BMX club. Furthermore, these cultural characteristics might seep into the executive officers and employees of the clubs. Since so many sporting organizations covet tradition and the accomplishments of the past, they also tend to be resistant to change. However, before any change can occur, an organization's culture needs to be accurately diagnosed.

In Practice 9.2 Changing Culture at Nike

Despite the success of Nike's aggressive, marketing-driven culture, the company was forced to re-evaluate its values and strategy, which had always given a central position to outsourcing the manufacturing of their products to inexpensive factories in Asia. However, negative media attention highlighted reportedly unfavourable conditions imposed upon offshore factory workers. Nike was subjected to hostile publicity, boycotts, protests and diminishing sales. In the face of such consternation about one of its key strategies, Nike resolved to reclaim their reputation as good corporate citizens and publicly modify their manufacturing approach. The founder and Chief Executive Officer at the time, Phil Knight, even claimed that the decision represented a sea-change in the company's culture.

As a corporation that relies on the brand reputation of sport consumers, Nike's approach was to change the cultural assumptions underpinning their manufacturing strategy. Where once cost, quality and distribution were the key factors in outsourcing arrangements, environmental impact, ethical codes and factory conditions became important new variables.

A cynical observer might suggest that Nike simply responded to poor press in the only way they could. While Nike may not have had much choice if it sought to address its declining brand reputation, the changes the company made were indicative of a long-term commitment to cultural change. Impelled by a new policy prioritizing working conditions in off-shore factories, Nike worked cooperatively with non-government organizations in order to ensure strict standards where manufacturing plant vendors were required to offer fair wages and social benefits for workers. Nike's supply chain code of social responsibility has taken nearly a decade to be deployed across hundreds of factories employing hundreds of thousands of workers, with over half now receiving an 'A' or 'B' rating in Nike's social responsibility reporting.

Continued

In Practice 9.2 Changing Culture at Nike—cont'd

According to Nike's public reporting documents, the company is determined to instill core values of trust, teamwork, honesty and mutual respect to all its factories and partners worldwide. As part of this process, social responsibility has become part of the management team's performance review. An individual manager's financial rewards are linked to their successful implementation and management of corporate social responsibility practices within their portfolio.

DIAGNOSING AND MANAGING ORGANIZATIONAL CULTURE

The central problem is that in order to grasp the concept of culture and its relationship to the individual, the group and the organization, an in-depth approach is required. Sport organizations create intentions and atmospheres that influence behaviour, routines, practices and the very thought systems of people. These systems and processes subsequently form patterns that are acquired primarily through socialization or learning over time from the reactions and behaviours of others. In essence, individuals within an organization are exposed to what researchers call 'culture revealing' situations, which might include the observable behaviour of other members, their organizational methods, 'artefacts' – the photos, honour boards and other memorabilia on show – and interactive communication, or the way in which individuals talk to each other. Some of these common superficial and observable representations of organizational culture are reproduced in Table 9.1. These are important to recognize because the driving values and belief systems behind them can never been seen as anything more than observable 'symptoms'.

Although the superficial aspects of culture can be observed, the difficulty comes in their interpretation because they are merely surface representations of deeper values. Thus, a useful cultural diagnosis will always seek to understand what drives the observable behaviour. For example, what does it mean if an employee makes a mistake and is severely reprimanded by his or her boss? What does common jargon imply? Why are certain rituals typical, like the celebration of employee birthdays?

The question remains as to how overt observations relate to deeper values. Most researchers recommend some form of classification system that describes organizational culture in the form of 'dimensions', each one a deeper, core value. These dimensions describe particular organizational characteristics as an aid to categorizing cultures. The summation of these characteristics is used to map an organization's culture, which can then allow

Table 9.1	Observable Symptoms of Sport Organizational Culture
Symptom	**Explanation**
Environment	The general surroundings of an organization, like the building it is housed in and the geographical location, like the city or in a grandstand
Artefacts	Physical objects located in the organization from its furnishings to its coffee machine
Language	The common words and phrases used by most organizational members, including gestures and body language
Documents	Any literature including reports, statements, promotional material, memos and e-mails produced for the purpose of communication
Logos	Any symbolic visual imagery including colours and fonts that convey meaning about the organization
Heroes	Current or former organizational members who are considered exemplars
Stories	Narratives shared by organizational members based at least partly on true events
Legends	An event with some historical basis but has been embellished with fictional details
Rituals	Standardized and repeated behaviours
Rites	Elaborate, dramatic, planned set of activities

for comparisons to be undertaken between varying organizations. For example, observable evidence in the form of an end of season awards night in a sporting club might be suggestive of the nature of the organization's reward/motivation values. Enough observable evidence can lead a sport manager to make some tentative conclusions about each dimension. Table 9.2 lists some common dimensions used to describe organizational culture (Smith and Shilbury, 2004). They can be seen as continua, an organization's position somewhere between the two extremes.

Any analysis that captures the complexity of organizational culture may have great difficulty in separating the interwoven strands of organizational history and personal relationships. As a result, concrete conclusions may be difficult to establish. It is therefore important to take advantage of the symbolism created by myth, ritual and ceremony that is abundant in sport organizations in order to gain a complete understanding of the full range of human behaviour within a complex organization. The traditions, folklore, mythologies, dramas, successes and traumas of the past are the threads that weave together the fabric of organizational culture.

A psychological approach is helpful in identifying and interpreting human behaviour in organizations as cultural phenomena. Psychologists, originally stimulated by the work of Carl Jung, suggest that there are different levels of behavioural awareness, from the conscious to unconscious. Organizational psychologists have appropriated this kind of thinking and transposed it to culture. The key analogy is that an organization is like a mind.

Table 9.2	Cultural Dimensions
Dimension	**Characteristics**
Stability/changeability	Disposition toward change: degree to which organization encourages alternative 'ways of doing things' or existing ways
Cooperation/conflict	Disposition toward problem resolution: degree to which organization encourages cooperation or conflict
Goal focus/orientation	Clarity and nature of objectives and performance expectations
Reward/motivation	Nature of reward orientation of organizational members: degree to which organization encourages seniority or performance
Control/authority	Nature and degree of responsibility, freedom and independence of organizational members
Time/planning	Disposition toward long-term planning: degree to which organization encourages short-term or long-term thinking

From the psychological viewpoint, the readily apparent and observable qualities of a sporting organization are the same as the conscious part of an individual mind. These include the physical environment, the public statements of officials, the way individuals interactively communicate, the form of language used, what clothes are worn and the memorabilia that fill the rooms and offices. Another of the most important observable qualities involves the place of sporting heroes. They are rich and are highly visible indicators of the culture that is sought. Heroes give an insight into the culture of an organization, since they are selected by the rank and file as well as the power brokers. In addition, they indicate those qualities in individuals which are respected and admired by a wider audience. The hero is a powerful figure in a sporting organization and may be simultaneously an employee and ex-player. The hero may also be charismatic, entrepreneurial or just plain administrative, which often characterizes business enterprises. By understanding the orientation of hero figures, both past and present, it is possible to map the trends in cultural change. Heroes can be both reactionary and progressive. Heroes that reinforce the dominant culture will not change the values and attitudes that the culture emphasizes. On the other hand, a hero that transcends and transforms the dominant culture will be a catalyst for change in the behaviours and values of a club. Often a hero is the most powerful medium for change management to be successful.

Tradition is another window into the culture of an organization. Like heroes, traditions are readily observable through memorabilia, but it is important to note that the underlying values and assumptions that give meaning to heroes and tradition reside in the deeper levels of a culture. Tradition may on one hand be preserved by the present cultural identity, while on the other hand the sporting organization may have developed a contemporary cultural personality. Thus, it is useful to acknowledge the importance of tradition and history to a sporting organization because it may be a cultural linchpin, or a stepping stone from which their contemporary cultural character has launched itself.

In order to bypass the obstacles (in the form of stereotypical views and superficial signs) that can block an assessment of culture, it is essential to analyse and explore natural, observable outcroppings of culture; places where the cultural understandings can be exposed. By analysing these sites, it is possible to gain a practical insight into the underlying culture of the organization. Thus, this level deals with organizational rites because, first, their performance is readily apparent and, secondly, in performing these rites employees generally use other cultural forms of expression, such as certain customary language or jargon, gestures and artefacts. These rites, which are shared understandings, are additionally conveyed through myths, sagas, legends or other stories associated with the occasion and, in practical terms, may take the form of barbecues or presentations. In order to actively assess this level of culture, not only must observational techniques be employed, but meanings must be attached to them. This requires more than a superficial level of analysis.

There are also 'unconscious' parts of organizations as well. In effect, it is the unconscious that controls the individual. This incorporates the beliefs, habits, values, behaviours and attitudes prevalent in a sporting organization. An accurate assessment of this level of culture is difficult and fraught with danger. For example, how employees say they behave and what they state they believe has to be compared to their actual behaviour.

As a cautionary note, it is relevant to be aware of the fact that there are different interpretations possible of the same evidence. For example, one way of looking at culture is to focus attention on consistency and congruence of

In Practice 9.3 The Emergence of Organizational Culture: The Barmy Army

Emerging during the 1994–95 Ashes series where the English Cricket team were struggling to make headway against their traditional Australian foes, a loyal and memorable group of English fans began to attract media attention. Colourfully labelled the 'Barmy Army', the group banded together to create their own supporter organization, registering their quirky moniker as a trademark. The Barmy Army is an unusual sport organization but it nevertheless demonstrates how a group of like-minded individuals with common values, beliefs and ways of doing things can form an organization and forge a strong and vibrant culture.

Continued

In Practice 9.3 The Emergence of Organizational Culture: The Barmy Army—cont'd

At the heart of the Barmy Army is a passion for English cricket. Travelling wherever the English Cricket team venture on tour, the Barmy Army strives to offer support at venues through songs, clothes and vocal support. Although a large group of largely male sport fans perhaps excessively fond of alcohol may be considered an unwelcome group at a sporting contest, the Barmy Army has fostered a culture that emphasizes a positive social contribution.

To begin with, the Barmy Army is not exclusive about its membership; anyone can join. The focus is on the fun, colour and spectacle of passionate cricket support. However, the infusion of commercial interests has added an unexpected side to the Barmy Army's activities. Barmy Army merchandise has become highly popular as a consequence of the group's media profile. What is interesting about this development is that the dominant cultural values of the Barmy Army have encouraged the group to use their exposure to support social and charitable causes, such as raising funds for victims of Pakistan's 2005 earthquake and those affected by the 2004 Christmas tsunami.

Now with sponsorship, the Barmy Army has become a sport organization with an unusual agenda driven by cultural beliefs that combine the fun and frivolity of sport fandom with a serious and substantial commitment to social welfare. Perhaps as much as anything else, the Barmy Army represents a case where the emergence of a formal organization was driven by the culture created by a handful of original members.

policies and practices within a sport organization as members are confronted with problems to solve. In contrast, it is also valid to consider ambiguities and inconsistencies in behaviour. These anomalies often represent the difference between espoused values and actual values. Cultural manifestations can be interpreted in multiple ways and change over time and location. It is important to look for both patterns and exceptions.

CHANGING ORGANIZATIONAL CULTURE WITH MAPPING

Cultural understanding stems from successfully translating information into meaning. Every aspect of a sporting organization is symbolically representative in some way of its culture. All information is not equal, however, yet all possible data must be analysed in order to establish the most comprehensive representation possible of the existing culture. In order for a culture to be created and bolstered, shared values and beliefs must in some way be reinforced and transferred to organizational members through tangible means.

A cultural map summarizes the predominant features of a sporting organization's culture and provides a means in which raw data can be interpreted into measurable criteria. It works by providing sets of categories in which information can be collected and summarized with the intention of identifying the main themes that continually emerge. Some researchers believe that this approach can also be used in a more statistical form, the numbers attached to responses from questions derived from the dimensions and answered by organizational members.

While the range and diversity of information available for cultural analysis is profound, many cultural studies ignore all but the most apparent and accessible data. A holistic cultural analysis will utilize every available piece of information, with the more obvious elements becoming vehicles for the transmission of less tangible, more subjective facets of culture. However, the culture of any one sporting organization cannot be classified into one of just a few categories, even though there are many models with a handful of neat categories. There are as many organizational cultures as there are sporting organizations and they cannot be generically categorized into one of a fixed number of groups. Sporting clubs are immersed in tradition, history, values and myths and these should figure prominently in any diagnosis. From an accurate diagnosis change is possible.

The main lesson for cultural change is that it cannot be tackled without a clear prior understanding of an organization's chief cultural traits and how they are manifested. Once an accurate diagnosis has been undertaken through some form of formal or informal cultural map, elements of culture can be managed. Since a sport manager cannot literally change peoples' minds, they instead have to change peoples' actions. To some extent this can be imposed or encouraged, but it is a slow process. For example, new rituals can be introduced to replace older, less desirable ones, like a club dinner instead of a drinking binge. Entrenched values and beliefs can be extremely difficult to change and even with the right introduction of new symbols, language, heroes, stories, employees and so on, genuine cultural change in an organization can take many years or even a new generation of organizational members before it takes hold.

SUMMARY

In the world of sport management, organizational culture has gained prominence as a concept useful in assessing and managing performance. Sport organizational culture can be defined as the collection of fundamental values and attitudes that are common to members of a sport organization and which subsequently set the behavioural standards or norms for all members. The difficulty is, however, that the deep values common to organizational members are not easy to access. As a way of getting around this inaccessibility problem, sport managers can use cultural dimensions which suggest some of the possible values that are present. A step further, cultural maps show the variables and observable manifestations of culture that need to be investigated. These maps use the tip of the cultural iceberg (the accessible aspects of culture like symbols and artefacts) to estimate the iceberg's underwater composition (the deep values and beliefs of organizational members). Once a thorough diagnosis has been completed, sport managers can work towards adapting and replacing undesirable cultural characteristics.

REVIEW QUESTIONS

1. Why is organization culture important to sport managers?

2. Explain how organizational culture can be manifested at different levels.

3. Describe the difference between superficial elements of culture and deeper elements of culture.

4. What is a cultural dimension?

5. How can organizational culture be measured in a sport organization?

6. How does measuring organizational culture help in changing it?

7. Select a sport organization you belong or have belonged to. Create a list of attributes or values that you believe embodies its organizational culture. Which are the characteristics that distinguish it from other similar sport organizations?

8. Select a sport organization you belong or have belonged to. Describe 10 artefacts that are on show in its premises and explain how each illuminates organizational culture.

FURTHER READING

Colyer, S. (2000). Organizational culture in selected Western Australian sport organizations. *Journal of Sport Management*, 14, 321–341.

Smith, A. and Shilbury, D. (2004). Mapping cultural dimensions in Australian sporting organizations. *Sport Management Review*, 7, 133–165.

Schein, E. (2004). *Organizational culture and leadership*, 3rd edn. Jossey-Bass, San Francisco.

Case Study: The All England Lawn Tennis and Croquet Club and the Wimbledon Tennis Championship

Like all organizations, those responsible for custodianship of a sport or sporting event are influenced by the cultural history and traditions of its products and services. For example, companies such as car manufacturer Ford and tea producer Twining make frequent reference to the values their foundation leaders held and use these as connections to a past that is the source of much admiration and respect. In the same way, the cultures of sport organizations are heavily influenced by their cultural histories. This means in the sporting context that the values, beliefs, norms and ideals associated with the sport itself remain powerful in forging the identities of the business organizations charged with their management. Perhaps there are few better examples of this phenomenon than in the Wimbledon Tennis Championship and its organizational steward, the All England Lawn Tennis and Croquet Club (AELTC).

The All England Lawn Tennis and Croquet Club is located at Wimbledon in London and is renowned for hosting one of the world's oldest and most prestigious sporting events, the Wimbledon Tennis Championships, the most coveted tournament in tennis. Consistent with the history of the AELTC, Wimbledon remains the only Grand Slam in tennis that is still played on grass and also at a private club. To say that the event has grown is a vast understatement. The first Lawn Tennis Championship in 1877 was held in the presence of a few hundred spectators and reported a profit of a few hundred pounds. The current Championship commands an attendance of nearly half a million spectators and is broadcast all over the world to hundreds of millions of tennis enthusiasts and delivers tens of millions of pounds in profit.

The organizational culture of the AELTC may be viewed and understood through the values and priorities laid down as a consequence of the club's historical context. For example, despite the obvious success and prestige that the club has cultivated, it has very few members. There are only 375 full members of the club, 100 temporary playing members and a handful of honorary members, of whom some are former champions. Of course, the number of members is not arbitrarily determined, but is the direct result of the club's structure and traditions. As is typical in sport, the club is faced with managing cultural tensions that accompany a changing environment. Membership carries with it the right to purchase two tickets to each day of the Wimbledon Championships. Expanding memberships would therefore either restrict the number of tickets available to the general public or end the convention of providing members with exclusive Wimbledon access. From an economic viewpoint, membership is a supply and demand equation where demand vastly outweighs supply leading to considerable exclusivity attached to membership and its privileges.

Some values embedded in the club's culture as a consequence of its historical attachment to exclusivity have caused controversy in the contemporary sport environment where inclusivity, equality and access have become standard expectations. An example can be found in the case of former 1956 Wimbledon doubles champion Angela Buxton who claims to have been on the waiting list since the 1950s. She believes that her failure to be invited to join along with other former champions is indicative of a pervasive elitism.

The opportunity for commercial expansion has been resisted by the AELTC in many instances as the club has attempted to preserve its cultural identity through a commitment to tradition. On the other hand, it is also possible to see how concessions to the business nature of professional sport have influenced the culture of the club. In fact, the Wimbledon Championship is organized by a committee of 12 AELTC members and seven nominees from the Lawn Tennis Association, the latter group and their administrative staff responsible for the operational management of the event. Like any well-financed sporting club, the AETLC is administered by a permanent and professional office staff comprising a Chief Executive, Championships Director, Financial Director, Marketing Director, Director of Television, Information Technology Director, Club Secretary and more than 40 other management staff. The courts, buildings and services are managed by a team of over 60 staff. Policy for the club is

Continued

supervised by a committee headed by a President, numerous Vice-Presidents and patronized by Her Majesty the Queen. There is no way around the fact that, in order for Wimbledon to maintain its image as the world's pre-eminent tennis event, its organization demands professional management.

Irrespective of the importance of the club's rich traditions, it has shown some business prescience in structuring its activities within a sporting context that has increasingly favoured commercialism. In 1920, the club formed a company, the All England Lawn Tennis Ground Ltd, with the intention of purchasing what is the current site at Wimbledon. In what was surely one of the first initiatives of its kind in the sporting world, the club issued debentures in order to raise capital. Another example occurred in 1993 when the club unveiled a long-term plan which sought to enhance Wimbledon's reputation as one of the world's premier sporting events by improving the quality of the Championship's experience for all of its stakeholders including the players, broadcasters, spectators, officials, members and the club's staff. As a result, the club's services and facilities represent a unique intersection of innovation and tradition. These include a new permanent broadcast centre, the Millennium Building housing facilities for players, media, officials, members and Lawn Tennis Association representatives, refurbishments to the Clubhouse and the Royal Box, redevelopments to the entry areas, shops, ticketing and offices and the opening of a new tennis museum. Perhaps most notably are changes to the historic centre court, which is undergoing renovation to allow more spectators to sit comfortably and where they shall imminently be protected from Wimbledon's notorious weather by a state of the art, transparent, concertina, retractable roof.

The impact of commercialism on the club is exemplified by the broadcast strategy behind the Wimbledon Championships. Wimbledon was one of the earliest televised sporting events, first broadcast in 1937. Currently, close to 9000 hours of footage are transmitted to media networks in over 175 territories. Some of the world's largest and most powerful broadcasters have signed long-term deals to televise the Wimbledon Championships including the BBC, the United States networks NBC and ESPN, Channel 9 in Australia, NHK in Japan, DSF in Germany and ESPN/Star in parts of Asia and China.

Although an extreme example, the AETLC exemplifies cultural traits indicative of many sporting clubs. It values the conventions, ideas, standards and behaviours reflective of the era in which it emerged. These Victorian values remain prominent in the club and the Wimbledon Championship today. For example, dress protocol is strict in the club with the expectation of jackets and ties for men and the equivalent for women. At the Wimbledon Championships, the tradition of bowing/curtseying to members of the royal family when entering or departing the centre court was not discontinued until 2003, with the ongoing exception of when Her Majesty the Queen and His Royal Highness, The Prince of Wales, are in attendance. Similarly, the language employed at the club is indicative of some salient artefacts revealing its dominant value codes and assumptions. The somewhat anachronistic terms 'ladies' and 'gentlemen' are still used in reference to the men's and women's competition. Such values are endemic to the Wimbledon championship: the prize money was different for the men's and women's competition until 2007, the seating is exclusively arranged so that members are afforded with privileged access and players are expected to compete wearing mostly white. To that end, inclusion is reinforced by adherence to the etiquette of the club, demonstrably evidenced by dress, speech and deference to tradition. There are certain parts of the club facility that cannot be accessed by non-members or non-champions, the latter conferred with special rights afforded only to members. Indeed, given the immense waiting list of more than half a century, winning the championship might in fact be the easier path to the highest level of social exclusivity that membership to the AELTC affords.

At the same time, the AELTC has been forced to modernize and accommodate to the commercial business context in which the Wimbledon championship is placed. As a result, the club has forged a delicate balance of prestige and exclusivity with professionalism and service. The result, like many sport organizational cultures, is one where tension and contradiction has to be managed with sensitivity to both the business imperative and historical precedence.

Case Study Question

1. Using the cultural map outlined in Table 9.3 as a guide, complete the third column highlighting the observable or overt features of the club/Wimbledon's organizational culture.

Table 9.3	Cultural Map	
Dimension	**Description**	**Observable features**
Stability/changeability	Disposition toward change: degree to which organization encourages alternative 'ways of doing things' or existing ways	
Cooperation/conflict	Disposition toward problem resolution: degree to which organization encourages cooperation or conflict	
Goal focus/orientation	Clarity and nature of objectives and performance expectations	
Reward/motivation	Nature of reward orientation of organizational members: degree to which organization encourages seniority or performance	
Control/authority	Nature and degree of responsibility, freedom and independence of organizational members	
Time/planning	Disposition toward long-term planning: degree to which organization encourages short-term or long-term thinking	

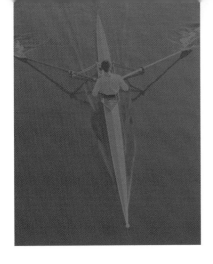

CHAPTER 10

Financial Management in Sport

OVERVIEW

This chapter examines the critical importance of sound financial management in ensuring effective outcomes for sport organizations. Throughout the chapter, incidents and cases will be used to illustrate both the theory underpinning the financial management of sport organizations and the practical things that should be done to sustain their financial viability.

After completing this chapter the reader should be able to:

- Understand the importance of effective financial management in sport

- Explain how sport has changed over the last fifty years and its implications for the source and use of funds

- Identify the ways in which sport organization financial arrangements can be reported

- Explain how assets are organized and how they differ from liabilities

- Explain how profits and or surpluses are calculated for sport organizations and the difference between operating profit and net profit

- Explain how budgets operate and explain why they are crucial to effective financial management of sport organizations.

THE FINANCIAL EVOLUTION OF SPORT

As the previous chapters have demonstrated, sport is quite a sophisticated institution with an often complex legal and financial structure. In many respects, it is a form of business where the consumers are the fans and the players, the producers are the clubs, associations and leagues and the distribution channels are the sport arenas and sport stadiums (Foster et al.,

201

2006). And, like all forms of business, it requires a strong system of financial management to make sure it can sustain itself into the future. However, this has not always been the case and sport around the world has gone through four phases of commercial and financial development over the last fifty years.

This metamorphosis of sport into a form of business, with its associated financial systems, begins in phase 1 with sport as a recreational and cultural practice where sport organizations are rudimentary, their revenue streams are small, sport was played mainly for fun and activities are organized and managed by volunteer officials. This model is often described as a kitchen-table approach to sport management, since the game is administered by a few officials making key decisions from a member's home. It has some strengths, since it not only ensures the involvement of grassroots players and members and provides a strong local community club focus, but it also nurtures a strong set of values that centre on playing the game for its own sake and the concomitant ideal of amateurism. At the same time, it perpetuates a simple system of management driven by an administrative committee made up of a few elected members and self-appointed officials. There is the president who is the public face of the club or association and a secretary who keeps things ticking over by maintaining a member register and organizing others to manage teams, run events and maintain the clubrooms and playing facilities. There is also a treasurer who looked after the financial affairs of the organization. The treasurer is more often than not unfamiliar with the theory and principles of accounting, but makes up for a lack of expertise with a mind for detail and a desire to ensure receipts run ahead of expenses.

The second phase is commercialization, where more revenue streams are utilized and both staff and players are paid for their services. Whereas the kitchen-table model depends on member subscriptions, player registration fees and social activities for their financial viability, the commercialized sport model uses sports' commercial value to attract corporate and other sponsors. In this phase, sports that have the capacity to draw large crowds increasingly understand that these crowds can be used to attract businesses who want to increases product awareness, secure a special and exclusive sales channel or obtain access to a market segment that will be receptive to their product. Sport is still a recreational and cultural practice, where the sport's overall development is the primary goal, but there is also an emerging or secondary strategy that focuses on elite development and the building of pathways by which players can move to the premier league or competition.

The third phase is bureacratization, where the structures of sport organizations become more complex, administrative controls are established and functional specialization increases. This phase is heavily dependent upon its antecedent phase, since an effective bureaucracy requires additional resources. In this phase, club, league and association structures are transformed so as to include a board of directors whose prime responsibility is to set the strategic direction and ensure compliance with government regulation. This then establishes an organizational divide between the steerers (the board) and the rowers (the chief executive officer and operational staff) who are expected to implement the board's plans and policies. In addition, a business-like set of functions and processes are created which are built around administrative support, marketing, finance, game development, coaching player development and the like. In this phase, less management space is given to the sport- as-recreation-and-cultural-practice model and more to the sport-as-business model.

The fourth and final phase is corporatization, where sport embraces the business model by valuing brand management as much as it does player and fan relations. Revenue streams are increasingly dominated by sponsorships and broadcast rights fees, merchandise sales are deepened and managers adopt a more professional outlook where the need to secure a competitive edge overrules the desire to hold on to old traditions. This is the phase in which players become full-time employees, player associations are established to protect their interests and the sport's governing bodies take on the role of employers. A formal industrial relations system is created that leads to detailed contractual arrangements, collective bargaining agreements and codes of conduct. The marketing process also becomes increasingly sophisticated as the sport club, association or league becomes a brand, members and fans become customers, sponsors become corporate partners and the brand name and image is used to strengthen its corporate partner arrangements and to build up a merchandising arm. This phase also features a move toward managerialism, whereby sport becomes more accountable to its stakeholders for its performance and use of resources. This is particularly evident in sport's relationship with government, where government funding becomes increasingly contingent upon sport meeting certain specific and agreed upon outcomes. This focus on managerialism also leads to greater transparency through an emphasis in performance measurement. Under this framework, it is no longer appropriate only to measure player performance, but also things like internal processes and efficiency, financial performance, market performance, employer and, in particular, player behaviour, and even social responsibility. Finally, sport becomes generally more regulated, with some being defined by government-framed parameters and legislation and others being internally controlled. The more government-bound controls involve venue safety, anti-discrimination programmes and crowd control policies. Internal regulation is highly visible within professional sport leagues and competitions, where player recruitment is governed by drafting rules,

Table 10.1	Sport as Business: Evolutionary Phases and Features			
	Values	**Revenue Focus**	**Structural Focus**	**Management Focus**
Stage 1 Kitchen table	Amateurism Volunteerism	Member funds Social club income	Management committee	Sustaining operations
Stage 2 Commercial	Viablility of sport Member service	Gate receipts Sponsorship	Management portfolios	Marketing the club
Stage 3 Bureaucratic	Efficient use of sport resources Accountability	Corporate income Merchandising	Divisions and departments	Improving club efficiency
Stage 4 Corporate	Delivering outputs Building the brand	Brand value Broadcast rights	Board policymaking Staff operations	Increasing club value Regulating constituents

player behaviour is constrained by a combination of collective agreements and codes of conduct, salaries are set within a total wage ceiling, revenues are redistributed from the most wealthy to the most needy clubs and associations and games are scheduled to ensure the lowest cost and greatest revenue. While this type of corporate regulation can be problematic because of its heavy emphasis on bureaucratic control and detailed performance measurement, it also ensures a disciplined system of management by creating a common purpose, setting a clear strategic direction and securing strong leadership (Stewart, 2007a). A summary of each phase in the sport-as-business evolution is provided in Table 10.1.

FUNDING SOURCES FOR SPORT

It is clear that the new business-based, corporate model of sport involves a massive expansion of income. However, it is important to not throw the baby out with the bath water and so traditional forms of revenue have been maintained, although in a slightly more sophisticated form. Member fees are still important, as are fundraising from social activities and gate receipts. However, as was touched upon previously, new and varied revenue streams have opened up over the last thirty years which have transformed sport and the way it operates (Szymanski and Kuypers, 1999). The funding of sport organizations begs a number of questions, the main ones being listed here:

1. Where does the money come from?

2. Where is the money spent?

3. How are the movements of money monitored?

In answering these questions, it is important to distinguish between funds that are used to create infrastructure and facilities and funds for use in managing the day-to-day activities of a sport organization. So, there are two types of basic funding uses. The first is funds for investment in capital development and the second is funds for recurrent and operating activities.

Capital funding

Capital funding, which is money to finance investment in assets, can come from a number of sources listed here:

1. Government grants, which may be federal, state/provincial or local. The point to note is that there are differences between sports which reflect not only their scale of operation but also their likelihood of generating international success. Funding may also be subject to certain conditions being met, like adopting certain policy requirements or working within a legislative framework.

2. Loans and borrowing, which could be short term (up to a year) or long term (up to twenty years). Loans and borrowings are known as debt finance. The points to note are that it provides ready cash for investment in facilities and income producing assets. On the other hand, it also incurs an interest burden and may not always generate an increase in income.

3. New share issue or a public float, which is known as equity finance. The points to note are that, like borrowings, it provides ready access to cash but, unlike borrowing, does not impose the burden of interest payment or repayment of the principle to lenders. However, it does hand over control to shareholders and there is an expectation that a dividend will be delivered.

4. Retained earnings, which is money re-invested in the sport organization. In this case, there is no interest payment and control is retained over funds used. For non-profit sport organizations, the retention of earnings is mandatory, since this is a legal requirement.

Recurrent funding

The recurrent funding of sport involves money to fund day-to-day operations, which comes from a variety of sources depending on the type of sport enterprise. The main revenue sources are:

1. Membership fees, which may be full adult, associate, family and similar categories. They are usually upfront and relatively stable and

therefore provide an immediate source of cash. Membership also serves a marketing function by establishing a core customer base.

2. Spectator admission charge, which includes the categories of full adult, family, special groups and premium. There is a high degree of flexibility as it is subject to significant variation because of changing attendance patterns and differences in the scheduling of games.

3. Corporate facilities including boxes and hospitality. Usually a large investment is required but the strengths are that business connections are made and premium rental can be charged.

4. Player fees and charges include entry fees, facility charge and equipment hire. This type of revenue is dependent on demand and the user pays for the experience.

5. Special fundraising efforts are another source of recurrent funding and may include a dinner dance, rage-party, auction night, a trivia night and so on. The points to note are that the burden is on staff and members to arrange and attend functions. However, these types of events can be profitable through large markups on food and drink.

6. Lotteries and gaming such as raffles, bingo and gaming machines. Permits are often required, margins are low and there is solid competition from other venues.

7. Merchandising such as memorabilia, scarves, T-shirts, jackets and autographed equipment. While it can produce a significant short-run increase in revenue, it can plateau out with a fall in on-field success.

8. Sponsorships and endorsement are another good source and may include naming rights, partnerships, signage, product endorsements and contra deals. However, the points to note are that the organization can lose control and become dependent on sponsor income and defer to their partnership demands.

9. Catering may include take away or sit down food or drink. This is labour intensive but, because it is delivered in a non-competitive environment, higher profit margins can be sustained.

10. Broadcasting rights such as television and radio and, more recently, Internet and mobile phone streaming rights. These focus on elite sports with a large audience base and may be irrelevant for most sports

associations and clubs. At the same time, it provides the single largest revenue source for professional sport leagues.

11. Investment income such as interest earned and share dividends. However, share prices can vary at short notice and losses can be made which increases the level of risk. In addition, interest rates may be low.

12. Government grants, which may be federal, state or local. There are often marked differences between sports, they can vary from year to year and, like government capital funds, are subject to certain conditions being met.

The expenses incurred in running a sport enterprise are also varied. They include:

1. Wages and salaries such as permanent, contract or casual administration staff and players. This is usually the largest expense item and is subject to inflation and competitive bidding as clubs aim to secure the best playing talent.

2. Staff on-costs, which include insurance, training, leave and superannuation. The points to note here are that they are legally required, ongoing and linked to the employment contract.

3. Marketing costs include advertising, sales promotion, site visits, trade displays and give-aways. In this case, it is easy to exceed budget estimates since there is always a tacit assumption that too much marketing and promotion is never enough.

4. Office maintenance includes power and light, phone and fax, postage and stationery and printing which are ongoing and tight control is required.

5. Venue maintenance includes the playing area, the viewing area and member facilities. Maintenance expenditure is ongoing and frequently absorbs a significant amount of revenue.

6. Player management includes equipment, clothing and footwear, medical services, fitness and conditioning and travel. While they constitute an essential investment in improved performance, they also require tight budgeting.

7. Asset depreciation includes facilities, buildings, cars and equipment. Assets lose value and must be replaced. Also, depreciation is a non-cash expense and it is essential that assets be amortized as expenses over their lifetime.

KEY FINANCIAL MANAGEMENT QUESTIONS

At the same time, it is important to note that, while significant segments of sport are now big businesses, most sport organizations are relatively small and depend on the support of club members, volunteer officials, community businesses and local government to sustain their operations. While high profile professional sport leagues turn over millions of dollars a year, the majority of sport clubs and associations are unlikely to secure more than a million dollars to fund their operations. A majority of sport is really a form of small business. A suburban supermarket turns over more money than most sport clubs and associations.

However, no matter what the scale or size of sport organizations, they all need to be managed in a sound and responsible manner. Many sport administrators do not feel comfortable handling money or planning the financial affairs of clubs and associations, which often arises out of poor background knowledge and a lack of experience in managing complex financial issues. In practice, there are many financial questions that sport managers need to answer. They include:

1. What do we own?

2. What do we owe?

3. What did we earn?

4. What did we spend?

5. Did we make a profit?

6. Do we have enough cash to pay debts when they fall due?

7. How big is our interest bill?

8. Are we borrowing too much?

9. Did we improve upon last year?

10. How do we compare with other similar sport organizations?

There is also the problem of making sense of the vocabulary of accounting. The distinction between assets and liabilities is mostly clear, with assets amounting to all those things we own and liabilities being all those things we owe to others. However, the distinction between tangible and intangible assets and current and non-current liabilities may often be less clear. The concepts of owners' equity, shareholders' funds and net worth can also cause confusion, while further difficulties can arise when contrasting operating profit with net profit, exploring financial ratios or dealing with depreciation and amortization issues.

Consequently, the effective management of any sport organization requires not only a sound knowledge of the principles of financial management, but also the support of a financial recording and reporting system that allows a quick and easy reading of the club or association's financial health (Hart, 2006). It is now taken for granted that a professionally managed sport organization will produce three integrated annual financial reports. The first document is a statement of performance, or profit and loss, which reports on the revenues earned for the period and the expenses incurred. The second document is a statement of position, or balance sheet, which reports on the current level of assets, liabilities and equity. The third document is a statement of cash flows, which identifies the cash movements in and out of the organization. The cash flow statement is divided into activities related to day-to-day operations, activities that involve the sale and purchase of assets and activities that involve the securing and borrowing of funds and their repayment. The balance sheet and profit and loss statement are discussed in more detail below.

THE BALANCE SHEET

The balance sheet measures the wealth of a sport organization. Assets are placed on the left hand side of the balance sheet, while liabilities are placed on the right hand side. Proprietorship (also known as owners' equity, net worth or accumulated funds) is located on the right hand side and represents the difference between assets and liabilities. The balance sheet gives a clear picture of a sport organization's wealth by contrasting its assets (things it owns) with its liabilities (things it owes). The balance sheet can therefore be seen as a snapshot of the wealth of a sport club or association at a point in time. The balance sheet also indicates how the assets of the organization have been funded. It can be though equity, (i.e. the capital of the owners) or from borrowed funds from some other organization or individual.

It is important to note that not all assets are the same. They can be broken down into a number of categories (Hoggett et al., 2006). So too can liabilities. As a result, a balance sheet will be set up to provide a clear picture of the level of both current and non-current assets and current and non-current liabilities. The level of owner's equity or shareholders' capital (or accumulated funds as it is usually called in non-profit organization statements) will also be identified in the balance sheet since it is effectively the difference between the two. This is because assets can be accumulated through either the owner's capital, reinvested profits or borrowed funds.

Assets

As noted above, assets are all those things owned by an organization. To put it more technically, they constitute resources owned and controlled by an entity from which future benefits are expected to flow. The assets of a balance sheet are not only broken down into their various categories, but they are also listed according to their degree of liquidity, with the most liquid coming first and the less liquid coming later in the statement. The measure of an assets liquidity is the ease with which it can be converted to cash and all those assets which can easily converted are listed under the current assets heading. The most frequently cited currents assets are cash in bank, accounts payable or debtors (which include those short-term invoices or bills for which payment has not yet been received), investments in the share market (which can be converted to cash through quick sale) and stocks of material and merchandise (which at a pinch can be sold for cash). Items like prepaid expenses (i.e. bills paid in advance) can also be included here. The level of current assets is an important indicator of the financial health of a sport organization since it is the means by which bills are paid and creditors' demands for payment are met.

Assets are also listed as fixed or non-current. These assets include everything that cannot be easily and quickly converted to cash. Some stock and materials will be listed here when they do not have high turnover. The main items will be all those tangible or material assets that are essential for generating revenue, but are difficult to sell at an appropriate price in the short term. These items include office furniture and equipment (including all sorts of sports equipment), motor vehicles, buildings and land. Building improvements (e.g. a stadium upgrade) are also examples of fixed assets. The main categories of assets are listed in Table 10.2.

The balance sheet of a sporting organization can be complicated by a number of other factors. For example, assets can either increase in value over time (i.e. appreciate) or decrease in value over time (i.e. depreciate). Property, stocks and shares and various scarce artefacts and forms of memorabilia are particularly prone to increase in value. On the other hand, there are other assets that can lose value quickly and include those things that incur constant use and wear and tear, become obsolete or both. Moreover, there are assets that, while not tangible, clearly add value to the organization and should be accounted for. Accountants have recognized these financial facts of life for many years and have consequently devised strategies for managing these phenomena (Atrill et al., 2006).

Table 10.2 Balance Sheet – Types of Assets

Asset Category	Degree of Liquidity	Example
Cash in bank	High (current)	Trading account balance
Accounts receivable	Medium (current)	Monies owed by club members
Prepaid expense	Medium (non-current)	Payment of next year's insurance
Company shares	Medium (current)	Ownership of shares
Inventory	Medium (current)	Stock of sports equipment
Office equipment	Low (non-current)	Computer system
Other equipment	Low (non-current)	Office furniture
Motor vehicle	Low (non-current)	Ownership of vehicle
Property	Low (non-current)	Ownership of office building
Building improvements	Low (non-current)	Stadium renewal

Depreciation

Depreciation is based on the principle that all non-current assets represent a store of service potential that the organization intends to use over the life of the asset. Assets therefore have a limited life as a result of their ongoing wear and tear and probable obsolescence. Accounting for depreciation is the process whereby the decline in the service potential of an asset, such as a motor vehicle, is progressively brought to account as a periodic charge against revenue. That is, the asset is devalued in response to its purchase price or market value and offset against income. In order to allocate the cost of the asset to the period in which it is used, an estimate must be made of the asset's useful life. This will usually be less than its physical life. For example, in the case of a motor vehicle, it may be decided that after three years it will not be operating as efficiently and therefore will be worth less after this period, even though it is still running. If an asset has a residual, or resale value, then this amount will be subtracted from the asset cost to establish the actual amount to be depreciated.

The simplest method for depreciating an asset is the straight-line or prime cost method. This method allocates an equal amount of depreciation to each full accounting period in the asset's useful life. The amount of depreciation for each period is determined by dividing the cost of the asset minus its residual value by the number of periods in the asset's useful life. Take for example, a computer system that was purchased for $11 000. It is anticipated that the system will have a resale value of $1000 after five years. Using the straight-line method of depreciation the annual depreciation will be $2000. This figure is obtained by dividing the difference between the purchase price and the residual value ($10 000) by the five years of antici-pated useful life. This annual depreciation will then be posted as an expense in the profit and loss statement for the following five years. This process of spreading the cost of an asset over a specific period of time is called amortization. The idea behind this process is that there needs to be a clear way of showing the relationship between spread of benefits from an asset's use and the costs involved in creating those benefits.

Asset valuation

Asset values can also be change to reflect current conditions and prices. Unless otherwise stated, assets are valued at their purchase price, which is known as historical cost. However, many assets, particularly land and buildings, can increase in value over time. Unless this is periodically done, the true values of assets can be seriously understated. This problem can be overcome by a revaluation of the assets by a certified valuer, with a note to this effect accompanying the annual statement of financial operations and standing.

In Practice 10.1 Players as Assets

Professional sporting clubs are also confronted by the issue of how players might be counted as assets and, if they can, how they will be valued. This problem arises in professional sport leagues where teams are able to trade players through a transfer market. In the English Premier League, where large transfer fees are par-for-the-course, this issue is dealt with by listing the transfer fee as an asset and amortizing the fee over the contract life of the player. Take for instance Manchester United Football Club (MUFC) player Christiano Ronaldo, who transferred from Portugal in 2003. His transfer fee was just under GBP 12 million and he signed with Manchester United for five years. Using the straight-line method of depreciation his fee would amortize at around GBP 2.4 million a year and be charged as an expense for each of the five years of his contract. After two years, he would therefore be valued at GBP 7.2 million (i.e. 12 less 4.8). At the end of his five-year contract his value would be technically zero. However, in practice his transfer price would still be positive, unless he was cut down by injury. Indeed, if he improved over this time, his transfer fee could even be higher than his purchase price of GBP 12 million. The value of a sample of Manchester United FC players is listed in Table 10.3.

Under this arrangement, MUFC can therefore allocate a proportion of players' transfer fees as an annual expense, thereby reducing its taxable income. The bonus here is that, unlike other assets that lose value over time and are depreciated, many players will in fact have increased in value. However, the balance sheet will show them as having zero value at the end of their contract. Under these conditions clubs assets will be seriously undervalued.

Table 10.3	Manchester United Football Club – Player Valuations 2005		
Player	Contract Period (years)	Transfer Fee Cost (GBP million)	Annual Expense Charge (GBP million)
Ferdinand	7	31	4.5
Howard	6	2.5	0.4
Smith	5	7	1.4
Rooney	6	25	6.1
Ronaldo	5	12	2.4

Source: Manchester United Football Club, (2005). Annual Report 2004–2005, Financial Statement, p.13.

Intangible Assets

For sporting clubs, there is also the issue of how intangible assets should be treated and how they cam be valued. Intangible assets are by their very nature difficult to quantify and their definition as non-monetary assets without physical substance merely confirms their ambiguity. A good starting point is to note that there are two types of intangible assets. They are first, identifiable intangibles that include things like trademarks, brand names, mastheads, franchises, licences and patents. Some of these intangibles like franchises, licences and patents have a purchase price and they can be amortized over their expected life. The second type of intangible assets is labelled as unidentifiable, the best example being goodwill. Goodwill arises from a combination of things like superior management, customer confidence and a favourable location. Goodwill is seen to possess value since it can produce future economic benefits that cannot be directly attributable to some other material asset. Goodwill is relevant to sport organizations, since the ability to attract fans often originates from often vague, but strong historical attachments between club image and fan identity. While few clubs have attempted to identify a goodwill value, it is often visible when a privately owned team is sold to a new owner. The difference between the sale price and the asset value of the team will in large part be attributable to the goodwill factor.

Liabilities

Simply put, liabilities are those things that an organization owes others. To be more exact, they are the present obligations of an entity which, when settled, involve the outflow of economic resources (Hoggett et al., 2006). Like assets, liabilities can be categorized into current and non-current.

Current liabilities included monies that are owed to people in the immediate future for services and goods they have supplied. For example, a club may have purchased some sporting equipment on credit for which payment is due in thirty to sixty days. This is called accounts payable or debtors. Other current liabilities include short-term borrowings, member income received in advance and taxes payable in the short term. Income received in advance is an interesting case because it is often intuitively viewed as revenue or asset and not a liability. However, under the accrual accounting model, it is clearly not relevant to the current flows of revenue and expenses. But, as monies received, it has to be accounted for. So, what happens is that it is debited to cash in bank and credited as something we owe to members in the future. That is, it is a liability which is listed as income received in advance.

Non-current liabilities include long-term borrowings, mortgage loans, deferred tax liabilities and long-term provisions for employees like superannuation entitlements. The accumulation of liabilities is not of itself a problem, so long as the debt is used to build income earning assets. However, if increasing debt is associated with losses rather than profits, then the gap between assets and liabilities will increase. It is not uncommon in sport for clubs to have liabilities that exceed the value of their assets. For example, in 2005, in the Australian Football League, the net worth of the Western Bulldogs and Carlton clubs was both negative and in excess of $5 million in each instance. These figures indicate a lengthy period where expenses constantly exceeded revenues and assets were used to pay debt. In the long-run these sorts of trends are unsustainable.

Balance sheets can say a lot about a sport organization's financial health. However, balance sheets do not tell us much about a sport club's earnings, profits and losses over the course of a month, quarter or year. For this information we must turn to the profit and loss statement or, as it is often called in the non-profit area of sport, the income statement.

PROFIT AND LOSS STATEMENTS

It is not just a matter of examining a sport organization's assets and liabilities at a point in time in order to diagnose its financial health, it is also crucial to shift one's attention to the financial operation of sport clubs and associations over time (Atrill et al., 2006). The first thing to be said about the profit and loss statement is that it can go under a number of names. It can also be called an income statement, which is the non-profit sector terminology, and is also referred to as a financial statement of performance. The point to remember about most sport organizations is that they do not focus on profits and losses, but rather surpluses and deficits (Anthony and Young, 2003). In any case, it does not alter the fact that these statements look at the revenue earned during a period (say three or twelve months) and compare it with the expenses incurred in generating the revenue. Profit and loss statement are straightforward to compile and moderately easy to understand.

While profit and loss statements contain many cash movements, they do accurately represent the total cash movements in and out of the organization, since they are essentially about earned income and incurred expenses. As a result, they will include many transactions that do not include the movement of cash. In other words, revenue can be earned, while the cash may come much later. But it is still a revenue item that needs to be identified in the profit and loss statement. For example, a sport consulting business may have completed a strategic planning exercise for a large national sport association and invoiced it for $50 000. If, at the end of the accounting period, the invoice has not been paid, it will still be included in the profit and loss statement as income. The adjustment or offset in the accounts will be an equivalent (i.e. $50 000) increase (or debit) in the accounts receivable asset account. If the invoice had been immediately paid, the adjustment would have been made as an increase (or debit) of $50 000 to the cash in bank asset account.

Revenue, or income as it is frequently called, is typically divided into operating and non-operating items. Operating items include all those revenues like member income and merchandise sales that provide the funds to support the day-to-day running of the club or association. Non-operating items include funds that are irregular, or even out of the ordinary. An asset sale, a special government grant or a large donation are examples of non-operating income. As noted earlier, sport organization revenues have expanded dramatically over recent years but, for the non-professional clubs, the main sources are member fees, gate receipts, government grants, fundraising activities and sponsors.

Expenses should also be treated cautiously. The profit and loss statement should include all incurred expenses rather than just paid expenses. Buying something on credit or by cash is an expense. On the other hand, paying for something that will not be used until next year, for example, should not be listed as an expense for the period under consideration. It is an asset (i.e. a prepaid expense). For example, rental or insurance paid in advance involves a movement of cash out of the club or association, but does not constitute an expense incurred for the current period.

Depreciation

Depreciation is an estimate of the wear and tear of working assets. In an office setting, computers are quickly depreciated for two reasons. First, they are heavily used and, second, they quickly become out of date and obsolete. Depreciation is therefore recognized as an expense and should be included in a profit and loss statement. Depreciation can be calculated in a number of ways, the most simple being the straight-line method. If, for example, a motor vehicle is purchased for $30 000 has an estimated life of five years and no residual value, then the depreciation expense for the following five years will be $6000 per annum. Some sporting club finance mangers make the mistake of listing the full cost of the motor vehicle in year 1 as an expense, but this is clearly misleading. The correct way to treat this transaction is to list it as an asset and then depreciate (i.e. amortize) it over its estimated lifetime. Interest paid and interest earned also appear on profit and loss statements. Interest paid will be classified as an expense while interest received will be classified as revenue.

Operating versus net profits

As already noted, when analysing profit and loss statements, it is important to distinguish between operating profit (or surplus) and net profit (or surplus). The differences between these two terms comprise abnormal revenue and expenses and extraordinary revenue and expenses. A transaction will be classified as abnormal if it is a regular occurrence but, in a specific case, is significantly higher than normal. In the case of a sporting club, an abnormal item might be an accelerated depreciation of office equipment or a supplementary government grant. A transaction will be classified as extraordinary if it is a significant transaction and does not regularly occur. A sporting club example includes a fine for breaching a salary cap regulation. (This happens frequently in the Australian Football League and the National Rugby League) or the sale of an asset (this occurs in the English Premier League, where players can be traded under certain conditions).

Operating profit does not include the abnormal and extraordinary items and is confined to those transactions that are directly related to day-to-day activities that regularly recur over the standard accounting cycle. So, operating profit is the difference between operating income and operating expenses. Net profit is something else again and will take into account all abnormal and extraordinary items. If the sport club happens to be part of profit-making entity, then it may be required to pay tax on its profits. This item will be subtracted from operating profit to get to a net profit figure.

Depreciation is also frequently listed as a non-operating item and can also make a significant difference to the level of profit. An operating profit can be transformed into a net loss by the inclusion of depreciation as a non-operating expense. Sometimes claims are made that depreciation can distort the real profit of a sport organization but, in fact, the opposite is the case. Depreciation is a legitimate expense since it takes into account that amount of assets used up to generate revenue. In the context of the above discussion a typical profit and loss or income statement is illustrated in Table 10.4.

In Practice 10.2 The Financial Health of the International Cricket Council

The international governing bodies for sport, otherwise known as International Sporting Organizations (ISOs), depend for their financial viability on the revenues they can secure from major sport events. One of the most highly credentialed ISOs, which recently shifted its headquarters from London to Dubai in the Middle-East, is the International Cricket Council (ICC).

The ICC, which has 96 member countries, runs two major competitions, the World Cup and the Champions Trophy. The World Cup was last run in 2007, while the Champions Trophy was last run in 2005. The success of the Champions Trophy was reflected in the sharp increase in its operating income. The ICC's financial indicators for 2004 and 2005 are listed in Table 10.5.

The ICC depends for its financial strength on the revenue from its international tournaments. Its surpluses are used to promote the game around the world and to assist national governing bodies develop the game locally.

BUDGETING SYSTEMS

Budgeting is a crucial part of the financial management process (Hoggett et al., 2006). It is one thing to construct some simple accounts and diagnose the financial heath of sport clubs, associations and leagues. It is another thing to make sure resources are available for allocation to the various parts of their operations. No matter how wealthy a sport organization is, its resource base will always be limited and decisions have to be made as to not only where the resources are allocated (facility maintenance, player salaries, coaching staff, equipment upgrade), but also how much each operational activity will receive. Moreover, budgets are finite and the constraining factor will always be the amount of available funds.

Budgets are really financial plans that involve the allocation of funds to strategically important operations and activities. Budgets are essential for

Table 10.4	Profit and Loss Statement Template	
Item	**Amount ($)**	**Total ($)**
Operating income		
Member fees	50 000	
Events	10 000	
Grants	30 000	
Total operating income		**90 000**
Operating expenses		
Administration	50 000	
Events	20 000	
Insurance	10 000	
Total operating expenses		**80 000**
Operating profit		10 000
Non-operating income		
Special government grant	10 000	
Non-operating expenses		
Depreciation	20 000	
Net profit		**0**

Table 10.5	Financial Indicators for International Cricket Council	
	2005 (USD million)	**2004 (USD million)**
Operating income	**49.4**	**11.9**
Event income	37.9	2.0
Member subscriptions	11.1	9.7
Operating expenses	**29.8**	**19.4**
Cricket development	7.2	8.2
Total assets	**77.6**	**86.8**
Cash assets	44.5	69.5
Total liabilities	**61.0**	**79.9**
Current liabilities	30.7	75.5

ensuring costs and expenses are contained and do not exceed the planned revenue. Good budgets act as a constraint on spending and also provide a clear picture of the anticipated sources of revenue. Budgets come in different shapes and forms but all share the desire to control spending patterns and make sure the spending is grounded in an appropriate level of funding and financial backing.

A good system of budgeting is crucially important for sport clubs and associations. As already noted, the sport world has become increasingly complex and the need to manage money effectively is stronger than ever. In addition, a well-planned budget is the basis for efficient management and ensuring viability over the long term. The benefits of budgeting are many. They can:

1. help anticipate the future and thereby assist the strategic planning process

2. give a clear picture of resource needs and programme priorities

3. signal where there may be revenue shortfalls

4. allow management better to mange and monitor spending

5. communicate the club or association's financial plans to key stakeholders

6. enable precise measures of financial performance to be made.

As already noted, budgets indicate the spending limits on different activities over particular periods. On one hand, there is the operational budget (which is sometimes called a recurrent budget) and, on the other hand, there is the capital expenditure budget (which is sometimes called an investment budget). Whereas an operating budget refers to spending on the day-to-day operations of the sport club, association or league, a capital budget refers to spending on buildings, facilities and equipment and other tangible assets.

Operational budgets

An operational budget is a statement of the anticipated levels of revenue for a period of time and how the revenue will be spent. The figures are estimates only, since there will always be unforeseen circumstances that will change the financial parameters in which a club or association conducts its affairs. As a result, the financial projections that underpinned the budget figures may not be realized due to changing economic and social conditions. For example, a sponsor may want to renegotiate its agreement, membership income may fall because of poor on-field performance and coaching and support staff costs may blow out because of an increased demand for skilled specialists.

An operational budget aims to estimate accurately the likely level of revenue that a club or association will have to play with and the anticipated expenses associated with the earning of that income. For every sport club and association, it is crucial to ensure that revenue and expenses will balance and, at best, work towards the generation of a healthy surplus. Table 10.6 illustrates what an operational budget will look like and what items might be included.

Table 10.6 Sleepy Meadows Table Tennis Club: Operating Budget

	March Quarter ($)	June Quarter ($)	September Quarter ($)	December Quarter ($)	Year Total ($)
Revenue					
Donations	500			1000	1500
Sponsor	6000				6000
Member fees	1400	200	200	200	2000
Gaming	1400	1300	1100	700	4500
Total	**9300**	**1500**	**1300**	**1900**	**14 000**
Expenses					
General administration services	2000	2000	2000	2000	8000
Coaching					0
Event administration		1000	1000		2000
Travel		500	500	500	1500
Table tennis supplies	2000				2000
Total	**4000**	**3500**	**3500**	**2500**	**13 500**

The simple budget in Table 10.6 immediately reveals a number of important things. First, it identifies the main items of revenue and spending. Clearly, in this fictitious case, the Sleepy Meadows Table Tennis Club (SMTTC) is heavily dependent on the local sponsor which just so happens to be the main hotel in town. It also shows that the day-to-day administration expenses are significant, although it would be good to have a breakdown of this item, since it might reveal specific activities like marketing or office rental that need to be monitored. Second, it also shows when the revenue is earned and the expenses are being incurred. While this is a not a cash budget, it does indicate possible times of cash flow problems. However, this is unlikely to be a problem here since most of the revenue is expected to arrive early in the year. The budget consequently allows the SMTTC to monitor the balance between expense commitments and revenue collections for different parts of the financial planning period.

Operational budgets can be organized in different ways as well. For example, an operational budget may be structured as a line-item budget, which is illustrated in Table 10.6. This involves breaking down spending and income into specific categories like administration, travel, marketing and entertainment and applying overall spending limits to each item. All of the different activities or programmes in the organization will work to these limits. The SMTTC budget uses the line-item method in setting its forecast figures. At the same time, operational budgets can be re-jigged as programme budgets or performance budgets.

In Practice 10.3 Customizing Budgets

A budget can also be organized as a programme budget. This involves allocating a designated amount of funds to each activity or programme. Each programme area is then allowed to spend on what they want, up to, but not beyond, the designated limit. For example, the SMTTC may allocate funds to each of its junior, regional and veterans' league programmes along the lines shown in Table 10.7.

Each programme manager can then decide how best to distribute the funds to each of its programme activities. Programme budgets can be converted into performance budgets without too much difficulty. The strength of a performance budget is that it links the budget to the club or association's strategic plan. It forces the programme manger not only to work within the budget parameters, but also ensure that the funds are directed to the achievement of relevant outcomes. In the case of the SMTTC, a performance budget could take the shape shown in Table 10.8.

Table 10.7 Sleepy Meadows Table Tennis Club: Programme Budget

	Junior League Programme ($)	Regional League Programme ($)	Veterans League Programme ($)
Budget	4000	8000	2000

Table 10.8 Sleepy Meadows Table Tennis Club: Performance Budget

Junior League Programme	Regional League Programme	Veterans League Programme
Goal: to provide activities that attract young children to the club	*Goal*: to provide activities that attract quality players through access to elite competition	*Goal*: to provide activities that balance social and competition table tennis
Anticipated outcome: increase in registered juniors	*Anticipated outcome*: all teams finish in top half of league table	*Anticipated outcome*: viable competition
Budget ($)	**Budget ($)**	**Budget ($)**
4000	**8000**	**2000**

SUMMARY

The above discussion demonstrates that sound financial management is essential for the ongoing viability of sport organizations. The importance of having a proper system of financial planning, record keeping, monitoring and evaluation becomes increasingly crucial as sport becomes more commercialized and corporatized. A basic starting point is to identify the different ways in which funds can be raised to underwrite the operation of a sport club, association, event or league. It is also essential that sport managers are able to design detailed budgets that provide clear and transparent information that makes it clear as to not only what an activity, programme or event will cost to mount and operate, but also where the money will be coming from. It is equally important for sport managers to be able to understand financial statements, use them to diagnose the financial health of a club, association, event or league and subsequently manage costs and revenues to ensure a regular surplus or profit. It is particularly important to be able to distinguish between the different ways of measuring surpluses and profits and, in particular, the difference between operating and net profit.

REVIEW QUESTIONS

1. Identify the different commercial stages sport has gone through in the last fifty years and the implications it has for sport's financial operations.

2. Explain the essential features of corporate sport and what makes it increasingly challenging to manage from a structural and financial perspective.

3. Why are budgets so fundamental to the effective management of sport clubs, associations, events and leagues?

4. Distinguish between a capital budget and an operating budget.

5. Balance sheets are an important tool for monitoring and measuring the financial health of a sport organization. What comprises a balance sheet and what does it measure?

6. Identify the main asset categories of a professional sport club and explain under what circumstances players can be treated as assets.

7. Identify the main liability categories of a professional sport club and explain under what circumstances long-term borrowings can be seen as either a drain on resources or, alternatively, a crucial means of generating revenue and profits.

8. Surpluses and profits are important to the long-term development of sport organization clubs since they indicate that not only were all costs covered for the period under consideration, but that there are funds available for re-investment in the club or association's future

activities and programmes. What is required for profits and surpluses to be generated and under what circumstances can an operating profit end up leading to a net loss.

9. What is the easiest way of distinguishing a wealthy sport organization from a poor sport organization?

10. What must a sport organization do if it aims to increase its wealth and financial health over the long term?

FURTHER READING

A great deal of the material in this chapter is drawn from various parts of Stewart, B. (2007). *Sport funding and finance*, Butterworth-Heinemann, Oxford, and is recommended as an excellent introduction to financial management issues in sport.

The four-phase model of sport's economic and financial development was first developed by Stewart (2007b). For an extensive discussion of the finances of North American professional sport leagues see Howard and Crompton (2004) where they provide a chapter-by-chapter breakdown of revenue sources, with special attention to ticket sales and broadcasting rights' fees. See also Foster et al. (2006). One of the most detailed analyses of English Premier League finances is contained in Szymanski, S. and Kuypers, T. (2000).

For a simple introduction to the structure and function of balance sheets and profit and loss statements and cash flow statement see Hart, L. (2006). For a more detailed and technical review of financial statements and what they say, see et al. (2006). See also Atrill et al. (2006). For a succinct discussion of financial statements of non-profit organizations see Anthony and Young (2003).

For an extensive introduction to the budgeting process see Hoggett et al. (2006). A detailed analysis of costing and budgeting processes is also contained in Anthony and Young (2003).

RELEVANT WEBSITES

For details of Manchester United FC financial position and the general financial operations of the English Premier League, see <www.footballeconomy.com/stats2/eng_manutd.htm>

For more details on the financial operation of the International Cricket Council see <icc-cricket.yahoo.com/about-icc/mission-statement.html>. Then click on 'annual reports' to secure finance details.

To secure a detailed evaluation of the London Olympic games budget see the National Audit Office (NAO) Report at <www.nao.org.uk/publicatgions/nao.reports/06-07/0607252.pdf>

For an alternative assessment of the London Olympic Games budget, with a breakdown of the costs of various venues, see <www.thisislondon.co.uk/standard-mayor/article-23484734-details/Mayor+seeks+City+financial+expert+to+check+growing+cost+of+Olympics/article.do>

Case Study: Budgeting for the London 2012 Olympic Games

In 2005, London won the right to host the 2012 Olympic Games. The bid was impressive and there is little doubt that the Games, as a spectacle and as a major sporting event, will be a success. However, it is not as clear as to whether it will be a financial success. Like all bids before it, the London Bid Committee created a budget that has since quickly escalated in scale. It is therefore instructive to undertake a detailed analysis of just how the budget was formulated, what the key budget items are, why the budget has blown out and where the money will ultimately come from to fund the London 2012 Olympic Games.

The city of London has staged the Games twice before, in 1908 and 1948 but, on both occasions, it stepped in at short notice when others could not do the job. In 2005, it won the hosting rights for 2012 despite finding itself up against the most competitive field in bidding history, with Paris being the initial favourite to secure the Games. The other bidding cities were Madrid, New York City and Moscow. The successful London bid also banished the memory of recent failed British bids for Manchester and Birmingham.

The plan for 2012 focuses on the regeneration of a 500-acre site around Stratford in the east of the city, one of the most deprived areas of the UK. It is also only six miles (or ten kilometres) from Trafalgar Square, which is in the centre of London. Lord (Sebastian) Coe and his Olympic organizing committee plan to transform the area into a futuristic Olympic Park, straddling four London boroughs. It will include an 80 000-seat athletics stadium, an athletes' village and a string of other key sporting venues, creating a strong case for a valuable Olympic legacy. According to Lord Coe, the aquatics centre, cycling velodrome, BMX track and hockey centre would all have been built even if London had not got the Games. In addition, 9000 new homes will be created now that London has secured the Games.

Existing venues to be used for the Games include the new Wembley stadium for football finals, Wimbledon for tennis, Lord's cricket ground for archery and the Dome for gymnastics and basketball. Beach volleyball will be staged in Horse Guards Parade, baseball and softball in Regent's Park and triathletes will cycle past the gates of Buckingham Palace. The football competition will take in Cardiff, Glasgow, Manchester, Newcastle and Birmingham, and sailing will be held at Weymouth in Dorset. Overall, the venues sound very impressive, but they will come at a high cost.

Costing the Bid

Costing a large-scale sport event can become quite complicated and, as with all events of this type, it is important to note that the costs of running the Games (the recurrent or operating costs) are separate to those for building the venues and residential facilities and redeveloping the land for the Olympic Park (the infrastructure or capital costs). And it should also be noted that while the running of the Games will be privately funded, the venues and parks and other infrastructure costs will be met largely by public (i.e. taxpayers') money.

The other point to note is that the budget for an Olympic Games always seems to escalate in the lead up to the big occasion. Sydney 2000 and Athens 2004 both suffered from this problem. In the initial draft bid document of 2003, the costs of staging the London Games were estimated to be just under 2 billion pounds, which by previous Games standards was significant. In 2006, the budget was re-set at around 3.5 billion. However, in March 2007, the minister for the Olympics, Ms Tessa Jowell, announced an up-dated budget of 9.3 billion pounds. This is a massive increase and it raises the questions of just what capital and operational activities the budget will cover, what specific costs have been identified and why they have escalated so much in such a short space of time. While the then Mayor of London, Ken Livingstone, optimistically confirmed that the Games Organizing Committee would aim to make a profit, there was growing concern that the Games budget was spiralling out of control.

The first thing to be said about the budget is that the initial forecast was wildly off the mark and was never realistic. The

Continued

second point is that the London bid involved a large urban renewal project and this was always going to be very expensive. Other costs that were substantially underestimated in the first budget draft included the cost of building the main stadium, the cost of building the cycling arena and the cost of ensuring a safe event.

So, at this point it is worth identifying the main cost and expense items and to find out how they will be funded. The main cost and expense items are:

- Main stadium: 530 million pounds (up from initial estimate of 280 million pounds)
- Additional venues and infrastructure: 4.8 billion pounds
- Security and policing: 600 million pounds
- Contingency fund to cover additional cost increases: 1 billion pounds
- Operating costs of Games: 2 billion pounds.

The important point to note is that the 9.3 billion pound budget not only takes into account the direct funding of the Games and its facilities, but also the regeneration of the East London region. Three bodies will have responsibility for making sure the Games are in time and on budget. They are the Government Olympic Executive (GOE), which is the main government agency involved in the project, the London Organizing Committee for the Olympic Games (LOCOG), which is responsible for making the Games happen and the Olympic Delivery Authority (ODA), which will manage the construction of the venues and all other infrastructure. The overall budget will be managed by LOCOG.

According to Games organizers, the funding for venues, infrastructure and regeneration will broadly break down as follows:

- 63% from the Central Government;
- 23% from National Lottery
- 14% from the Mayor of London and the London Development Agency

As already noted, the costs for staging and running the Games are estimated to be 2 billion pounds and will be funded from the private sector by a combination of sponsorship, merchandising, ticket sales and broadcast rights.

Public Concerns

According to some commentators, the euphoria gained from securing the Games was dissipated when it was realized what costs were involved in creating facilities for the athletes. Moreover, there were rumours that grass-root sport cuts would be used to help fund the Olympics. Critics were also saying that the massive budget blow-out would undermine public support and one member of Parliament suggested that the Games organizers had either 'acted in bad faith or were incompetent'. Things got worse in early 2008 when a local 'culture and sport' committee report expressed concerns that the Games funding would take away money from London's community sports and arts groups. There were additional allegations that the Olympics had been to the detriment of other development programmes around the nation. In Wales, there was criticism about the Games depriving Wales of money by using UK-wide funding rather than English funding.

Other Problematic Issues

There is no dispute, though, that the London Olympic games will be both a massive mega-sport event and a huge international festival. It will also be a gigantic urban-renewal project that will rehouse hundreds of thousands of people. It will give people great pleasure, but will also create significant disturbance and disruption which all come with costs. At the same time, a number of initiatives are already being taken to reduce the level of community trauma, as the following examples show.

Games Partners

To help fund the cost of the games, the LOCOG has agreed to a number of partnership deals with major companies. 'Tier One' partners already announced include Lloyds TSB, EDF Energy and Adidas.

Ticketing

Organizers estimate that more than eight million tickets would be available for the Olympic Games and 1.6 million tickets for the Paralympic Games. They will be going on sale in 2011, with at least 50% priced under £20. To reduce traffic congestion, ticketholders will be entitled to free use of London's public transportation network on the day of the event. It is estimated that 82% of available Olympic tickets and 63% of Paralympic tickets will be sold. There will also be free events: for example, the marathon and road cycling.

many instances it is difficult to quantify many of them. This is also why a detailed and transparent budget is so important.

Event Scheduling

Some representatives of Muslim countries have expressed concern that the month of 'Ramadan', which goes from mid-July to mid-August in 2012, will clash with the Games. During Ramadan, Muslims are expected to fast from sunrise to sunset, which may put Muslim athletes at a disadvantage during the Games. As a result, some Muslims have called for the Olympics to be rescheduled outside this period.

Where to from here?

Of course, all of this discussion raises the question as to whether the Games are worth the cost. But the answer is not easy, since we also need to understand just what the net value of the games will be and what the real costs of staging them will be. It all comes back to the balance to be struck between the benefits and costs, although in

Case Study Questions

1. What was the initial budget estimate for the staging of the 2012 London Olympic Games?

2. What were the main line items in the initial budget?

3. To what extent did the organizers distinguish between capital or infrastructure spending and recurrent or operating spending?

4. Was this a problem?

5. What did the revised 2007 budget estimate look like?

6. What caused the budget apparently to spiral out of control?

7. Could the organizers have done more to control the budget and, if so, what?

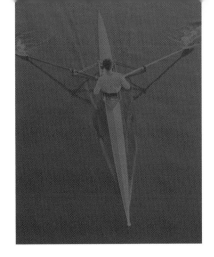

CHAPTER 11

Sport Marketing

OVERVIEW

The principles and tools of sport marketing are essential knowledge for sport managers to be able to position their sport club, player, code or event in the highly competitive sport market. This chapter examines the marketing of sporting organizations, sport leagues and codes, players and athletes, sporting equipment and merchandise and sporting events. The purpose of this chapter is to overview the key concepts of sport marketing, with special emphasis on the process of sport marketing as outlined in the Sport Marketing Framework provided.

After completing this chapter, the reader should be able to:

- Explain the key concepts of sport marketing

- Describe the process of sport marketing using the steps of the Sport Marketing Framework

- Define the role of strategy, positioning and branding in sport marketing

- Understand how to deploy the sport marketing mix.

DEFINING SPORT MARKETING

Marketing generally refers to the process of planning and implementing activities which are designed to meet the needs or wants of customers with particular attention on the development of a product, its pricing, promotion and distribution. Marketing seeks to create an exchange, where a customer or consumer relinquishes money for a product or service that they believe is of equal or greater value. Sport marketing is focused on satisfying the needs of sport consumers, or those people who use sport-related goods or services through playing sport, watching or listening to sport, buying merchandise, collecting memorabilia or using sporting goods. There are two dimensions to

229

sport marketing: the marketing *of* sports and marketing *through* sports. The first dimension is the marketing *of* sport products and services directly to consumers such as sporting equipment, professional competitions, sport events and facilities and recreational clubs. The second dimension involves the marketing of other, non-sport products and services *through* sport. Some examples include a professional athlete endorsing a food or fashion brand, a corporation sponsoring a sport event or even a drinks manufacturer arranging to have exclusive rights to provide their products at a sport event.

In order for a sport organization to be successful, it must mean something to sport consumers. In practice, this demands that a consumer is aware of the sport organization, its brand and the products or services it offers, and has responded to them in a positive way. The process of cultivating such a response is known as branding and, when a sport brand has carved out a firm place in the market and in consumers' minds, then it is said that it is positioned. The consequence of successful branding and the acquisition of strong market positioning is an ongoing relationship between a sport brand and its users.

Sport marketing is therefore best understood as the process of planning how a sport brand is positioned and how the delivery of its products or services are to be implemented in order to establish a relationship between a sport brand and its consumers. This may be achieved by the marketing *of* a sport brand or marketing *through* a sport brand.

THE SPORT MARKETING FRAMEWORK

The Sport Marketing Framework puts the sport marketing definition into practice by providing an approach to meeting sport consumers' needs. The Framework outlines a step-by-step process for planning and implementing the key principles of sport marketing. The Sport Marketing Framework involves four stages:

1. Identify sport marketing opportunities

2. Develop a sport marketing strategy

3. Plan the marketing mix

4. Implement and control the strategy.

Stage one of the Sport Marketing Framework, Identify sport marketing opportunities, involves analysing the conditions of the external marketplace, considering the conditions within the sport industry specifically and examining the activities of competitors. This stage also involves studying the internal capabilities of a sport organization by identifying its goals and limitations. Finally, in order to identify marketing opportunities, it is necessary to collect information about market circumstances with a particular emphasis on existing customers and other potential consumers. After all of this information has been collected and analysed, stage two of the Framework, Develop a sport marketing strategy, may be undertaken. Stage two involves determining the direction of the sport marketing programme, taking into account what was learned during stage one. It is important at this stage to document the strategy with both objectives and performance measures in order to keep it on track and, ultimately, to evaluate whether the strategy was successful. Once the direction is set, the specific tactics of the strategy can be specified revolving around how to distinguish or 'differentiate' the sport organization's brand and products in the market, deciding on whom the strategy is targeted (segmentation) and what marketing mix (the product offering, pricing strategies, promotional strategies and distribution systems) will be employed. Stage three of the Framework involves the precise determination of the sport marketing mix and how they will be combined to achieve the strategy set out. Finally, stage four, Implement and control the strategy, involves measuring outcomes and taking remedial action so that the plan stays on target. Figure 11.1 provides an illustration of the Sport Marketing Framework.

STAGE 1: IDENTIFY SPORT MARKETING OPPORTUNITIES

This step shows that it is important to collect information and conduct research before introducing sport marketing activities. It is essential to know what opportunities exist in the marketplace, what competitors are doing, what can be delivered and what consumers actually want. Identifying sport marketing opportunities involves three elements:

1. analysing the internal and external environment
2. analysing the organization
3. analysing the market and consumers.

Analyse the internal and external environment

The first element in identifying sport marketing opportunities involves assessing the internal and external environments of the sport organization.

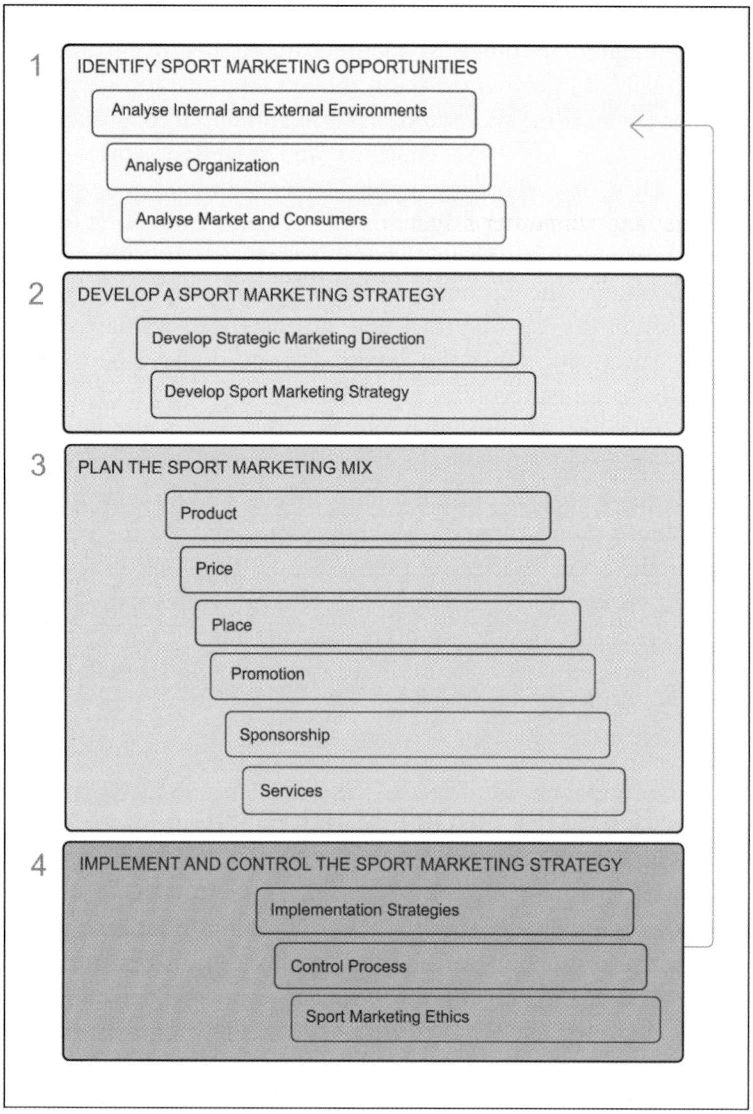

FIGURE 11.1   *The Sport Marketing Framework.*

The internal environment refers to the conditions in which a sport organization undertaking the marketing process is placed. The external environment refers to the market in which the sport organization is operating, including the broad national/global environment, the sport industry and the sport organization's competitors. There are five main tools for conducting an internal and external analysis:

1. SWOT analysis

2. competitor analysis

3. five forces competitor analysis

4. organizational analysis

5. market and consumer research.

Given that these aspects of internal and external analysis overlap with those conducted for any strategic planning and are covered in more detail in Chapter 5, they will only be mentioned briefly here.

The term SWOT is an acronym for the words strengths, weaknesses, opportunities, threats. The SWOT analysis can be divided into two parts. The first part represents an internal analysis of an organization, which can be summarized by its strengths and weaknesses. Strengths are those things an organization does well and weaknesses are the things an organization finds difficult to do well. The second part of the SWOT technique is concerned with external factors, or opportunities and threats. Opportunities could include environmental situations which could be used to the organizations' advantage. The SWOT analysis influences what a sport organization is capable of achieving in their marketing plan and highlights potential areas in which there might be an opportunity.

A competitor analysis focuses on the external environment by revealing opportunities or threats associated with other organizations in the same marketplace. A competitor analysis should examine several kinds of competitors: *direct* competitors who produce a similar product or service; *secondary* competitors who sell *substitute* products that meet similar customer needs but in a different way; and *indirect* competitors who sell completely different products and services that might satisfy consumers' needs. A competitor analysis should consider a wide range of variables, including their strategies, strengths, vulnerabilities, resources as well as their next likely actions.

In addition to conducting a competitor analysis, it is possible to conduct a five forces analysis which focuses on five forces which drive competition in the sport industry. It is used to help work out whether the industry is an attractive one in which to conduct business and whether there is scope for existing or new products to be developed. The five forces are described in detail in Chapter 5.

Analyse the organization

The second component of stage one involves understanding the purpose, aims and goals of the sport organization developing the plan, as well as understanding the needs of its stakeholders. The first three of these elements can be determined by locating (or if necessary developing) the mission statement, vision statement and objectives of the sport organization. More about these can be found in Chapter 5.

Stakeholders are all the people and groups that have an interest in a sport organization, including, for example, its employees, players, members, the league, association or governing body, government, community, facility owners, sponsors, broadcasters and fans. A marketing strategy can be strongly influenced by the beliefs, values and expectations of the most powerful stakeholders. As a result, careful analysis of the goals and objectives of each stakeholder must be completed before a strategic direction can be set.

Conduct and examine market and consumer research

The final step in the first stage is to conduct and examine market research. Market research means gathering information about the market and the consumers it contains. It is the process of learning about the marketplace and what consumers want, listening to their desires and expectations and determining how to satisfy them. It is also used to determine whether consumers have reacted to a marketing plan as expected.

In general, there are two broad types of market research: quantitative and qualitative. Quantitative research gathers statistical information, which is superficial but diverse. The most common method of gathering quantitative information is to conduct a survey or questionnaire. Qualitative research gathers non-numerical information (such as words from an interview of a person). Qualitative information is in-depth and usually gathered from a narrow and relatively small sample of people. Common types of qualitative research in sport include focus groups, suggestion boxes and complaint analysis. This information is pivotal in deciding what kinds of products and services should be offered to sport consumers.

STAGE 2: DEVELOP A SPORT MARKETING STRATEGY

The second stage of the Sport Marketing Framework involves two components:

1. develop strategic market direction

2. develop a sport marketing strategy.

With the information-gathering stage completed, the direction of the sport marketing strategy can be determined and documented in the form of objectives and performance measures. These act as a guide through all the coming stages of the Sport Marketing Framework. Next, the actual sport marketing strategy can be decided in the form of a positioning approach that differentiates the sport organization's brand and product offerings from competitors and segments the market into target groups.

Develop strategic marketing direction

A marketing objective is a goal that can realistically be achieved as the result of the marketing strategy. It can be expressed as a sentence which highlights what will occur as a result of marketing activities. There are basically four different types of marketing objectives that sport organizations might wish to pursue: higher levels of participation or involvement, on-field performance, promotion of messages about the sport or its benefits, and profit.

For each objective set it is important to add a performance measure. In this case, the term means a way of objectively estimating, calculating or assessing whether the objective has been achieved. It usually involves finding a way to quantify or put a number to the objective.

Develop a sport marketing strategy

Assuming that sport marketing objectives and performance measures have been set, the second part of stage two can be undertaken by developing the actual sport marketing strategy. The process of developing a sport marketing strategy requires four steps. Step one and two are associated with market segmentation, step three is the choice of market positioning strategy and step four involves determining the marketing mix.

Market segmentation is a term which describes the process of categorizing groups of consumers together based on their similar needs or wants. A market is the total group of potential consumers for a product and includes retailers, businesses, government, media and individuals. Market segmentation is a process of breaking this total group down into smaller groups based on a characteristic that the consumers have in common like age, gender, sporting interests or attendance levels. Once a particular segment or segments of the market have been targeted, it is possible to customize the product and marketing strategies to meet their specific needs.

The process of market segmentation involves two steps. First, the market must be divided into sub-groups based on a common feature or features. This can be done with the help of market research. There are six common factors that are often used to divide a market into sub-groups: demographic, socio-economic, lifestyle (psychographic), geographic, product behaviour and product benefits. After the market is divided into sub-groups, the segments to be targeted must be specified. The segment or segments chosen must be big enough and different enough from the others to justify the effort.

There are three approaches to segmentation: focused segmentation, multiple segmentation and undifferentiated segmentation. Focused segmentation occurs when one segment only is chosen and one marketing mix is customized for it. Multiple segmentation involves choosing more than one segment and then developing one marketing mix for each segment. Finally, undifferentiated segmentation involves no choice at all where the entire market is considered a legitimate and worthwhile target.

Once decisions have been made about market segmentation, the next step is to choose a market positioning strategy for each segment identified. Market positioning refers to how a sport organization would like consumers to think and feel about their brand and its product offering when compared to competitors. For example, does a sport organization want to be thought of as offering luxury, high quality or basic, value-for-money products? Do they see it as conservative and reliable or exciting and changeable? There are many different positioning strategies that can be selected that may suit the segment that is being targeted. It is important that the positioning strategy reflects a form of differentiation. That is, the positioning strategy must communicate to each target segment that the sport organization's brand and product offerings are special or different in some way from others available. It may be on the basis of the components of the product offerings, the quality of the products or services, the price at which they are offered, or even the method that they are delivered. If stage one has been completed carefully, there should be many possibilities for capitalizing on market opportunities that align strongly with the internal capabilities of the sport organization. Like all strategic decisions, market positioning and differentiation should reflect a match between external opportunities and internal competitive advantages.

The idea of branding is closely linked with positioning. A brand is like an identifying badge (often a name or a logo) that helps consumers recognize a product or an organization. A brand becomes linked with the consumers' opinions and views of the sport organization. Because branding and positioning are linked, it is important to keep branding, segmentation and positioning strategies closely related.

STAGE 3: PLAN THE SPORT MARKETING MIX

The marketing mix is a set of strategies which cover product, price, promotions and place (distribution) and are commonly referred to as the 'four

In Practice 11.1 Sport England Segmentation

Sport England is a Government funded organization which promotes community sport with the intention of encouraging a more active population. They undertook a research project to segment the sport participation market in England so that they could understand better why people play sport and why they don't. The research has helped them to understand the attitudes and motivations that people who are living in England have toward sport. Sport England are providing the results of their research freely on the Internet so that sport organizations in England can use it to help them to get more people involved in sport.

The research project has yielded 19 different sporting segments, each representing a group that holds a common set of attitudes and motivations concerning participation in, and watching, sport. Not only is each segment profiled in detail in terms of its typical social and demographic features and activity preferences, each can be examined according to the habits of specific geographic regions. Some of the key demographic variables used to differentiate the categories were: gender (male, female); age (18–25, 26–35, 36–45, 46–55, 56–65, 66+); marital status (single, married, unknown/missing); tenure (owner occupied, private rented, council/ha rented); employment status (employed full-time/other, student/unemployed, employed part-time/housewife, retired); and households with children (no, yes). The categories are reproduced in Table 11.1.

Source: www.sportengland.org

Ps'. They are collectively identified as a 'mix' because they should be combined and coordinated together in order to deploy the market positioning strategy. To the traditional four Ps it is necessary to add an additional two elements of the marketing mix: sponsorship and services. Both are already

Table 11.1   Sport England Demographic Categories

A01: Competitive Male Urbanites	C11: Comfortable Mid-Life Males
A02: Sports Team Drinkers	C12: Empty Nest Careerists
A03: Fitness Class Friends	C13: Early Retirement Couple
A04: Supportive Singles	C14: Older Working Woman
B05: Career Focused Females	C15: Local 'Old Boys'
B06: Settling Down Males	C16: Later Life Ladies
B07: Stay at Home Mums	D17: Comfortable Retired Couples
B08: Middle England Mums	D18: Twilight Year Gents
B09: Pub League Team Mates	D19: Retirement Home Singles
B10: Stretched Single Mums	

part of the marketing mix; sponsorship is part of 'promotions' and services are considered through 'product'. However, both are of central importance to sport marketing and are therefore given elevated status here.

Product

A product can include:

1. a good (physical item being sold)
2. a service being delivered
3. an idea
4. a combination of any of these.

A sport product can be defined as the complete package of benefits that a sport organization presents to sport consumers through offering goods, services and/or ideas. Sport goods are physical items that can be touched. Sport shoes, tennis rackets, memorabilia, golf-balls and skateboards are examples. These goods are all tangible, meaning that they exist as physical objects. Sporting goods usually have a high degree of reliability in their quality does not change much from one product to the next. They can also be stored after they are made because they are not perishable. Sport services will be considered independently in a forthcoming section.

A sporting product can be made up of a mixture of both goods and services. One important principle in sport marketing is to try to design products to have a mixture of tangible and intangible elements in order to help it stand out from competitors. To do this sport marketers think of the sport product as having three important variables:

1. the core benefit
2. the actual product
3. the augmented product.

Figure 11.2 shows that the core benefit represents the main advantage that consumers receive from buying the product. The actual product refers to the features of the product itself. As long as the core benefit of the product is wanted by consumers, then developing the right features can help to make it fit their needs perfectly. The augmented product refers to any extras or extensions that are added to the features of the product. These may be additional benefits, bonus extras, or even the image of a product and how people see it.

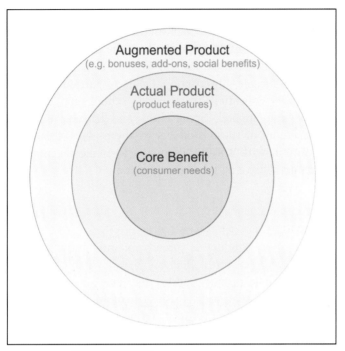

FIGURE 11.2 *Sport product features.*

Branding

Branding is one of the key strategies that sport marketers use to augment their products by associating them with certain ideas. The added value that a product has because of its brand name is called brand equity. Branding is much more than choosing a good name or having a good logo designed; it revolves around building the brand. Once potential consumers are aware of a sport brand, it is important to help them connect certain ideas about what it stands for that reflect an intended positioning strategy. Sport marketers achieve this by manipulating the brand image, which encompasses all of the symbols and ideas that influence the image of a brand such as its name, logo, product features, product quality/performance, packaging, price, advertising, promotion, customer service and distribution channels. The ultimate goal of branding is consumer loyalty. Brand loyalty is improved through high levels of product quality, convenience of distribution, keeping up regular contact with customers and customer loyalty programmes.

Related to the idea of branding is licensing. Licensing occurs when a sport organization allows another organization to use their brand name or logo for a fee. The company who buys the right to use the brand (called the licensee) will then produce a good, service or promotion and will give a percentage of the money they make back to the real owner of the brand (called the licensor). Licensing is a common product strategy in sport and each year it generates billions of dollars in sales internationally. It is particularly popular with merchandising (toys, collectible cards, games, school supplies, videos, DVDs and magazines) and apparel. Sport clubs and leagues do not have the resources to make all of these products by themselves. Instead, they may make an agreement with another company to make the merchandise for them and agree to share a percentage of profits.

Price

The way that a sport product is priced not only influences it financial impact, but also has a powerful affect on the way that consumers perceive it. The price of a sport product represents what a consumer gives up in exchange for using or owning it. Price is usually thought of in financial terms, but may include other things that a customer has to give up in order to obtain the product, such as time (e.g. waiting in a queue) or social costs (e.g. being in an aerobics class with others instead of a one-on-one instruction). A useful way to think about pricing decisions is to consider them in terms of value. In sport marketing, the value of a product is a factor of how its price relates to the benefits that consumers believe they will receive in exchange.

There are six main steps involved in setting the right price for a sport product:

1. setting a pricing goal

2. determining price sensitivity

3. conducting a break-even analysis

4. assessing pricing variables

5. selecting price tactics

6. setting a price point.

First, because different pricing strategies will achieve different things, it is important to determine what outcome is being sought and should be specified in the form of pricing goals. These may range from those focused on maximizing profit to those designed to provide the product or service to as many different sport consumers as possible. Second, it is necessary to determine how sensitive consumers are to price changes. Consumers are sensitive to price if they do not buy a product when the price is high or if they buy more of it when the price is lowered. The more sensitive they are, the more they will change their buying habits when the price changes. Third, a break-even analysis should be conducted to ascertain how many sales are needed in order to recover the costs of producing the product. Fourth, other variables that might affect price should be considered including the pricing strategies of competitors, legal or regulatory limitations that may be relevant and the impact of the other marketing mix variables. Fifth, a pricing strategy should be selected that underscores the overall market positioning strategy. There are many different types of pricing strategies that sport organizations might use including those designed to maximize profit, following competitors, setting a low introductory price, adding a flat margin to costs, using market demand as a guide and pricing according to the segment of consumers being targeted. Sixth, and finally, a price point is selected. It is important to realize that price needs to be re-considered constantly and should always remain consistent with a market positioning strategy.

Promotion

Promotion is concerned with communicating with consumers, providing them with information about product offerings and trying to persuade them to buy. Ultimately, promotion is pivotal in shaping and cultivating brand image. Sport promotion can be defined as the way that sport marketers communicate with potential consumers to inform, persuade and remind them about their product offerings.

There are four main promotional activities known together as the promotions mix because they are typically used in concert to create an integrated promotional strategy. The promotion mix elements are:

1. advertising

2. personal selling

3. sales promotion

4. public relations.

Advertising is a form of one-way communication where a sport marketer pays someone else to have their product or company identified. Common examples include television commercials, magazine and newspaper advertisements, radio spots, Internet pop-ups, posters, billboards and advertisements on public transport. Personal selling involves one-to-one communication between a consumer and a salesperson such as talking to a customer on the phone, talking face-to-face or even telemarketing. Endorsements and sponsorships are two forms of personal selling that are common in the sport industry. Sales promotions are short-term programmes that aim to stimulate an increase in sales. They give consumers an incentive (or a bonus) to use the sport product. Common examples include 'two-for-one' offers, prize give-aways, competitions and free trials or samples. Public relations programmes try to build a favourable image for a sport organization, its brand and product offerings in the community. It is not paid for by the sport organization and usually involves publicity in the media in the form of a news item.

In Practice 11.2 Marketing with NASCAR

In the post World War II popularity of stock car racing, the National Association for Stock Car Auto Racing (NASCAR) was the first to bring together the diverse range of drivers, venues, locations and cars into an organized competition. NASCAR began officially in 1949 and has become the premier stock car racing division in the USA. Now, every season, millions of fans attend races all over the country, commanding the enviable position of being the country's most attended spectator sport presiding over 17 of the top 20 most attended sporting events in the USA. But the real success story is in NASCAR's media popularity. The sport is broadcast in 150 nations and is the second most watched sport on television in the USA, behind the National Football League.

Corporate sponsorship of NASCAR began in 1971, when the R.J. Reynolds Tobacco Company through its Winston brand, assumed naming rights to what became the Winston Cup series. It proved to be one of the most longerous sponsorship arrangements ever, only coming to a close in 2004, after 33 years. Today, a visit to the nascar.com website reveals that the organization has 51 'official sponsors', 14 'promotional partners', three 'entitlement' sponsors and endorses 28 'automotive aftermarket companies'. The interest of this vast range of sponsors stems from the surprisingly diverse target market NASCAR enjoys. The majority of NASCAR fans range from 18 to 54 years of age with incomes from US$30 000–US$100 000. Forty percent are female and 21% are from minority backgrounds.

Aside from the obvious speed and excitement, there is much for fans to be interested in. For example, electronic sensors are installed every 100 yards on each track to provide accurate statistics for fans to access. Through its web service 'Track Pass', non-attending fans can follow cars in real time through global position satellite data, 'FanScan' allows enthusiasts to eavesdrop on communications between drivers and their pit crews and 'FanView' enables spectators in grandstands to access video, audio, race statistics and driver data during events.

Place

Place refers to the location where a sport product or service is delivered or the method of distributing a product. As a result, the terms 'place' and 'distribution' are interchangeable. Both describe how a sport product or service gets from the producer to the final consumer. The process of distribution can be explained through the concept of a sport distribution channel, which comprises a series of organizations or individuals through which a sport product must pass. There are both direct and indirect distribution channels. A direct distribution channel is short where the producer sells the product directly to the consumer. Examples include Internet sales of sporting merchandise and sport services like live matches and coaching lessons. An indirect distribution channel is longer where there are a number of organizations or people (called intermediaries) involved along the way. Examples include sporting goods products like athletic shoes and equipment.

Ticket sales are one of the most important sources of revenue for sport organizations that run competitions or events. Ticket distribution is therefore an extremely important issue for sport marketers that relates to the 'place' element of the sport marketing mix. When consumers contact a ticket distributor to buy a ticket for a sport event, they are often looking for more than just a ticket. They want convenience, fast and friendly service, questions answered and a reasonable price. If a consumer becomes unhappy with the service or price they receive from a ticket distributor, they can feel dissatisfied about the sport event or club as well. It is essential that sport organizations carefully control their contracts with ticket distributors.

The sport facility is perhaps the most important distribution channel in the sport industry. There are numerous features of sport facilities that affect their success as a distribution vehicle for sport products. The important features of a sport facility can be summarized into four main areas:

1. location and accessibility

2. design and layout

3. facilities

4. customer service.

Table 11.2 summarizes the variables influencing distribution in sport facilities.

Sport marketers do not always have control over the features of sporting facilities and may be able to do little to enact change without substantial resources. For this reason, it is important that sport marketers attempt to bolster the distribution of sport by managing a number of other aspects of the

Table 11.2 Distribution Variables of Sport Facilities

Location and accessibility	Attractive location
	Convenient to get to
	Good signage and directions
	Enough parking
	Accessible by public transport
	Accessible by different forms of public transport
	Easy to enter and exit facility
	Disabled access (ramps, lifts, washroom facilities)
Design and layout	Fits in with local area
	Attractive design (size, colour, shape and light)
	Ambience and atmosphere
	Easy to get from one area to another
	Good direction signs
	Seating arrangements with good viewing
	Weather protection
	Control of noise levels
	Areas for non-smokers and non-drinkers
	Lighting of playing area
	Protection from heat and cold
	Air circulation
	Adequate storage
	Safety issues (emergency procedures, fire detection, stand-by power, emergency communication, exits)
	Security (surveillance, control room, entrance security)
	Spectator control (zones, safe barriers, security, police)
Facility infrastructure	Variety of food and drink outlets
	Overall seating quality
	Premium seating available
	Corporate boxes and special services
	Toilets – number and location for convenient access
	Child-care facilities
	Scoreboards and screens
	Message centres and sound systems
	Emergency medical services
	Merchandise areas
	Broadcasting and media requirements
Customer service	Queuing and waiting times
	Prominent information stands/booths
	Efficient, friendly and helpful staff

Table 11.2	Distribution Variables of Sport Facilities (*continued*)
	Sufficient security and emergency staff
	Entrance staff, ushers
	Services for elderly, disabled and children
	Telephone enquiry service

venue. First, seating selection influences sport consumers' experience and can be used to enhance their viewing comfort as well as the marketing messages they are exposed to. Second, scoreboards and signage are an essential method of communicating marketing messages irrespective of the size of a venue and can enhance sport consumers' experience of the event. Third, lighting and sound systems can be used to attract sport consumers at attractive times and can also improve the atmosphere of a venue and event. Fourth, transport can be used to assist sport consumers in accessing a facility and can be marketed as a special customer service. Fifth, media facilities can encourage broadcasting and general media interest in events that occur in a sport facility. Sixth, the provision of child-care facilities can be important in attracting sport consumers during non-peak periods or to special events. Seventh, selling merchandise in sport facilities is a powerful marketing tool because it provides sport consumers with a convenient way of spending more money on items that emphasize the sport product's brand image. Finally, the supply of food and beverages is among the most lucrative of all services that can be offered at a sport facility.

Sponsorship

Although sponsorships and endorsements are part of the promotional mix, they are so important to sport that they deserve special treatment. Sport sponsorship is a business agreement where an organization or individual provides financial or in-kind assistance to a sport property (the sport organization or person being sponsored such as an athlete, team, event, association or competition), in exchange for the right to associate itself with the sport property. Sponsorship is an example of marketing through sport. The objectives of sponsorship can vary greatly, depending on the size of the partners, the type of sponsorship and the type of sport property being supported. Some common objectives for the sponsor are to promote the public image of their organization, to increase customer awareness, to manage their brand image and to build business relationships. In general, sponsorship helps to generate goodwill among consumers. The amount of goodwill generated can vary depending on the kind of sport property being sponsored, the degree of involvement that consumers have in the sport property, the time at which the sponsor becomes involved and when/how the sponsor ceases the sponsorship.

Sponsorship works through an image transfer from the sport property to the sponsor. This image transfer works best when there is a strong sponsorship affinity, or a good fit or match between the sponsor and the sport property. Two elements are particularly important for ensuring a good match:

1. an overlap of target markets

2. an overlap of brand positioning strategies.

As a result, sponsorship works best when the two partners are linked to the same group of consumers and have a similar kind of message. Most sponsors support their sport sponsorship programmes by leveraging them with additional marketing activities. For a sponsor to make the most of a sponsorship they usually need to undertake other promotional activities drawing attention to it. Sometimes sponsorship leveraging can cost several times the amount that is spent on the sponsorship itself. Sponsors also have to be careful about ambush marketing, where another company (other than an official sponsor and often a competitor to the official sponsor) creates marketing

In Practice 11.3 Sponsorship and the Tour De France

Even before television, the Tour de France provided a commercial marriage between bicycle manufacturers sponsoring the cyclists and print journalists covering the event. However, sponsorship radically escalated when the Tour first appeared on television in 1948. By 1960, footage from motorcycles and helicopters was being broadcast, the popularity of which shortly led to full television coverage. By 1973, there were 50 million television viewers making it a genuine global opportunity for sponsors. Presently, the Tour de France is one of the world's most broadcast sporting events with 150 million television viewers in 170 countries.

Sponsorship of the Tour began to change after 1929 as corporate supporters began to finance teams and provide prize money. International sponsors responded to the growth of media coverage and the Tour became an attractive and lucrative opportunity for promoting brand awareness and recognition. In 1995, Tour sponsors, Coca-Cola and Nike, were ranked first and fifth in a consumer poll that recognized French sport sponsorship. This level of exposure has attracted some of the world's leading companies to invest in teams. Today, there are between 20 and 22 teams bearing their primary sponsor as a team name, with approximately nine riders per team. Former seven times winner, Lance Armstrong, helped increase the popularity of the Tour de France in the USA, but his retirement also had a negative impact on viewing figures in that country.

The danger of such a well-publicized event is the potential for unfavourable brand associations. Sponsors of the Tour de France have been faced with alleged doping incidents leading to doubts over future sponsorships. Dutch financial company,

Rabobank, Swiss bike manufacture, BMC, and German truck company, Man, made news headlines when they publicly considered dropping out as team sponsors in the wake of the doping scandals revealed in the 2007 Tour. German broadcasters, ARD and ZDF responded to the drug scandal by ceasing coverage part way through the Tour. The competitive nature of sport sponsorship suggests that corporations may invest elsewhere if the negative publicity does not subside.

communications that give the impression that they are associated with the sport property. While evaluating sponsorships can be difficult, it is important that a careful evaluation strategy is implemented. Being able to demonstrate that sponsorship has a positive outcome for corporations is the best way to legitimize it as a marketing technique and to attract and retain sponsors.

Services

Sport services cannot be seen, felt or tasted; they are intangible because they exist only as an experience, inconsistent in terms of quality and perishable in that they can only be offered and experienced once at any point in time. Sport services are inseparable because they are consumed at the same time as they are produced. Sport organizations offer services where their staff, team or athletes provide an experience to consumers. For example, services are offered through fitness centres, local participation-based competitions, professional sport matches and support services like sport physiotherapists.

It is a common view that, when it comes to marketing a service, there are three additional Ps that should be added to the standard four. These are participants, physical evidence and process. Participants are those individuals who are involved in delivering and receiving a service. Physical evidence refers to the tangible or visual elements of a service such as a sporting facility. Process is concerned with the steps involved in delivering a service. All three of these new Ps revolve around service quality and customer satisfaction. Sport consumers are more likely to be loyal users of a service if they perceive it to be of high quality with consistent levels of delivery, leading to satisfaction.

Service quality may be seen as the degree to which a service meets the needs and expectations of customers. For example, if a customer expects a level of service that is higher than what they feel they actually receive, they are likely to believe that the service is lower quality and will tend to be dissatisfied. One key method of focusing on service quality is to work hard on ensuring that five aspects of its delivery are present. These five areas are reliability, assurance, empathy, responsiveness and tangibles. Reliability refers to the ability to offer a service in a consistent and dependable way.

Responsiveness refers to a willingness to help customers and to provide them with the service on time. Assurance refers to the level of confidence and trust that a customer has in the service. Empathy refers to the ability to get to know customers and their needs and to deliver a personalized service. Tangibles refer to the physical features of the service such as information booklets, equipment, appearance of staff, facilities and characteristics of a sport venue. If these aspects of service quality are emphasized, then customer satisfaction is likely to be maximized.

STAGE 4: IMPLEMENT AND CONTROL THE SPORT MARKETING STRATEGY

The final stage of the Sport Marketing Framework is to implement and control the sport marketing strategy. Implementing a sport marketing strategy means putting the plans into action. Many sport organizations discover that it is harder to implement a marketing strategy than it sounds. There are, however, two important actions that sport marketers can perform in order to help them to implement a marketing strategy more effectively. These are to use implementation strategies and to use a control process.

A sport marketing plan is more likely to be successful if there is a clear leader or group of leaders who take responsibility for its implementation. In addition, it is important that all members of the sport marketing team have a good understanding of the marketing plan and, where possible, have all made a contribution according to their unique skills and knowledge. This demands a team comprising a combination of staff and volunteers who have the right mix of skills, experience and attitudes in the first place. Whether the implementation of marketing strategy will be successful depends on the individual and team efforts of staff and volunteers. The final part of implementing a marketing strategy is to review and evaluate its outcomes on a regular basis. It is vital to keep track of how well the plan is going and to make changes if things are not going as intended. A control process provides the structure to this feedback.

The sport marketing control process has five main steps. The first step involves setting performance measures. These should already be in place in accordance with stage two of the Sport Marketing Framework. The second step is to put the performance measure into action by evaluating performance before and after the marketing strategy has been implemented, leading to the third step, a comparison of results to determine gaps, shortfall and performance successes. With these variations in the fore, the fourth step is to determine whether the variance is favourable or not and whether intervention needs to occur. The final step is to make remedial changes to the marketing strategy and mix in order to bring it back in line with marketing objectives.

While the implementation of a sport marketing plan should align with a sport organization's objectives, it should also fit within the broader boundaries of ethical behaviour. Ethics in sport marketing typically refers to whether the traditional four Ps of the marketing mix are deployed within a moral and professional code. Mostly, these include issues associated with unsafe or poor quality products, deceptive or predatory pricing, misleading or dishonest promotions and exploitative or collusive distribution. In the sporting world, other major ethical issues are concerned with publicizing the private lives of athletes, exploiting passionate fans and children who idolize sport stars through athlete endorsements of commercial products, the use of venues with unsafe facilities, unrealistic promises associated with health, fitness and weight loss products, the use of performance-enhancing drugs and the over-pricing of high profile matches and special sport events. In short, informed, autonomous consumer decisions based on the faithful representation of the product features and its price lie at the core of responsible and ethical sport marketing.

SUMMARY

This chapter was structured around the Sport Marketing Framework. Stage one is to identify sport marketing opportunities, which involves undertaking several kinds of assessments: a SWOT analysis, a competitor analysis, a five forces competitor analysis, an organizational analysis and market and consumer research. All of these analyses allow sport marketers to better understand market circumstances, consumer preferences, the sport industry, competitors' activities and the internal organization context.

Stage two of the Sport Marketing Framework is to develop a sport marketing strategy. This stage begins with decisions about the direction of the marketing programme, which is subsequently documented using marketing objectives and performance measures. Stage two also involves deciding on the basic theme of the marketing strategy. To that end, it requires the identification of the target market/s (segmentation), the positioning strategy (differentiation) and the composition of the marketing mix to deploy the strategy.

Stage three of the Sport Marketing Framework requires planning the sport marketing mix in detail. Here, decisions about the four Ps of marketing, the product, price, promotions and distribution (place) are determined, along with specific approaches to sponsorship and the management of sport services.

Finally, stage four is to implement and control the plan. Plans are put into action, facilitated by implementation strategies. It is also essential to keep the plan on track by using a control process that emphasizes the comparison of the results from marketing activities with the performance indicators and objectives set in stage two. Remedial action is then taken to correct the plan where it has been unsuccessful, has strayed off course or needs supplementation in order to capitalise on some unexpected opportunity.

Sport marketing revolves around the premise of satisfying the needs of sport consumers, in so doing cultivating a relationship with them that leads to a strong brand loyalty. Sport marketing lies at the intersection of strategy, where sport organizations focus on what they are good at and market opportunities, where sport consumers are offered what they want. The best way of finding this intersection is to use a systematic approach like that outlined in the Sport Marketing Framework.

REVIEW QUESTIONS

1. Explain the difference between the marketing of sport and marketing through sport.

2. What are the steps in the Sport Marketing Framework?

3. What is the relationship between sport marketing objectives and performance measures? How are these relevant to controlling the marketing plan?

4. What is the purpose of market positioning?

5. What is the difference between a sport product and a sport service?

6. What effect does pricing have on positioning? Provide an example of how price can influence a consumer's perception of a product.

7. What are the four tools of the promotions mix? Provide an example of each.

8. Provide a good example of a sponsor and sport property relationship that enjoys a high level of affinity.

9. What is the relationship between service quality and customer satisfaction?

FURTHER READING

American Marketing Association (2004). *Code of ethics*, revised edition. American Marketing Association, Chicago.

Amis, J. and Cornwell, T. B. (2005). *Global sport sponsorship*. Berg, Oxford.

Mason, D., Andrews, D., Silk, M. (eds) (2005). *Qualitative methods for sports studies*. Berg, Oxford.

Rein, I., Kotler, P. and Shields, B. (2006). *The elusive fan: reinventing sports in a crowded marketplace*. McGraw-Hill, New York.

Shilbury, D., Quick, S. and Westerbeek, H. (2003). *Strategic sport marketing*, 2nd edn. Allen & Unwin, Melbourne.

Smith, A. (2008). *Introduction to sport marketing*. Elsevier, Oxford.

RELEVANT WEBSITES

Sport England: www.sportengland.org
National Association for Stock Car Auto Racing: www.nascar.com
Tour de France: www.letour.fr

Case Study: The Dallas Cowboys and Lessons in New Media Sport Marketing

The Dallas Cowboys are the most valuable (worth around US$1.5b) and globally prominent team competing in one of the world's most lucrative sporting leagues, the US National Football League. They are also the most successful team in the modern era of the NFL, a performance level that has earned them unprecedented media coverage. As a result, the Cowboys have cultivated an extraordinarily vast and loyal group of supporters as evidenced by their NFL record for the most consecutive sold-out games. However, given the demand for tickets and the immense nationwide and global supporter base, there is an increasing need for teams like the Cowboys to be able to engage with all of its disparate supporter community. New media have provided the opportunity for the Cowboys to employ cutting-edge technologies to communicate with their fans irrespective of their location and to facilitate the interaction of non-local Cowboys supporters through novel channels. The Internet is no longer just the place to obtain the latest scores or locate some specific game statistics. In many ways, the Internet has subsumed the traditional media as the hub of sport fan engagement.

To begin with, it does not matter if a Cowboys fan cannot attend a game or even find the time to watch it on television. For the geographically displaced fan, it is possible to view highlights or watch an entire game streamed through the Internet. In addition, it is possible to acquire scores, player updates and statistics, watch interviews, download sport or team-related games, podcasts and vodcasts, view historical archives or even download some highlights to a phone. For example, the NFL.com video gallery is packed full of media content, while subscriptions are available for access to Internet-delivered, real-time game broadcasts.

The importance of new media for a team like the Cowboys is difficult to underestimate. Technology is a mainstay of their fan engagement strategy. In the centre of their new stadium scheduled for completion in 2009, will hang what will be the largest video board in the world to complement three additional panels with a total high definition viewing area of 13 000 square feet. Innovative new media are noteworthy throughout the Cowboys' Internet network. Their 'True Blue' fan club used an online interactive game to entice new users to engage with the site. 'Pigskin Toss' employs a training camp style football challenge to encourage visitors to the site to linger and explore other online activities, such as discussions, media content and insider information. Game players are enticed to involve friends, with the intention of increasing the web-flow traffic further. For the serious Cowboys fan, there are also invitations to visit MySpace pages of fellow supporters and even visit them in online virtual worlds such as Second Life, where there is a burgeoning trade of Cowboys memorabilia for avatars to wear such as player jerseys.

One of the emerging platforms for the Cowboys is the use of Really Simple Syndication (RSS) software. RSS provides an easy way for fans to access news, discussions and media content from multiple other websites. The RSS 'feed' on the Dallas Cowboy's dedicated RSS web page contains headlines and links to Cowboy's related content. Fans do not need to surf through a range of sites; they can access everything they need through the Cowboy's own RSS page which has already aggregated all the information a fan could want, from media content to weblogs. It also, of course, ensures that the Cowboy's website is crammed with traffic which will inevitably branch off into other features of the site.

Another benefit of RSS technology for the Dallas Cowboys is that it enables the organization to monitor the kind of information that is being published and posted about it. In a marketing context, where it is increasingly difficult for sport organizations to control what is being said about them, RSS may provide one tool to help watch out for and respond to both positive and negative press.

The Dallas Cowboys website shows an extensive range of ideas that sport marketers can use to communicate with fans using new media technology. The site gives fans the opportunity to access video and audio information as well as standard text. Importantly, it also allows fans to connect and talk with one another. The site is set up so that fans can easily read and create blogs, chat on the fan forum, receive instant e-mail alerts, watch live broadcasts, download audio podcasts (of games highlights, interviews, press conferences) and even watch video of game highlights and replays.

The Dallas Cowboys case demonstrates the impact that new media are having on the way products are being delivered in the sport market. Consumers can watch sport in completely new ways thanks to advances in digital television, which allows a choice of camera angles, the personalization of menus and settings and the ability to rewind live television. Not only is new media revolutionizing the delivery of sport, the reverse is also true; sport represents essential content for new media technologies. For example, organizations such as phone companies are eager to use sport content (such as games results) for mobile phone services. Other new media providers are keen to use sport in other ways such as to create editorials and articles, generate opportunities for customer participation, set up discussion forums, as well as for gambling and merchandising opportunities. These examples highlight the fact that sport and the media enjoy a symbiotic relationship, meaning that, although sport and media organizations are very different, they have come to be dependent on one another. Sport provides the content and new media provide the distribution. New media technology is a central part of this relationship.

In addition to well-known services like MySpace and FaceBook, there are other innovative sites that give sport consumers a chance to interact and network with other fans who share their interests. The two websites Furl (from File Uniform Resource Locators) and Flickr are excellent examples. Furl (www.furl.net) offers people a way to organize and share a personal file of websites and content they have enjoyed. A similar site (http://del.icio.us) also offers social bookmarking so that participants can see what other people have bookmarked. Flickr (www.flickr.com) provides a visual networking forum, where people can post and share photographs of subjects that interest them. Even a cursory visit to these sites demonstrates that teams like the Dallas Cowboys generate a tremendous volume of content, all of which represents free marketing exposure.

While most sport fans can still venture to their local sporting venue to experience live sport every weekend, only a decade ago, few had the opportunity to access much desired information about teams like the Dallas Cowboys without the aid of television, radio or newspapers. The emergence of new media as prominent access points has led to major teams such as the Cowboys to become converging locations of social networking. Geography is less important than technological literacy and the new breed of young fans are the vanguard of the new media movement. The most powerful opportunity for sport marketers is in using new media platforms to communicate simultaneously with their supporters irrespective of their location, while facilitating engagement between supporters. In other words, new media have enabled sport marketers to help fans talk to each other and this 'word of mouse' has exponential capacity for encouraging fan growth.

Case Study Questions

Log on to the NFL team, Dallas Cowboys website: www.dallascowboys.com. Navigate through the various toolbars on the site to learn about the new media tools the team uses to communicate with fans and consumers. Click on 'Fans' in the top toolbar and then select 'RSS'. Read about what RSS (Really Simple Syndication) means and how it can be used. New media have significant applications for sport marketing. Consider how each of the following is pivotal to new media and how they each might be employed to further the goals of sport marketers:

1. Internet Driven Platforms
2. Mobile Communications
3. Up-graded Conventional Technologies
4. Hardware
5. Software.

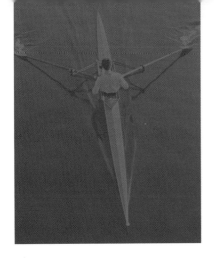

CHAPTER 12

Sport Governance

OVERVIEW

This chapter reviews the core concepts of organizational governance, explores the unique features of how sport organizations are governed and summarizes the key research findings on the governance of sport organizations. The chapter also provides a summary of principles for governance within community, state, national and professional sport organizations.

After completing this chapter the reader should be able to:

- Identify the unique characteristics of organizational governance for corporate and non-profit sport organizations

- Differentiate the various models and theories of governance relevant to sport organizations

- Understand and explain the role of boards, staff, volunteers, members and stakeholder groups in governing sport organizations

- Understand some of the challenges facing managers and volunteers involved in the governance of sport organizations

- Identify and understand the drivers of change in governance systems within sport organizations.

WHAT IS GOVERNANCE?

Organizational governance is concerned with the exercise of power within organizations and provides the system by which the elements of organizations are controlled and directed. Governance is necessary for all groups – nation states, corporate entities, societies, associations and sport organizations – to function properly and effectively. An organizational

255

governance system not only provides a framework in which the business of organizations are directed and controlled but also 'helps to provide a degree of confidence that is necessary for the proper functioning of a market economy' (Organization for Economic Cooperation and Development, 2004). Governance deals with issues of policy and direction for the enhancement of organizational performance rather than day-to-day operational management decision-making.

The importance of governance and its implied influence on organizational performance was highlighted by Tricker (1984) when he noted, 'if management is about running business, governance is about seeing that it is run properly'. The Australian Sports Commission (ASC) defines governance as, 'the structures and processes used by an organization to develop its strategic goals and direction, monitor its performance against these goals and ensure that its board acts in the best interests of the members' (ASC, 2004). Good organizational governance should ensure that the board and management seek to deliver outcomes for the benefit of the organization and its members and that the means used to attain these outcomes are effectively monitored.

A 1997 report to the Australian Standing Committee on Recreation and Sport (SCORS) identified a major concern among the sporting community, which was the 'perceived lack of effectiveness at board and council level in national and state sporting organizations' (SCORS Working Party on Management Improvement, 1997). Major sport agencies in the UK, New Zealand and Canada have also identified improving governance of sport organizations as a strategic priority. Failures in the governance of national sport organizations such as the Australian Soccer Association and Athletics Australia in 2003 and 2004 respectively, together with reviews of professional sport governance such as those conducted by the Football Governance Research Centre at the University of London, continue to highlight the importance of developing and implementing sound governance practices in both amateur and professional sport organizations.

CORPORATE AND NON-PROFIT GOVERNANCE

The literature on organizational governance can be divided into two broad areas:

1. corporate governance that deals with the governance of profit-seeking companies and corporations that focus on protecting and enhancing shareholder value

2. non-profit governance that is concerned with the governance of voluntary-based organizations that seek to provide a community service or facilitate the involvement of individuals in social, artistic or sporting activities.

Studies of corporate governance have covered 'concepts, theories and practices of boards and their directors, and the relationships between boards and shareholders, top management, regulators and auditors, and other stakeholders' (Tricker, 1993). The literature in this field focuses on the two primary roles of the board in first, ensuring conformance by management and, second, enhancing organizational performance. Conformance deals with the processes of supervision and monitoring of the work of managers by the board and ensuring that adequate accountability measures are in place to protect the interests of shareholders. Enhancing organizational performance focuses on the development of strategy and policy to create the direction and context within which managers will work.

The unique characteristics of non-profit organizations demand a governance framework different to that of the corporate firm. Non-profit organizations exist for different reasons than do profit-seeking entities and generally involve a greater number of stakeholders in their decision-making structures and processes. The relationships between decision-makers – the governance framework – will therefore be different to that found in the corporate world. The management processes employed to carry out the tasks of the organizations might well be similar, but a fundamental difference between non-profit and corporate organizations is found in their governance frameworks.

While many sports organizations, such as major sporting goods manufacturers, athlete management companies, retail companies and venues, can be classed as profit seeking, the majority of sport organizations that provide participation and competition opportunities are non-profit. These organizations include large clubs, regional associations or leagues, state or provincial governing bodies and national sport organizations.

IS THERE A THEORY OF SPORT GOVERNANCE?

Clarke (2004) provides a unique overview of the development of theories of corporate governance. Some of the important theories applied to the study of organizational governance include agency theory, stewardship theory, institutional theory, resource dependence theory, network theory and stakeholder theory. In this section, we shall examine each of them in turn and assess how relevant they are to understanding the governance of sport organizations.

Agency theory proposes that shareholders' interests should prevail in decisions concerning the operation of an organization. Managers (agents) who have been appointed to run the organization should be subject to extensive checks and balances to reduce the potential for mismanagement or misconduct that threatens shareholders' interests. This has been the predominant theoretical approach to the study of corporate governance and has focused on exploring the best ways to maximize corporate control of managerial actions, information for shareholders and labour in order to provide some assurance that managers will seek outcomes that maximize shareholder wealth and reduce risk. In relation to corporations operating in the sport industry that have individual, institutional and government shareholders, this theory helps explain how governance systems work. For the majority of non-profit sport organizations, which have diverse stake-holders who do not have a financial share in the organization (aside from annual membership fees), agency theory has limited application.

Stewardship theory takes the opposite view to agency theory and proposes that rather than assume managers seek to act as individual agents to maximize their own interests over those of shareholders, managers are motivated by other concepts such as a need for achievement, responsibility, recognition and respect for authority. Thus, stewardship theory argues that managers' and shareholders' interests are actually aligned and that managers (agents) will act in the best interests of shareholders. This theoretical view can also be applied to sport corporations such as Nike, FoxSports or a listed professional football club franchise. The application of either agency or stewardship theory is dependent on the actions of the managers (who choose to act as agents or stewards) and the view of shareholders (who create either an agent or stewardship relationship through their conscious choice of governance framework). Stewardship theory is arguably more applicable than agency theory to the study of non-profit sport organizations where managers may have a connection to the sport as an ex-player, coach or club official and therefore have a deeper sense of commitment to the organization and are more likely to act as stewards.

Agency and stewardship theories focus on the internal monitoring issues of governance. Three theories that seek to explain how organizations relate to external organizations and acquire scarce resources are institutional theory, resource dependence theory and network theory. Institutional theory argues that the governance frameworks adopted by organizations are the result of adhering to external pressures of what is deemed acceptable business practice, including legal requirements for incorporation. Such pressures reflect wider societal concerns for proper governance systems to be employed. Further, if all organizations of a similar type and size seek to conform to these pressures, they are likely to adopt very similar governance frameworks, a situation know as institutional isomorphism. Evidence of this is apparent throughout club-based sporting systems, such as in Canada, Australia, New Zealand and the UK, where most national and state or provincial sporting organizations operate under remarkably similar governance frameworks.

Resource dependence theory proposes that, in order to understand the behaviour of organizations, we must understand how organizations relate to their environment. Organizations paradoxically seek stability and certainty in their resource exchanges by entering into interorganizational arrangements which require some loss of flexibility and autonomy in exchange for gaining control over other organizations. These interorganizational arrangements take the form of mergers, joint ventures, cooptation (the inclusion of outsiders in the leadership and decision-making processes of an organization), growth, political involvement or restricting the distribution of information (Pfeffer and Salancik, 1978). Such arrangements have an impact on the governance structure adopted, the degree to which stakeholders are involved in decision-making and the transparency of decision-making.

A final theory that attempts to explain elements of governance based on how organizations relate to external organizations is network theory. Network theory posits that organizations enter into socially binding contracts to deliver services in addition to purely legal contracts. Such arrangements create a degree of interdependency between organizations and facilitate the development of informal communication and the flow of resources between organizations. This is particularly true of sport organizations that, for example, rely on personal contacts to facilitate the success of major events by securing support from high profile athletes, using volunteers in large numbers from other sports organizations and depending on government support for stadium development of event bidding. Network theory can help explain how governance structures and processes, particularly concerning the board of sports organizations, evolve to facilitate such informal arrangements.

These three theories emphasize the need to examine governance in terms of the external pressures that organizations face and the strategies, structures and processes they put in place to manage them. Such an approach offers a more realistic view of how and why organizations have a particular governance framework than agency and stewardship theories.

Stakeholder theory provides another perspective for examining the relationship between organizations and their stakeholders. It argues for conceptualizing a corporation as a series of relationships and responsibilities which the governance framework must account for. This has important implications for corporations acting as good corporate citizens and particularly for sport organizations that need to manage a myriad of relationships with sponsors, funding agencies, members, affiliated organizations, staff, board members, venues, government agencies and suppliers.

Much of the writing and research on organizational governance has been based on corporations rather than non-profit entities. Applying a particular theory to the study of sport organizations must be done with regard to the type and industry context of the sport organization being studied. Sport organizations and their governance frameworks have diverse elements that prevent the development of an overarching theory of sport governance. The value of the theories presented here is that each of them can be used to illuminate the governance assumptions, processes, structures and outcomes for sport organizations.

GOVERNANCE STRUCTURAL ELEMENTS

The governance elements of a corporate or profit-seeking sport organization are the same for any general business operation. These elements can include paid staff, including a CEO who may or may not have voting rights on a board, a board of directors representing the interests of many shareholders (in the case of publicly listed company), or directors who are direct partners in the business. The real differences in governance elements can be found in volunteer sport organizations (VSOs).

A simple governance structure of VSOs is depicted in Figure 12.1 and comprises five elements: members, volunteers, salaried staff, a council and a board. Normally, members meet as a council (usually once per year at an annual general meeting) to elect or appoint individuals to a board. If the

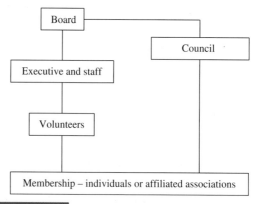

FIGURE 12.1 *Typical governance structure of a VSO.*

organization is large enough, the board may choose to employ an executive and other paid staff to carry out the tasks of the organization. Together with a pool of volunteers, these employees deliver services to organizational members. The board acts as the main decision-making body for the organization and therefore the quality of its activities is vital to the success of the organization.

Members of a VSO can be individual players or athletes or, in some cases, members are classified as other affiliated organizations such as a club that competes in a league provided by a regional sports association. Members can also be commercial facility providers such as basketball, squash or indoor soccer stadiums. The membership council comprises those people or organizations that are registered members and may be allocated voting rights according to membership status. The board comprises individuals who have been elected, appointed or invited to represent the interests of various membership categories, geographic regions or sporting disciplines in decision-making. The senior paid staff member, often designated the CEO, is employed by and reports directly to the board. Other paid staff are appointed by the CEO to assist in performing various organizational tasks. These staff must work with a variety of volunteers in sport to deliver essential services such as coaching, player and official development, marketing, sport development and event delivery. Finally, a wide range of stakeholders such as sponsors, funding agencies, members, affiliated organizations, staff, board members, venues, government agencies and suppliers must be consulted and managed in order for the organization to operate optimally.

The majority of national and state or provincial sport organizations that provide participation and competition opportunities in club-based sporting systems are governed voluntarily by elected office bearers, who fill positions on either committees or boards. Most of these VSOs operate under a federated delegate system with club representatives forming regional boards, regional representatives forming state or provincial boards and state or provincial representatives forming national boards.

This traditional governance structure has been criticized for being unwieldy and cumbersome, slow to react to changes in market conditions, subject to potentially damaging politics or power plays between delegates and imposing significant constraints on organizations wishing to change. On the other hand, the majority of sports organizations still use this model today and value its ability to ensure members have a say in decision-making, the transparency of decisions and the autonomy granted to organizations at every level of the system. In Practice 12.1 explains a typical governance structure of a VSO.

In Practice 12.1 Hockey Canada

Hockey Canada is the sole governing body for amateur hockey in Canada. More than 4.5 million Canadians are associated with Hockey Canada as players, coaches, officials, trainers, administrators or volunteers. In season 2007/08, there were more than 545 000 registered players and another 1.5 million casual or unregistered participants playing hockey at more than 3000 arenas throughout the country. Hockey Canada employs 75 staff and has offices in most Canadian provinces. The organizations that affiliate with Hockey Canada include 13 Branch associations, the Canadian Hockey League and Canadian Inter-University Sport. In conjunction with these member organizations, Hockey Canada facilitates participation in amateur hockey leagues, teams and games through player, coach and referee development, grading of competitions and establishing appropriate rules and regulations for amateur hockey across Canada.

Hockey Canada exists to:

- Foster and encourage the sport of amateur hockey throughout Canada
- Foster and encourage leadership programmes in all areas related to the development of hockey in Canada
- Recognize and sanction the establishment of governing bodies in Canada in accordance with the principles, philosophy and practices of the Association
- Support and encourage Branches and other members in the development of amateur hockey within their jurisdictions and areas of responsibility
- Establish and maintain uniform playing rules for amateur hockey
- Maintain national insurance programmes
- Affiliate with and cooperate with other national or international amateur hockey organizations
- Conduct Inter-Branch and international contests of amateur hockey
- Provide representation for international open hockey competition.

The governance structure of Hockey Canada reflects the nature of these activities and incorporates a range of decision-making groups to ensure the interests of all stakeholders are considered in relation to strategic planning and resource allocation by the national organization. The governance structure can be viewed at http://www.hockeycanada.ca/6/8/4/3/index1.shtml

The articles, by-laws and regulations for Hockey Canada are encapsulated in a 210 page document that sets out in detail the rights and responsibilities of the members of Hockey Canada and the processes used to govern its activities.

An important element of the structure to note is the large size of the Board of Directors which comprises Officers (eight), Branch Presidents (13), Council Representatives and Directors (eight) and Special Advisory Council Members (five). Each of these positions represents a specific constituent group within Hockey Canada. In addition, the Board of Directors receives reports from a Hockey Development Council of 24 members, again made up of individuals representing the specific interests of regional affiliates or membership types (i.e. coaches, officials). The Board of Directors has a number of policy subcommittees (five) that deal with areas such as elite competitions, women's programmes, policy development, programmes of excellence and junior development. Finally, there are 10 standing subcommittees that report to the Board on issues such as insurance, marketing, finance, management and other areas of activity. This appears to be a very cumbersome way to manage the affairs of a relatively simple activity like facilitating games of ice hockey, but the sheer scale and geographic spread of its constituents requires Hockey Canada to maintain a comprehensive governance structure that facilitates decision-making and communication among its 4.5 million participants.

Sources: Hockey Canada (website www.hockeycanada.ca) and Hockey Canada (2007). *Annual Report 2007*. Calgary, CA: Hockey Canada.

GOVERNANCE MODELS

There are three generic governance models that can be applied to non-profit sport organizations: the traditional model outlined by Houle (1960, 1997); the Carver policy governance model (Carver, 1997); and the Executive led model (after Drucker, 1990; Herman and Heimovics, 1990, 1994; Block, 1998). A governance model can be defined as a set of policies and practices that outline the responsibilities of the various governance elements and the processes used to carry out the governance function. All of the following models relate to organizations that are governed by boards that employ a paid executive and staff as opposed to more informal organizations that maintain a collective and informal structure. The models are more relevant to these organizations because boards that carry out the 'hands on' work of the organization, such as a small community club, are 'usually so strongly influenced by personalities and special circumstances that few generalizations can be made about their general nature or how they may be improved' (Houle, 1997).

Traditional model

Houle (1960, 1997) outlined a 'traditional model' for governance of non-profit organizations that is based on five elements. The first of these is the human potential of the board where the board ensures a systematic recruitment process is in place accompanied with on-going board member development. Secondly, the work of the board is structured according to a set of by-laws, policies are clearly defined and minutes of the board and committee meetings are consistently reported. Thirdly, the roles of and relationships between the board, executive and staff should be well defined and developed enabling clear decision-making to occur. Fourth, the operation of the board should be undertaken in a positive group culture and based on an annual work plan, regular meetings with well-managed agendas and on-going evaluation of the board and its work. Finally, the board has a focus on maintaining external relationships through formal and informal representation of the organization to the community. The model advocates that 'the work is done by the staff, the administration by management and the policy making by the board; in this traditional model, the board is truly in charge of the organization' (Fletcher, 1999).

This model has been and is probably the most widely used among non-profit sport organizations. It clearly separates the tasks of staff and volunteers and highlights volunteer board members as being accountable for the organization. The model has been criticized for the idealistic view that the board alone has ultimate responsibility for the organization (Heimovics and Herman, 1990) and the rather simplistic notion of the board making policy while the staff do the work (Herman and Heimovics, 1990), which does not reflect the reality of the working relationships that occur in most non-profit organizations.

Policy governance model

Carver (1997) outlines five elements of a 'policy governance' model for the effective governing board. The first of these is determining the mission and strategic direction of the organization, with a focus on the desired outcomes, rather than becoming immersed in the detail of the means to achieve them. Secondly, setting executive limitations or constraints for the work practices and the means that staff employ to achieve the mission set by the board. Thirdly, establishing clear board and executive roles and relationships. Fourthly, ensuring governance processes are clearly defined in areas such as board member selection and succession, the reporting of activities of the board and staff and ensuring the board focuses on the policies of the organization rather than cases or specific issues. Finally, the board's role should be more than simply ensuring conformance to financial procedures and ethical management practice; it should also develop clear performance measures related to strategic outcomes.

Like the Traditional model, Carver's model has been criticized for its 'idealized view of the board, operating above the messiness of the board–executive relationship as it really exists in non-profit organizations' (Fletcher, 1999). The model also does not address the important role of the board in managing external relationships and it 'clearly subordinates the CEO to the board and expects the board alone to set the parameters of the relationship' (Fletcher, 1999).

Executive led model

The executive led model, in contrast to the previous models, advocates the executive as central to the success of non-profit organizations. Drucker (1990) argued that the ultimate responsibility for the performance of a non-profit organization, including its governance, should rest with the executive. His views were supported by Herman and Heimovics' (1990) research that found that the reality of most boards was that they depended on their executive for information almost exclusively and looked to them to provide leadership. Hoye and Cuskelly (2003) also found this was the case in VSOs. Block (1998) argued that because the executive is working in an organization much more than the average board member, they have better access to information and therefore they must also 'be at the core of leadership and decision-making activities'.

BOARD STAFF RELATIONSHIPS

The gradual introduction of professional staff into VSOs over the last 20 years has created the need for volunteers and paid staff to work together at all levels, including the board table. This has led to some degree of uncertainty about what roles should be performed by each group and the extent to which staff and volunteers should be involved in strategic planning, policy development, performance evaluation and resource acquisition. The potential for tension between these groups as they negotiate their respective roles has been well established, as has the ongoing desire of volunteers to maintain a degree of involvement in decision-making while, at the same time, utilizing the expertise of paid staff to assist them in running their organizations. This then is the crux of board staff relationships: what areas do volunteers maintain control over and which do paid staff control?

Hoye and Cuskelly (2003) found that VSO boards perform better if a degree of trust exists between the board and staff and that board leadership was shared among a dominant coalition of the board chair, executive and a small group of senior board members. As mentioned earlier, the executive controls the flow of information to board members and so the quality, frequency and accuracy of this information are vital to their ability to make decisions. Ensuring the board and executive work together effectively enhances this information flow and therefore the performance of the board.

PRINCIPLES OF GOOD ORGANIZATIONAL GOVERNANCE

The notion of good organizational governance extends beyond ideas of monitoring to ensure conformance and developing to improve performance discussed earlier in this chapter. Henry and Lee (2004) provide a list of seven key principles for good organizational governance in sport organizations:

1. Transparency – ensuring the organization has clear procedures for resource allocation, reporting and decision-making

2. Accountability – sports organizations need to be accountable to all their stakeholders

3. Democracy – all stakeholder groups should be able to be represented in the governance structure

4. Responsibility – the board has to be responsible for the organization and demonstrate ethical stewardship in carrying out that responsibility

5. Equity – all stakeholder groups should be treated equitably

6. Efficiency – process improvements should be undertaken to ensure the organization is making the best use of its resources

7. Effectiveness – the board should establish and monitor measures of performance in a strategic manner.

This list of principles is not exhaustive, but it does give us a clear indication of the philosophical approach organizations should adopt in designing and implementing an appropriate governance framework. It may be somewhat surprising to find that even some of the more high profile sport organizations in the world struggle to implement good governance standards. Corporate governance of English Premier League football clubs has come under increasing scrutiny in recent years, due in part to the annual reviews of corporate governance undertaken by the former Football Governance Research Centre (FGRC) based at Birkbeck in the University of London. The Premier League (PL) is the flagship of the game's governing body in England, the Football Association (FA), which was explored in the Chapter 6 case study. The FA is in turn under the control of a European governing body, the Union of European Football Associations (UEFA), which in turn is a member of the world's governing body, the Federation of International Football Associations (FIFA).

The regulatory system for Premier league clubs comprises four elements:

1. regulation by the Football Authorities

2. regulation through the legal system in terms of company law, consumer law, labour law and competition law

3. regulation by a code of corporate governance developed by the Premier League

4. shareholder activism and stakeholder participation.

The Football Authorities (namely FA and UEFA) have developed criteria such as a 'fit and proper person' test aimed at improving the quality of individuals appointed or elected to govern Premier League (PL) clubs and the development of a code of corporate governance that provides guidelines for good governance. These actions are largely designed to ameliorate the effects of poor financial management within the Premier League clubs (since 1992 50% of PL clubs have been in hands of administrators or insolvent) and to improve the sustainability of clubs that are promoted or relegated between the FA leagues. The FGRC noted that the PL clubs that regularly compete in the UEFA Champions' League hold a distinct financial advantage over other PL clubs. As a consequence, the governing body of the PL must be cognizant of the more powerful clubs and their potential to influence decision-making at the board table.

The English legal system requires PL clubs to fulfil a number of obligations for communicating with shareholders, consultation with fans, the use of customer charters and dialogue with Supporters' Trusts. The FGRC noted that while the majority of PL clubs do an adequate job in this area, there was room for improvement. In addition, PL clubs that are listed public companies must follow a Combined Code that sets out principles for the activities of directors, directors' remuneration, accountability and audit requirements, relations with shareholders and institutional shareholders. The FGRC found that, while PL clubs are moving towards having more independent directors, they fall short compared to other listed companies.

There are now more than 70 Supporters' Trusts for clubs in the FA and about 60% of PL clubs have a Supporter's Trust. The trusts fulfil an important governance role, with 25% of PL clubs having a trust representative on their board. This representation means that committed fans have the chance to participate in decision-making at the highest level in regard to the future of their club and, in return, support the club in sport development, marketing and fundraising activities.

While there are signs that PL clubs have generally accepted good governance practices and abide with the majority of codes of conduct and principles for good governance, they do fall down in certain areas of governance practice. These include the lack of performance evaluation of individual directors or the overall board in a small number of clubs and a significant portion of clubs failing to adopt standard strategic planning practices. While the English PL enjoys enormous global profile as a leading football competition, the governance of the member clubs does not reach such exalted heights. The importance of good governance for a sport is highlighted via In Practice 12.2.

In Practice 12.2 British Horseracing Authority

The sport of kings – thoroughbred horseracing – is governed in Britain by the British Horseracing Authority (BHA). The BHA exists primarily to regulate and govern the sport on behalf of the many stakeholders and aims to:

- provide the most compelling and attractive racing in the world
- be seen as the world leader in raceday regulation
- ensure the highest standards for the sport and participants, on and away from the racecourse
- promote the best for the racehorse
- represent and promote the sport and the industry.

The stakeholders involved in racing include owners, breeders, trainers, jockeys, racecourses and bookmakers. The eight-member Board of the BHA meets monthly and is comprised of the Chairman and Chief Executive, two Independent Regulatory Directors, two Independent Directors and two Member Nominee Directors, nominated by the Racecourse Association and the Racehorse Owners Association, Thoroughbred Breeders Association and Licensed Personnel.

The BHA lists its responsibilities as including:

- Compilation of the fixture list
- Setting and enforcing the rules and orders of racing
- Race planning, including the supervision of race programmes and the employment of handicappers
- Licensing and registering racing participants – jockeys, trainers, horses, owners and stable staff
- Strategic planning and policy for racing
- Setting and enforcing standards of veterinary and medical care
- Protecting the integrity of the sport on and off the racecourse
- Setting and enforcing common standards for British racecourses
- The conduct of a day's racing
- Central promotion of racing
- Encouraging and fostering the breeding of bloodstock
- Developing and maintaining programmes of training and education
- Representing racing in dealings with government
- Liaison with the betting industry

- Representing British Racing abroad, which includes membership of the Executive Council of the International Federation of Horseracing Authorities.

Racing is almost entirely dependent on betting revenue to provide prize monies and operating costs for racecourse development, horse breeding and training and to sustain the significant numbers of people employed throughout the racing industry. As such, the BHA is focused on maintaining high standards of integrity throughout racing and governs a sophisticated set of rules for racing, codes of conduct, licensing and disciplinary procedures and security measures. The proper governance of racing is crucial to preserve the high standards of integrity necessary in order to maintain public confidence and interest in the sport.

Source: The BHA website at www.britishhorseracing.com

BOARD PERFORMANCE

Board performance has been found to be related to the use of appropriate structures, processes and strategic planning, the role of the paid executive, whether the board undertakes training or development work, personal motivations of board members and the influence of a cyclical pattern in the life cycle of boards. How to measure board performance, however, is a subject of ongoing debate. Herman and Renz (1997, 1998, 2000) support the use of a social constructionist approach to measure board performance based on the work of Berger and Luckmann (1967). Their view is that the collective judgements of those individuals directly involved with the board can provide the best idea of its performance. A widely used scale, the Self-Assessment for Non-profit Governing Boards Scale (Slesinger, 1991), uses this approach and provides sporting and other non-profit organizations with an effective way to gauge board performance.

Aspects of board activity that are evaluated using a scale of this type include: the working relationship between board and CEO; working relationships between board and staff; CEO selection and review processes; financial management; conduct of board and committee meetings; board mission statement and review of the mission; strategic planning; matching operational programmes to the mission and monitoring programme performance; risk management; new board member selection and training; and marketing and public relations. The performance of the board in undertaking these activities is then rated by board members, executives and the chair of the board. While this approach is open to criticisms of self-reporting bias, the fact that the whole group makes judgements on performance and then compares perceptions is an aide to board development and improvement.

The evaluation of individual board member performance is more problematic. Research into the human resource management practices related to board members shows that smaller sports organizations may struggle to find board members, while larger sports have an element of prestige attached to them so the problem is the opposite – how to engage in succession planning within a democratic electoral process. Very few board members are inducted, trained, provided with professional development opportunities and evaluated at all in regards to their role and the role of the board, a potentially serious problem for non-profit sport organizations given the significant responsibilities with which board members and board chairs are charged.

DRIVERS OF CHANGE IN GOVERNANCE

VSOs are increasingly under pressure from funding agencies to improve the delivery of their core programmes and services. Funding agencies recognize that sports' capacity for this delivery depends to a large extent on sport organizations being appropriately governed and, as a result, have implemented a range of measures to improve the governance of VSOs. For example, the Australian Sports Commission has a dedicated programme of management improvement for NSOs that provides advice on governance issues, funding to undertake reviews of governance structures and provides information on governance principles and processes. Sport England has negotiated detailed strategic plans with NSOs to improve the delivery and coordination between regional sport organizations.

The threat of litigation against sport organizations, their members or board members, has forced sport organizations to address issues such as risk management, fiduciary compliance, incorporation, directors' liability insurance and board training and evaluation. The heightened awareness of the implications of governance failure due to several much publicized corporate cases of impropriety worldwide has also forced sport organizations to improve their governance systems. Legislative changes to address issues of equity and diversity are additional pressures sports organizations must face and their governance systems, particularly membership criteria, voting rights and provision of information must change accordingly.

The threat of competition in the marketplace also has forced sports organizations to become more commercial and business focused, primarily through employing paid staff. Large clubs and regional sports associations that in the mid-1990s were exclusively run by volunteers are increasingly investing in paid staff to manage the increased compliance demands from government and their members and customers. As discussed earlier, the employment of paid staff changes the governance structures, the decision-making processes and the level of control exerted by volunteers. Maintaining governance structures devised decades ago creates many problems for sports organizations. In Practice 12.3 highlights some of the problems that result from poor governance and how one organization has been forced to change.

In Practice 12.3 Soccer Australia

In August 2002, the Australian Federal Minister for the Arts and Sport, Senator Rod Kemp, announced that Soccer Australia (SA) had agreed to a major structural review of soccer in Australia to be managed by the Australian Sports Commission. The review was undertaken after almost two decades of crises in the sport with the result that, in mid-2002, SA was $AUD2.6 million in debt, had reduced staffing levels at the national office, was racked by political infighting, had a lack of strategic direction and had enjoyed mixed results in the international arena. The review examined the structure, governance and management of soccer at all levels across Australia.

During the course of the review, it was found that many of the constituent bodies at state and regional levels suffered from similar financial difficulties, political infighting and inappropriate governance systems. These created problems of mistrust and disharmony, a lack of strategic direction, inappropriate behaviour and factionalism that hampered national decision-making. While the sport enjoyed a large grass roots participation base, a good talent pool for national teams, good training programmes, strong growth in female participation and passionate public support, its governance system was preventing it capitalizing on these strengths.

The review found that the governance system needed to change in four key areas:

1. Ensure independence of the governing bodies
2. Separate governance from day-to-day management
3. Change the membership and voting structures for the national and state organizations
4. The relationship between SA and the National Soccer League.

In all, the review made 53 recommendations aimed at improving the structure, governance and management of SA. The first three recommendations in the report illustrate the parlous state of affairs that existed in the organization in 2002. The review recommended that:

1. the membership of SA be changed to recognize key interest groups and reduce the power of larger states and the NSL
2. a new constitution be developed
3. that each state affiliate adopt a model constitution and membership agreements.

These recommendations alone represent wholesale change in the governance system, but the review went on to recommend a further 50 changes to governance processes and structures throughout the sport.

Continued

In Practice 12.3 Soccer Australia—cont'd

The sweeping changes made to the governance systems of Soccer Australia as a result of the review and the subsequent appointment as Chief Executive Officer of John O'Neil (ex-CEO of the Australian Rugby Union who has subsequently returned to the ARU) ushered in a new era for the sport. On the 1 January 2005, Soccer Australia changed its name to Football Federation Australia as part of the ongoing process of repositioning the sport. These changes in governance enabled the sport to:

- relaunch successfully a national league – the Hyundai A-League with eight new teams and a lucrative Pay TV rights deal that has enabled it to attract some of the top European-based Australians back to play in Australia
- have the financial capacity to employ a super coach in Guss Hiddink who managed to get the Socceroos to the second round of the 2006 World Cup before being beaten by the eventual champions Italy
- be in a position to bid for the future rights to host the World Cup.

Source: Australian Sports Commission, (2003). Independent soccer review: Report of the independent soccer review committee into the structure, governance and management of soccer in Australia. Australian Sports Commission, Canberra.

SUMMARY

Organizational governance has been described as the exercise of power within organizations and provides the system by which the elements of organizations are controlled and directed. Good organizational governance should ensure that the board and management seek to deliver outcomes for the benefit of the organization and its members and that the means used to attain these outcomes are effectively monitored.

A distinction is made between corporate governance that deals with the governance of profit-seeking companies and corporations that focus on protecting and enhancing shareholder value and non-profit governance that is concerned with the governance of voluntary-based organizations that seek to provide a community service or facilitate the involvement of individuals in social, artistic or sporting activities.

Sport organizations and their governance frameworks have diverse elements that prevent the development of an overarching theory of sport governance. A number of theoretical perspectives, namely agency theory, stewardship theory, institutional theory, resource dependence theory, network theory and stakeholder theory can be used to illuminate parts of the governance assumptions, processes, structures and outcomes for sport organizations.

The traditional governance structure for VSOs outlined earlier has been criticized for being unwieldy and cumbersome, slow to react to changes in market conditions, subject to potentially damaging politics or power plays between delegates and imposing significant constraints on organizations wishing to change. On the other hand, the majority of sports organizations still use this model today and value its ability to ensure members have a say in decision-making, the transparency of decisions and the autonomy granted to organizations at every level of the system.

A number of models for sport governance exist, each emphasizing different levels of responsibility for the chair of the board and paid executive. VSO boards perform better if a degree of trust exists between the board and staff and that board leadership is shared among a dominant coalition of the board chair, executive and a small group of senior board members. While evaluation systems for board performance are still relatively simplistic, they do cover a wide range of board activities. Evaluation of individual board member performance is more problematic and is the subject of ongoing research.

Finally, VSOs are increasingly under pressure from funding agencies to improve the delivery of their core programmes and services. The threat of litigation against sport organizations, their members or board members, has forced sport organizations to address issues such as risk management, fiduciary compliance, incorporation, directors' liability insurance and board training and evaluation. The heightened awareness of the implications of governance failure due to high profile corporate cases worldwide has also forced sport organizations to improve their governance systems.

REVIEW QUESTIONS

1. Explain the difference between corporate and non-profit governance.

2. What theory would you apply to the study of negligence on the part of a board of directors of a sport organization?

3. Explain the role played by boards, staff, volunteers, members and stakeholder groups in governing sport organizations.

4. What criteria would you apply to gauge the performance of a non-profit VSO? How would these criteria differ for a professional sport club?

5. What are the important elements in developing good relationships between boards and paid staff in VSOs?

6. Compare the governance structures of a multidisciplinary sport (e.g. gymnastics, canoeing, athletics) with a single discipline sport (e.g. field hockey, netball, rugby league). How do they differ? What impact does this have on volunteers involved in governance roles?

7. Review the governance performance of a VSO of your choice using Henry and Lee's (2004) seven principles of governance presented in this chapter.

8. What issues does a potential amalgamation present for a VSO?

9. How are board performance and organizational performance linked?

10. Interview the CEO and the Board Chair of small VSO. Who do they perceive to be the leader of the organization?

FURTHER READING

Carver, J. (1997). *Boards that make a difference: a new design for leadership in non-profit and public organizations*, 2nd edn. Jossey-Bass, San Francisco.

Clarke, T. (ed.) (2004). *Theories of corporate governance*. Routledge, Oxford.

Football Governance Research Centre (2004). *The state of the game: the corporate governance of football clubs 2004*, Research paper 2004 No. 3, Football Governance Research Centre, Birkbeck, University of London.

Henry, I. and Lee, P.C. (2004). Governance and ethics in sport. In J. Beech and S. Chadwick (eds) *The business of sport management*. Prentice Hall, London.

Hindley, D. (2003). Resource guide in governance and sport, Learning and teaching support network in hospitality, leisure, sport and tourism at http://www.hlst.ltsn.ac.uk/resources/governance.html.

Houle, C.O. (1997). *Governing boards: their nature and nurture*. Jossey-Bass, San Francisco.

Hoye, R. and Cuskelly, G. (2007). *Sport governance*. Butterworth-Heinemann, Oxford.

Organization for Economic Cooperation and Development, (2004). *Principles of corporate governance*. OECD, Paris.

RELEVANT WEBSITES

The following websites are useful starting points for further information on the governance of sport organizations:

Australian Sports Commission at http://www.ausport.gov.au

Sport and Recreation New Zealand at http://www.sparc.org.nz/

Sport Canada at http://www.pch.gc.ca/progs/sc/index_e.cfm

Sport England at http://www.sportengland.org

Sport Scotland at http://www.sportscotland.org.uk

Case Study: Governance Reform in Basketball Australia

Basketball Australia (BA) is recognized as the national sporting organization for basketball in Australia by the Federation Internationale de Basketball (FIBA), the Australian Sports Commission (ASC) and the Australian Olympic Committee (AOC). Like other national governing bodies for basketball, BA promotes competitive and recreational basketball throughout Australia. During 2006 to 2008, it was the subject of two separate but intertwined reviews of its high performance pathways and governance.

In early 2006, BA approached the ASC and requested a review of its high performance pathways. This might have seemed somewhat unusual given the high regard in which BA's high-performance pathway and programmes were held by most other Australian Olympic sports. The review was completed in January 2008 and made some interesting observations about the success of BA's existing programmes:

> They have successful elite teams; successful junior teams; a professional national men's league (NBL); semi-professional national women's league (WNBL); an internationally regarded national intensive training centre program (NITCP) for 14 to 17 year olds (men and women); support of the State Institute and Academy (SIS/SAS) network; and a strong Australian Institute of Sport (AIS) development program for men and women; as well as healthy underpinning state programs and competitions. Australian basketball is very well regarded internationally. The Australian women's team, the 'Opals', are the current world champions (2006) and have medalled at every World Championship or Olympic Games since 1996. As a nation, Australia (senior and junior men and women) is ranked number two in the world behind the USA. The senior men ('Boomers') are consistently in the top 10 in the world, but despite medals at under 19 and under 21 world championships, they are yet to win a medal at world or Olympic level (ASC, 2008).

Despite this seemingly positive picture of elite basketball in Australia, the review noted that while Australia had developed organized structured elite programmes in the late 1980s, other countries have now caught up and are injecting higher levels of funding into elite high performance basketball programmes. The review concluded that there was widespread support for the notion that the high performance pathways in Australian basketball were becoming static and/or outdated and were significantly under-resourced relative to other nations. One of the key problems identified was the inability of BA to secure additional funding to support the increased costs of maintaining an effective suite of high performance and community-based programmes. Indeed, BA is dependent on the ASC for approximately 90% of the total budget for high performance programmes.

The other major issue identified was the misalignment between the athlete pathway and the competition structure. While BA includes the elite national league for women, the Women's National Basketball League (WNBL), it does not formally include the men's national league, the National Basketball League (NBL). In March 2007, BA, the NBL and the ASC set up a review into the structure and governance of basketball in Australia (ASC, 2007). In the introduction to the report that emerged from the review, the relationship between BA and the NBL was described as follows:

> The NBL is run by NBL Management Limited which is granted a licence by BA to conduct the national elite men's competition. BA owns the intellectual property of the NBL and theoretically retains powers in relation to: approval over admission of new teams; the requirement for the NBL to follow FIBA international rules; the number of import players; and player availability for national duties. BA is a member of NBL Management Limited along with the 11 NBL clubs. A representative from BA along with representatives from each of the 11 Clubs comprises the Board. Due to both the structure and governance of the NBL, in practical terms BA has limited influence over the running of the NBL.

Continued

Concurrently the NBL has poor links with BA membership and the broader basketball community (ASC, 2007).

Both the high performance pathways review report and the report into the governance of basketball noted that BA and the NBL were separate bodies with very different objectives and were not necessarily working together for the betterment of the sport and optimal international results. Both reports recommended that BA and the NBL should merge under a single national basketball structure, to enable a unified approach to delivering and coordinating the sport in Australia. The governance review stated that the dominant view of stakeholders in 2007 was that:

- The current structures for BA and the NBL are ineffective for delivering and building basketball in Australia
- The sport lacks strategic direction and focus
- There is no shared vision
- Objectives and focus of the different entities has resulted in fragmentation
- There is a lack of consistency and trust in delivering the sport
- And the sport is significantly undercapitalized (ASC, 2007).

The benefits of creating a new single integrated national body for the sport were cited as:

- One voice for the sport that can make whole of sport decisions
- One brand for the sport
- Integration deemed to be the last chance to get the sport right
- Better links between BA, the state and territory associations and the NBL Clubs – and with it, an opportunity to increase the links to grassroots and the broader relevance of the sport.
- Improved pathways for athletes, coaches and officials (ASC, 2007).

The arguments against merging the NBL with BA included increased financial risks for BA, the differing objectives of each body and the historical lack of trust between the NBL and BA (ASC, 2007).

The principles for creating a single national governing body were outlined in the governance review as:

1. The new body constituting as a company limited by guarantee under the Corporations Act 2001 (Cth). (Name of the body to be decided)
2. Governed by a seven person Board made up of five elected and two appointed who are all independent directors
3. The CEO of The Company would not be a director but would attend Board meetings at the invitation of the Chairperson
4. A membership made up of the current member state and territory associations and the NBL Clubs (see below)
5. A revised voting structure that ensures current member state and territory associations hold 60% of the votes, with NBL Clubs holding the remaining 40%
6. The integration of all national competitions under the new Company
7. Formalized franchise agreements between the new Company and each of the NBL clubs. This agreement would involve payment of annual membership and franchise fees to The Company (ASC, 2007).

In referring to independent directors, the word 'independent' is defined to mean that a director could not concurrently hold a position in the sport that would be deemed as a conflict of interest. Such positions would include an elected official of a state or territory association, an owner or director of a professional club, a management position with the Company, state or territory association or professional club or a material supplier of goods and services to the sport of basketball (ASC, 2007).

The issue of establishing voting rights within the new entity proved a difficult proposition. The following is an edited extract from the report that outlined the arguments around voting rights between BA, the NBL, NBL clubs and other stakeholder groups.

The BA membership [as at 2007] currently comprises the eight state and territory associations and the NBL, WNBL and ABA. In terms of voting rights, New South Wales and Victoria each have three representatives; Queensland, South Australia and Western Australia two representatives each; and Tasmania, Northern Territory, Australian Capital Territory, NBL, WNBL and ABA one representative each. Each representative is entitled to one vote.

The Ernst & Young report [from an earlier review in 2001] agreed that the state and territory associations should be the members of The Company and recommended a 'one state one vote' voting structure in line with that suggested in the ASC Good Governance Principles for a total of eight (8) state votes. Further, Ernst & Young recommended membership and one (1) collective vote for the Owners of NBL Clubs, as these private owners are the only group not represented by the state and territory associations (they are not covered by any 'membership' however they are significant investors in the sport). Taking into account the history and context of the sport, the Steering Committee [in 2007] did not see this as a workable solution and has proposed an alternate solution which is outlined below.

The recommended membership structure is that each NBL Club would become a member of The Company by virtue of its participation or franchise agreement. Each NBL Club would, in addition to its annual NBL franchise fee, make a further financial contribution toward the development of basketball through a 'membership fee' to The Company. The existing state and territory associations would retain their membership of The Company through a Service Agreement relationship and pay capitation fees based on participation

numbers, monitored through a national player database. As under the new structure, the national 'League Associations' are fully integrated into The Company, there would be no membership status for the NBL, WNBL, ABA or any of the underpinning Leagues. The NBL, WNBL and ABA are represented through Commissions of The Company under its governance structure. By nature of their current structure, individual clubs participating in the WNBL, ABA or underpinning leagues are presently represented through their state or territory associations.

The number of votes exercised by the NBL Clubs in General Meetings of The Company will be equal to one vote per Club, set at 40% of the total votes. The state and territory associations will distribute the remaining 60% of the votes between them with each receiving a minimum of one vote. The distribution shall be determined based on registered members and related capitation fees contributed to The Company. Currently, there are 13 NBL Clubs [which became 11 in mid 2008, so 13 votes would constitute 40% of the votes, leaving 60% = 20 votes to be distributed among the eight state and territory associations. The relative 40:60 percentage votes will be written into the constitution of The Company as a constant. If the number of NBL clubs change, the number of state and territory association votes will change accordingly to preserve the relative weighting.

The membership fee payable by the NBL will also be fixed at the 40:60 ratio relative to the state and territory associations. Thus the total annual NBL membership fee will be equal two thirds of the total capitation fee paid by the state and territory associations. Each state and territory member's voting entitlement shall be cast by one representative of that member. Each NBL Club's one vote shall be exercised by its representative (ASC, 2007).

The restructuring of BA and the NBL illustrates the competing interests of stakeholders that exist within a sport and the need to align these interests through an appropriate

Continued

governance structure that will facilitate the development of both elite and community-based sport.

Case Questions

1. Summarize the main arguments for merging Basketball Australia and the NBL.

2. Why did the Steering Committee report recommend distributing voting rights in a different way to what the ASC recommends?

3. Why is it important that the new governing body has 'independent directors' rather than representatives elected directly from the various stakeholder groups?

4. What are the advantages and disadvantages of merging the national governing body of a sport with its professional league?

Sources: Australian Sports Commission, (2007). Report of the steering committee into the structure and governance review of basketball in Australia (November 2007). ASC, Canberra; and Australian Sports Commission, (2008). Review of high performance pathways in Australian basketball (January 2008). ASC, Canberra.

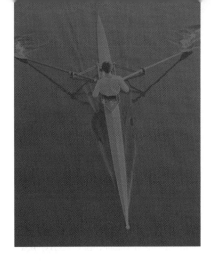

CHAPTER 13

Performance Management

OVERVIEW

This chapter examines the ways in which sport organizations can manage their operations and evaluate their performance. Particular attention will be given to the special features of sport organizations and how these features create the need for a customized performance management model. The imperative of using a multidimensional model of performance management will be highlighted, together with the need to accommodate the conflicting demands that arise from the claims of multiple stakeholders. Throughout the chapter, cases and incidents will be used to illustrate the concepts and principles that underpin effective performance in sport organizations.

After completing this chapter the reader should be able to:

- Explain the concept of performance management

- Describe how the special features of sport necessitate the formulation of a customized performance management model

- Identify the stakeholders that that need to be taken into account when building a performance management model for sport organizations

- Construct a multidimensional model of performance management that accommodates sport's special features and gives appropriate weight to financial factors, internal processes, market awareness and penetration and social responsibility

- Apply the model to a variety of sport situations and contexts.

SPORT AND PERFORMANCE

From a management perspective, sport is a very interesting institution to study since it is both similar to and different from traditional business organizations (Smith and Stewart, 1999). Its similarities have arisen out of its relentless drive over the last thirty years to become more professionally structured and managed. Large segments of sport have consequently copied the values and practices of the business world and, as a result, players and administrators are paid employees and strategic plans are designed. In addition, games and activities become branded sport products, fans become customers to be satisfied and surveyed and alliances with corporate supporters are developed (Slack, 1997).

At the same time, sport is also different from business (Smith and Stewart, 1999). First, it has a symbolic significance and emotional intensity that is rarely found in an insurance company, bank or even a betting shop. While businesses seek employee compliance and attachment, their primary concern is efficiency, productivity and responding to changing market conditions. Sport, on the other hand, is consumed by strong emotional attachments that are linked to the past through nostalgia and tradition. Romantic visions, emotion and passion can override commercial logic and economic rationality (Foster et al., 2006). Second, predictability and certainty, which are goals to be aimed for in the commercial world, partic-ularly with respect to product quality, are not always valued in the sporting world. Sport fans are attracted to games where the outcome is uncertain and chaos is just around the corner (Sandy et al., 2004). Third, sport is not driven by the need to optimize profit in the ways that large commercial businesses are. In practice, sport organizations face two conflicting models of organizational behaviour when deciding upon their underlying mission and goals. The first is the profit maximization model, which assumes that a club is simply a firm in a perfectly competitive product market and that profit is the single driving motivational force. The second is the utility maximization model, which emphasizes the rivalry between clubs and their desire to win as many matches as possible (Downward and Dawson, 2000). The utility view assumes that sporting organizations are by nature highly competitive and that the single most important performance yardstick is competitive success. These differences therefore beg the question of where to begin when setting up a performance management system for sport organizations.

WHERE TO BEGIN?

In many respects, sport is always subject to intense scrutiny. For example, in elite competitive sport, players and teams are rated and ranked continuously. In cricket, for example, an ever-expanding array of statistics is used to calculate not only batter scoring rates and bowling strike rates, but also patterns of scoring and fielding efficiency. Moreover, everyone has an opinion on the performance of coaches in various professional sport leagues, which range from win–loss ratios to how the game strategies impact on scoring efficiency and player movements. At the same time, many sporting clubs do not take the time to undertake a comprehensive evaluation of their off-field performance. And, if they do, they limit their analysis to just a couple of issues like operating profits and membership levels. We argue here that it is better to use an evaluation model that covers a range of performance dimensions and embraces a variety of measures.

A systematic approach to performance management is an essential tool for identifying strengths and weaknesses and revealing the ways in which overall organizational performance can be improved. It is also important for deciding where scarce resources should be allocated in order to achieve the best possible outcome. It can also give a picture of how one organization, club or league is doing in relation to other organizations, clubs or leagues. This performance snapshot can be used to identify weaknesses and design strategies that improve critical result areas in the next season or annual sporting cycle. In short, the use of some sort of performance management model is crucial to the long-term success of sport organizations. However, the question remains as to how best to go about implementing an appropriate model of performance management and where to begin?

A good starting point is to look at performance management from a strategic perspective. That is, we should initially focus our attention on what the organization wants to achieve. In other words, as we noted in Chapter 5, a performance management system should be linked to an organization's vision, goals and objectives (Robbins and Barnwell, 2002). These objectives can be used to identify what it needs to do well to improve its performance. It is at this point that the primary goals of sport organizations become quite different from those of business organizations. While commercial leisure centres and most American professional sport teams seem to be focused on maximizing profits, most other sports clubs, even with a large revenue base, are more concerned with priorities like winning more games than their rivals and servicing the needs of members. However, it is not always clear just what the primary goal of a sport organization is, or what is the best measure for deciding how well the organization has performed. In commercial terms, the most successful association football (or soccer) club is Manchester United, closely followed by Real Madrid. However, neither Manchester United nor Real Madrid got to the Champions League final in 2003, which was won by Porto, a relative pauper. However, this situation was reversed in 2008 when Manchester won the Champions League competition when it defeated its English Premier League rival, Chelsea.

In the USA National Football League, the Cincinatti Bengals rarely got to the end of season play-offs during the late 1990s and early part of the 21st century but, because of its frugal spending and League's income equalization strategy, made a greater profit than some of the better known teams. In this case, it was never clear just what the primary performance goal was but, in the end, the Bengals were probably best known for their ability to make a profit rather than their capacity for winning.

At the same time, it has to be said that there is a close correlation between revenue and success in most professional sport leagues. In other words, clubs that have a large resource base and the capacity to secure the best facilities, the best coaches and the best players will, on balance, have the best win–loss ratio. But this also begs the question as to whether there may be other ways of measuring performance and estimating the success and failures of a sport organization. In some instances, it may be important to consider what are called process factors, which include things like staff retention, player development and the overall level of morale and job satisfaction. However, despite these additional complexities and anomalies, it is clear that any performance management system must take into account and, indeed, should reflect, the primary goals of the relevant club, team, facility, event or league.

In Practice 13.1 Measuring the Performance of Sport Coaches

As noted above, the intuitive response to any question about sport team performance is to say that the obvious indicator of success is a good win–loss ratio. It would follow, then, that a team with a win–loss ratio of 0.80 or 80% has outperformed a team whose win–loss ratio was 0.60 or 60%. Alternatively, a current season win–loss ratio of 0.70 or 70%, when contrasted with a previous season win–loss ration of 0.50, or 50%, would also suggest an improved level of performance. Not only would fans be happy with this sort of result, but so too would the coach.

But that is not all there is, according to Joanne MacLean, in her publication, *Performance Appraisal for Sport and Recreation Managers*. Having examined in some detail the performance dimensions of sport coaches, she asserts that conceptually speaking, while the win–loss record is clean and precise, it is not the best measure of coaching performance. While coaches themselves would probably agree, MacLean notes that despite its unidimensional and simplistic nature, win–loss ratios continues to be used as a basis for evaluation and a main consideration when hiring and firing staff. This is partially because win–loss is an easy criterion to measure and to use. But it does not tell the whole story, as Maclean suggests when she says:

> The problem with the use of win–loss records as the ultimate criterion of success is that it produces two finite categories: one good, one bad. In reality, however, innumerable factors contribute to success. In other words, a loss may not be an indication of bad performance, and a win may not result from good performance (MacLean, 2001).

In order to provide a much broader framework for evaluating coaching performance in both team and individual player settings, MacLean comes up with a model that is premised on the assumption that coaching success is about much more than having teams and players winning as many games as possible. For instance, it could also be about player development and creating a culture built upon a good work ethic and respect and support for fellow players.

MacLean concedes, though, that winning cannot be dismissed as a performance measure and she includes it in what she calls a 'product factor'. Product factors include things like win–loss ratios, medals won and rankings achieved.

But this is just the first of a number of performance dimensions. The second dimension she identifies as 'process factors'. They include the actual tasks performed by the coach on the job, as opposed to the outcome of such tasks. These process factors can be further broken down into (A) 'task-related factors', which are those behaviours necessary to complete the main tasks of the job such as recruiting quality athletes, teaching new skills, managing drills and practices and utilizing effective game tactics and (B) 'maintenance-related factors', which are those behaviours required to maintain a positive work environment such as cooperating with staff, communicating effectively with athletes, conforming with organizational policies and adhering to timelines and other administrative procedures and requirements.

MacLean goes on to suggest that that all three of the above categories, being (1) product factors, (2) task-related process factors and (3) maintenance-related process factors, are important in the work of the coach and should form the basis for identifying the specific criteria against which coach performance is to be measured.

MacLean's model for measuring coaching performance is therefore very instructive in that it goes beyond a single product factor like the number of wins and on-field successes and, in addition, considers the importance of a variety of process factors that clearly impact on the internal operations of the team and/or player group. She also makes the very important point that all performance evaluation models should be situational. That is, they should be constructed to take into account the context in which the coaching is occurring (is it a professional sport league or, alternatively, a learn-to-play programme for children) and the special features of the sport being undertaken (is it a combat sport like judo or an aesthetic sport like rhythmic gymnastics). In other words, fine tuning of the performance measure criteria is essential.

BUILDING A PERFORMANCE MANAGEMENT MODEL FROM A STAKEHOLDER PERSPECTIVE

Performance management should also be linked to an organization's key stakeholders (Atkinson et al., 1997). If stakeholders are satisfied with the organization's performance, then clearly it is doing well. In a publicly owned sports retail business for example, a large profit and dividend will be good for management and shareholders alike. However, in a member-based sport club, success will be more about on-field performance and member services than massive profits. On the other hand, for a sport's governing body, the interests of its registered players may take the highest priority. In other words, different types of sport organizations will have their own unique goals and priorities, which will in turn reflect the ways in which they rank their stakeholders (Friedman et al., 2004).

Stakeholders may also have conflicting needs. Sponsors may want maximum media exposure and access to players, but the clubs have a primary interest in improving player performance, which may mean less, not more player involvement in sponsor activities. In the case of a national sporting body, the national government may want international success to justify its investment in elite training and coaching programmes, whereas the rank-and-file players who make up the bulk of the membership may want more local facilities. Sport organizations are therefore required to balance the often-conflicting needs and 'contradictory interests' of the various stakeholders (Chappelet and Bayle, 2005). The major sport organization stakeholders and their expectations are summarized in Table 13.1.

The key point to note here is that a sport organization will have multiple stakeholders and their interests will have to be integrated into its evaluation processes.

AN INPUT–OUTPUT APPROACH TO PERFORMANCE MANAGEMENT

In developing a model for evaluating a sport organization's performance, a number of additional principles should be utilized. A second approach is to focus on inputs and outputs. This involves looking at things like quality, quantity, efficiency, cost–benefit ratios and employee productivity (Bouckaert, 1995). This approach provides a checklist of essential performance dimensions that need to be addressed. It ensures that no one measure is dominant and also provides for measures that not only focus on internal

Table 13.1	Stakeholder Expectations of Sport Organizations
Stakeholder Type	**Expectations of Sport Organization**
Players	On field success
	Appropriate pay and benefits
	Low injury rates
Employees	Appropriate pay and benefits
	Job security
	Professional development
Equipment suppliers	Reliability of demand
	Player endorsement
	Brand awareness
Members	Services and benefits
	Overall satisfaction
Owners/shareholders	Return on investment
	Public recognition of club or association
Sponsors	Positive reputation of club or association
	Brand awareness and recognition
Player agents	High player morale
	Payment of market rates
Fans	Game quality and excitement
	High win–loss ratio
Community/society	Civic pride
	Provides role models for young adults
Media	Mass market
	High level of public interest

processes, but also look at the organization's relationships with key suppliers and customers. A summary of the ways in which input–output analysis can be applied to sport organizations is illustrated in Table 13.2.

A BALANCED AND MULTIDIMENSIONAL APPROACH TO PERFORMANCE MANAGEMENT

A third approach is to avoid the often obsessive emphasis that shareholders place on financial measures by balancing it against the benefits that might accrue to customers, suppliers and employees (Harvard Business Review, 1998). This approach is exemplified in the Balanced Scorecard (BSC) model designed by Kaplan and Norton (1992, 1996). The BSC has four dimensions, which are reviewed below.

Table 13.2	An Input–Output Approach to Performance Management in Sport
Dimension	**Measure**
Output: quantity	Premierships
	Attendance
	Membership
	Participation
Output: quality	Standard of play
	Features of venue/facility
	Standard of service
	Overall customer experience
Output: cost/benefit	Operating profit
	Costs of operation
	Net economic benefit
	Social benefit
Input: efficiency	Cost of providing service
	Administrative support cost
	Waiting time
Input: staff performance	Customer/member/fan satisfaction ratings
	Staff skills and experience
	Staff achievements

One of the first things Kaplan and Norton (1996) note is that a good performance measurement tool should not be a 'controlling system' obsessed with keeping 'individuals, and organizational units in compliance with a pre-established plan'. Rather it should be primarily a 'learning system' concerned with 'communication and informing'. To this end, Kaplan and Norton aimed to design a performance measurement system that balanced external and easily quantifiable measures like market share and return on investment against internal and more ephemeral factors like administrative processes and staff development.

Kaplan and Norton's first dimension is 'Financial Perspective'. Although they argue that too much emphasis has traditionally been given to the so-called bottom-line result, financial measures are, nevertheless, a funda-mental starting point for evaluating the economic sustainability of an organization. They can range from total sales, operating income and net cash flow, to return on assets, debt to equity ratio and net profit. This dimension answers the question 'how do we look to shareholders?'.

The second dimension is 'Customer Perspective'. In this instance, the emphasis is on identifying the 'customer and market segments in which the business will compete' and to develop measures that will indicate how well the organization competes in these segments. These measures will include total sales in each segment, market share, customer acquisition, customer retention and customer satisfaction. Kaplan and Norton also suggest that for this performance dimension attention should be given to the factors like short lead times and on-time delivery that actually underpin the levels of customer satisfaction and retention. This dimension addresses the question 'how do customers see us?'.

The third dimension is the 'Internal-Business-Process Perspective'. This perspective requires management to identify the 'critical internal processes in which the organization must excel' in order to secure a competitive advantage. Kaplan and Norton note that it is not just a matter of ensuring that current value-adding processes are efficient and streamlined, but that there are also systems in place to improve and re-engineer existing processes and products. This dimension addresses the question 'what must we excel at?'.

The fourth dimension is the 'Learning and Growth Perspective'. Kaplan and Norton see this perspective as crucial to the long-term success of organizations. In a turbulent business environment, there is an ever-increasing likelihood that the technologies and processes required to sustain a market advantage and competitive edge may race ahead of the technical and managerial skills of the staff who are responsible for managing those technologies and processes. In order to close this gap, organizations will 'have to invest in re-skilling employees, enhancing information technology and systems, and aligning organizational procedures and routines'. This dimension addresses the question 'can we continue to improve and create value?'.

Finally, Kaplan and Norton suggest that each of the above perspectives should be linked to a common over-arching objective that ensures consistency and mutually reinforcing conduct. In other words, the BSC is more than a 'dashboard' of 'critical indicators or key success factors'. In order to be effective, it must reflect the organization's mission and goals.

COSTS AND BENEFITS OF A PERFORMANCE MANAGEMENT SYSTEM

Planning and implementing a performance management system can be costly, since it involves a lot of time-intensive analysis of an organization's processes and activities. It can also become a bureaucratic nightmare since it can produce hundreds of microscopic statements about the ways thing should be done and how they must be measured. It should be remembered that the concept of performance management arose out of the mechanistic time-and-motion studies of Frederick Winslow Taylor in the early part of the 20th century. According to Taylor, the key to increasing productivity was to analyse systematically work practices in order to identify the most efficient process, which could then become a best-practice template (Stewart, 1989). Taylorism also underpinned the development of Management by Objectives (MBO) and Total Quality Management (TQM) which were later refined into a broader model of performance management (Bouckaert and van Doren, 2003). As a result, a rigidly structured performance management system can stifle initiative and creativity by setting narrowly defined work standards and strict standards of workplace behaviour.

At the same time, a well thought out performance management system can provide a number of long-term benefits (Williams, 1998). First, it makes sure that the core activities of an organization are directly linked to its primary aims and goals. Second, it can motivate employees by setting targets which are rewarded when they are attained. Third, it ensures greater accountability by clearly identifying not only what is to be achieved, but also who is responsible for making it happen. Fourth, it completes the management cycle by making sure processes are monitored and outcomes are measured against some sort of minimum performance standard. Finally, it forces management to come up with a quantifiable measure of its key outputs and eliminate ambiguous aims and nebulous objectives.

In Practice 13.2 Measuring the Performance of Football Leagues in Australia

The Australian Football League is the showcase competition for Australia's only indigenous game of any significance, Australian rules football. Australian rules football was invented in Melbourne in 1858 and went on become one the nation's most popular sports (Hess and Stewart, 1998). In 2007, it generated revenues of more than $280 million and drew a total season attendance of more than 7 million fans (Hess et al., 2008). However, unlike cricket and tennis, it really ever only embraced the southern states of Australia. Whereas it captured the hearts and minds of people living in Victoria, South Australia, Western Australian and Tasmania, its presence in New South Wales and Queensland was, for the most part, marginal. In these two states, rugby league was the most popular football code, with rugby union being the second most popular code. Association football, or soccer as it is more commonly identified in Australia, was very much a minor code in every state. During the 1950s and 1960s in particular, European migrants, who had been immersed in the soccer culture at home, were amazed that the world game had been relegated to the periphery of Australia's sporting landscape.

However, at the beginning of the 21st century, things had changed quite dramatically. The rapid commercialization of sport during the 1980s and 1990s had produced a number of national sport leagues, the most powerful being the football codes. The National Soccer league had the earliest beginnings, having been established in 1978. However, it went through many traumatic changes and clubs were rarely able to trade profitably. In 2003, the league was abandoned while the national governing body was reformed and a new eight-team league was set up. It was completely re-badged and clubs were stripped of their ethnic origins. The A-League, as it is now called, commenced in 2006. The National Rugby League competition (NRL) is far more robust. Although the competition was fractured with the establishment of a rival Super League in 1995, it is now solidly entrenched in New South Wales and Queensland and, to a lesser extent, Victoria. However, the competition no longer has teams in either South Australian or Western Australia, although this structural problem is slightly compensated for by having a team playing from Auckland in New Zealand. Rugby union is an interesting case because like League, it has only moderate support in Australia's southern states, but is a major code in New South Wales and Queensland. Union's Super-12 competition comprised five New Zealand teams, three Australian teams and four South African teams. However, in 2007 another two teams were added to the competition, namely Perth in Western Australia and a fifth South African team, thereby making it a Super-14 competition. Finally, there is the Australian Football League (AFL), which arose out of the Victorian Football League in 1986. The AFL, a 16-club competition, has teams in every state and, over the last ten years, has made significant inroads in the hostile rugby territory of New South Wales and Queensland.

Each of the above football codes has their own unique history and culture, but it is also the case that they are serious rivals in a highly competitive sporting marketplace. There are many arguments about the relative strengths of each code and which national competition is the most successful (Stewart, 2007b). In performance management terms, this is an interesting issue to address. Neither is it immediately clear as to how one should best go about doing a comparative evaluation of the performance of the leagues. This is because there are many different ways of undertaking the performance management task.

The management team of each national competition is very sensitive to developments in the rival leagues. They are also eager to trumpet and promote their successes, particularly if it means they have secured some type of strategic advantage over their competitors. At the same time, there are a number of critical success factors that are commonly used to rank the performance of the national leagues. These factors are first, total season attendance, second, total club membership, third, aggregate league revenue, fourth income from television broadcast rights and, finally, weekly television audiences. The five somewhat crude measures give a very good indication of just how well each league performs. However, over recent times some additional measures have been incorporated into their performance management models. First, there is the issue of the viability of teams and the ability to balance their budgets. Second, there is the competitive balance of the league and the extent to which it can guarantee fans a close and exciting contest. Third, there is the reputation of the league and the extent to which it is seen as a responsible sporting citizen. To this end, the leagues are eager to promote equal opportunity for players and administrators, put in place anti-harassment rules and have a strong anti-doping policy. In general, the leagues are very sensitive to criticism about player misconduct, particularly when it involves some sort of sexual assault. A sample of key indicators for measuring the performance of Australian national football leagues is listed in Table 13.3.

Table 13.3   Performance Measures for Australia National Sport Leagues

Item	Descriptor/measure	Examples
Financial stability	League turnover	Australian Football League (AFL) turnover is more than $280 million. National Rugby League (NRL)
	Net assets	Turnover is around $120 million
Corporate support	Sponsorship income	AFL supported by more national brands (e.g. Vodafone, Air Emirates, Toyota), than NRL
	Stadium suites	
Broadcasting rights fees	Fees from TV stations	AFL TV rights fee currently $150 million pa; NRL TV rights fee currently around $90 million pa
	Fees from radio stations	
Media exposure	Television rating	AFL grand final draws 2.9 million TV audience; NRL grand final draws 2.2 million TV audience
	Print media coverage	
Public interest	Brand awareness	AFL average match attendance 36 000; NRL average match attendance 16 000
	Match attendance	
Spread/coverage	Media coverage	AFL teams spread around five of six states; NRL teams spread around three of six states plus New Zealand
	Spread of teams and venues	
Competitive balance	Win–loss ratios for each team	NRL teams have slightly more closely aligned win–loss ratios (i.e. smaller standard deviation).
	Premierships won by each team	
Game development	Junior development programmes	AFL spends $30 million a year on community development; NRL spends $15 million on community development
	Regional development programmes	

Source: Stewart, B (ed.) (2007b).

DESIGNING A PERFORMANCE MANAGEMENT MODEL APPROPRIATE FOR SPORT

The BSC has many strengths, but it requires significant adjustment to make it better fit the special requirements of sport organizations. One approach is to maintain the four basis dimensions that underpin the BSC and use it to design a customized performance model that reflects the special features of sport organizations. To this end the following '9 point' model of performance management has been designed.

The first performance dimension focuses on wins, awards and successes. This dimension recognizes the fact that most sport associations and clubs want be seen to be doing well and producing winning players and teams. In other words, faced with the choice of winning a championship, or increasing profits, most clubs would prefer the winner's pennant or medal.

However, like all organizations, sport leagues, associations and clubs need ongoing funding to ensure their long-term viability, to pay their debts when they fall due and cover their operating costs from year to year. Therefore, the second dimension is concerned with financial sustainability. In this respect, measures of revenue growth will not be enough and more specific measures of profit, liquidity, long-term indebtedness, return on investment and net asset growth are all useful indicators.

The third dimension is market distribution, or the extent to which a sport league, association or club is able to facilitate the consumption of its particular sporting practice. If its major concern is with participation, then it needs to be aware of how many facilities it provides, their location and spread and the experiential quality they offer. If the major concern is the potential audience that can be attracted, then it needs to aware of the number of spectator seats it can provide, the radio exposure it will receive and the scale and breadth of any television broadcast.

The fourth dimension is market size and share. It is one thing to have a broad range and spread of facilities and venues and a large number of television-broadcast hours, but it is another thing to attract a consistently large number of participants, spectators and viewers. It is also important to compare the numbers for these indicators with the numbers for other related sports that are seen to be competitors.

The fifth dimension is customer satisfaction, which is really a measure how strongly participants, fans and members approve of the performance of the league, association or club. Sport organizations usually engender very passionate connections with their customer and member base, but there are also many instances when they attend games or activities less frequently, or more seriously downgrade their involvement. Surveys of participants, members and fans can reveal early signs of dissatisfaction or, alternatively, indicate what is sustaining the relationship.

The sixth dimension is internal procedures and processes. Like Kaplan and Norton's similarly labelled dimension, it aims to highlight the key links in the value chain and how each stage is performing relative to the others. For sporting organizations, it often begins with how well players are recruited, their numbers and overall quality. The recruitment and retention of members is also an important consideration and the question often arises as to the capacity of members to contribute time, expertise and money to the association and club's activities. The ability of players to improve their skill and overall performance is also a function of the support system and, in particular, the skill and abilities of the coaching staff. This leads to the capacity of the organization to ensure a safe environment where the management of risk is taken seriously and the incidence of litigation is slight. All the above processes are, of course, linked to administrative functions that can either enhance the player and member experience as poor training or sloppy systems can make the experience both unpleasant and costly. Many of the above factors can be difficult to quantify, but they nevertheless need serious consideration.

The seventh dimension is product improvement. In this respect, sport is no different from business in that it operates in a very competitive market-place and constant innovation and product improvement is essential to attract new customers and retain the old. Some sports have been very successful in modifying their games to suit the needs of special groups, while others have been unable to move beyond their traditional practices. In some spectator sports, there have been very slow improvements in venue quality while, in others, there has been a virtual revolution in terms of stadium design and spectator comfort. Progressive changes in the design of sporting equipment have also improved product quality. In tennis, for example, the use of carbon fibre racket frames and the creation of larger 'sweet-spots' have enabled average club players to improve their standard of play and overall skill levels.

The eighth dimension is staff development and learning. Sport is a very person centred, time-absorbing activity and, therefore, requires staff who have highly refined people-management skills and the capacity to create an organizational culture that retains players and members. The growing technical sophistication of sport also means that traditional administrative, officiating and coaching skills are no longer adequate and, therefore, large-scale retraining and education are necessary to ensure a proper fit between the staff competencies and the new technologies and infrastructure that underpin contemporary sport.

The ninth dimension covers the economic, social and environmental impact that a sport league, association or club has on its surrounding community. Increasingly, the level of support a government will provide a sport organization is contingent upon the organization's ability to produce a positive economic, social or environmental impact. This trend has been exaggerated by the growing popularity of the triple-bottom-line accounting concept, which highlights the importance of going beyond profitability and wealth creation as the sole measure of an organization's contribution to society to include environmental and social impacts (Norman and Mac-Donald, 2004). In this case, sport organizations also have a responsibility carefully to manage and sustain their environment and establish an organizational culture that values things like diversity, equal opportunity and the fair treatment of gays, lesbians and religious minorities.

This nine-dimensional model has the advantage of being broad and inclusive and geared to the needs of sport in general. But, it needs to be customized to fit different sporting organizations. As we indicated before, an organization's strategic intent and stakeholder interests will shape the design of a performance evaluation model (Atkinson et al., 1997; Williams, 1998; Robbins and Barnwell, 2002). For example, the evaluation model for a national sporting body should be different from the model used to evaluate a professional sport club. The national sporting body will be more interested in participation rates, club development and the provision of quality local facilities. On the other hand, a professional sport club will be more concerned with its win–loss ratio, sponsor income, television ratings and membership levels.

PERFORMANCE MEASURES

Once a model is in place, it is then crucial to design performance measures. These measures should be able precisely to identify and quantify specific indicators of success or failure. Sometimes it is difficult to 'put a number' on a measure. Customer and fan 'satisfaction' readily comes to mind in this respect, but there are often ways of converting a subjective opinion into a measurable indicator.

It is one thing to identify some key performance indicators and to collect some data under each heading. However, it is another thing to make sense of the data. It is, therefore, important to develop some sort of benchmark or standard by which to measure the performance of a sport organization. There are two ways of doing this. The first is to undertake a longitudinal study that examines the progress of a sport organization over time. Take for example the performance of Athletics Australia (AA), the national governing body for athletics in Australia. A 10-year analysis of its financial performance would show it has been increasingly unable to balance its books over the last few years. By 2003, it had accumulated a seriously worrying level of debt which brought on an organizational crisis. By any financial measure, AA's performance had fallen dramatically over this period. The same sort of longitudinal analysis could be applied to its participation levels and elite international performance. In each, the data indicated very little improvement over the last 10 years.

Another way of looking at AA's performance would be to compare it with other national sport bodies to see how it ranks. That is, it will also be important to undertake a comparative study by which the performance of AA is stacked up against a number of other national sport organizations. There are two ways of doing this. The first way would be compare it with similarly funded Australian national sport bodies like Swimming Australia or Rowing Australia. In this case, AA has not performed well, since both swimming and rowing have achieved regular gold medal winning performances at both World Championships and Olympic Games over the last ten years. The second way is to compare AA's performance with an equivalent national athletic association from another country. An appropriate point of comparison here might be the Canadian Athletics Federation since both countries have similar populations and the national athletic associations have a similar resource base. In this case, the comparison would yield an elite performance outcome substantially better than the one with Swimming Australia.

The lesson to be leant here is that the performance of a sport organization cannot be measured in a vacuum or without some yardstick and point of comparison. At the minimum, either some form of longitudinal or comparative analysis should be undertaken. Ideally, a mixture of both methods would provide the best set of results.

In Practice 13.3 Measuring Performance in a Community Leisure Centre

As we indicated in the early part of this chapter, performance management systems have infiltrated their way into every nook and cranny of the business environment and public sector (Robbins and Barnwell, 2002; Bouckaert and van Doren, 2003). Moreover, they are not only applied to corporate performance, but also to many of the so-called micro activities that comprise the day-to-day operations of business enterprises. Community leisure centres in particular lend themselves to micro measurement. In the first place, they provide an array of person-centred activities that are subject to strong user responses and perceptions. Second, their services are not only rated on the scale, range and quality of its tangible facilities, but also on the quality of the service provided by the staff. Third, many community leisure centres are funded and subsidized through local government rates and taxes and, therefore, need to ensure that scarce community resources are utilized as efficiently as possible (Graaff, 1996).

It is useful to examine the performance of community leisure centres from two perspectives. The first perspective focuses on the efficient use of funds, staff and space. To get some idea of how funds are being used, it is always good to start with some idea of the relationship between operating costs and income. This will generate an operating profit indicator and an expense recovery rate. And, where more detail is needed, something like fees (admission charges) per visit or fees per unit of space can be calculated. It is also very important to identify not only the gross subsidy that may apply, but also the subsidy per visit. There are also a number of sales and marketing related measures that can be used to indicate how well funds are being used in attracting visitors. They include things like total visits per space used and promotion cost per visitor. It is also important to measure facility usage. In this instance, measures include visit per metre of space, maintenance cost per unit of centre expenditure and energy cost per metre of space. Finally, there are a number of measures that provide an indication of how well staff are being utilized. They include staff cost as a percentage of total income, staff costs as percentage of total centre expenditure and the ratio of desk staff to programming staff. A sample of performance indicators for community leisure centres is listed in Table 13.4.

The second perspective focuses on the level of service quality. In this instance, it is a matter of finding out what visitors think of their experiences in the centre (Beech and Chadwick, 2004). Their experiences are usually divided into five categories. They are first, the quality of the tangible product or service itself; second, the reliability and dependability of the service; third, the responsiveness of staff and their willingness to assist; fourth, an assurance that staff will be trustworthy and courteous; and, finally, the degree to which staff are empathetic and provide individual attention. There are many models to choose from and many rating tools. Some of the more sophisticated tools aim to calculate a service delivery gap, which is nothing more than the difference between what customers expected and what they experienced (Graaf, 1996). In the end, all they are doing is providing a customer rating of the facilities and personal service provided. Typically, this will be done by a survey or questionnaire that asks visitors to score the specific services on a rating scale of 1–5. Ratings of 1 usually indicate low levels of satisfaction, while ratings of 5 will indicate high levels of satisfaction.

SUMMARY

The above discussion suggests that, while the introduction of performance management systems into sport organizations can be costly and sometimes create an administrative strait-jacket for its staff, officials, volunteers and members, it can also bring substantial benefits. In fact, a sport organization that does not provide a systematic evaluation of its performance would be derelict in its duty to stakeholders. The question is really one of what form and shape the performance management system should take. At

Table 13.4 Sample of Efficiency Indicators for a Community Leisure Centre

Indicator	Description	Examples
Expense recovery rate	Ratio of total centre income to total centre expenses	Income of $5 million, expenses of 4.5 million, Expense recovery rate is 111
Admission fees per visit	Total fees divided by number of visits	1000 visits per week, $6000 in fees, admission fee per visit is $6
Visits per space available	Visits divided by amount of space	1000 visits per week, 50 square metres of space, visit per metre-space is 200
Promotion costs per visitor	Promotion costs divided by number of visitors	1000 visits per week, $1000 of promotion per week, promotion cost per visit is $1
Maintenance costs rate	Ratio of total centre maintenance costs to total centre income	Maintenance cost are 1.5 million, centre income is $5 million, maintenance cost rate is 0.30 or 30%
Staff costs per unit of space	Staff costs divided by space	Staff costs are $3 million, space is 50 square metres, staff cost per unit of space is $6000

this point it is important to say that there is no one best performance management system. It all depends on the particular sport organization being studied, its primary strategic goals and the environment in which it operates. A good starting point is to use Kaplan and Norton's BSC as the foundation and customize it to the fit the sport organization's specific needs. The nine-point model described above gives a number of possibilities but, at all times, the measures should be quantifiable, linked to the sport organization's primary goals and consistent with stakeholder expectations.

REVIEW QUESTIONS

1. What does a performance management system aim to do?

2. What are the origins of performance management, and what do these origins tell us about its possible strengths and weaknesses?

3. What might prevent a sport organization from implementing a system of performance management?

4. What are the benefits that will follow from the implementation of a performance management system?

5. What are the key components of Kaplan and Norton's BSC?

6. How might you go about modifying the BSC to make it better fit the special features of sport organizations?

7. What specific measures can best reveal the financial performance of a sport organization?

8. How can the intrinsically vague concept of customer satisfaction be 'hardened-up' to provide a quantitative, concrete measure of the service quality in a community leisure centre?

9. What would you advise a sport club or association to do in order to ensure it was delivering its sport services in a fair, equitable, and environmentally friendly way.

FURTHER READING

To get a more detailed picture of the fundamentals of performance management, and how it has been used in both private and public sectors, see Williams (1998) and Bouckaert and van Doren (2003). In order to obtain a fuller appreciation of the theoretical foundations of performance management, its relation to organizational effectiveness and problems of implementation, refer to Chapter 3 of Robbins and Barnwell (2002) and Bouckaert (1995). Chappelet and Bayle (2005). A comprehensive comparative evaluation of the four professional football leagues operating in Australia can be found in Chapter 8 of Stewart (2007b). One of the most revealing books written about Nike and its branding, marketing and strategic initiatives is Goldman and Papson (1998).

RELEVANT WEBSITES

For an update on the balanced scorecard approach to performance management, go to <www.balancedscorecard.org>

Japan's professional soccer (i.e. association football) league, the J.League is one of Japan's most popular sport competitions. To obtain a general picture of its overall level of performance, go to <www.j-league.or.jp>.

In Australia, the Australian Football League is highly profitable but, paradoxically, some of its member clubs have had to fight severe financial turbulence over many years. The Institute of Chartered Accountants undertakes an annual survey of club finances. For further details go to www.icaa.org.au/news/index

For a detailed discussion of the Global Reporting Initiative (GRI) and related indicators go to <www.cisco.com/web/about/ac227/ac333/cisco-and-citizenship/global-reporting.html>

Nike has developed a strong corporate social responsibility programme in recent years. For a detailed discussion of their programme go to <www.socialfunds.com/csr/reports/Nike_FY05-06_Corporate_Responsibility_Report.pdf>

Case Study: Measuring Corporate Social Responsibility (CSR) At Nike

Businesses are often criticized for thinking only of the profits they make and ignoring the social consequences of their strategic decisions and the outputs they deliver. This dilemma is particularly striking in the case of tobacco companies. On one hand, there are profits to be made but, on the other hand, there is evidence that links smoking cigarettes to lung cancer and heart disease. Sport has for many years had a close relationship with tobacco producers, who have provided millions of dollars of sponsor funds to both community and professional sport.

There is now growing pressure from both government and the public in general for businesses to move beyond the bottom line and take into account the effect their decisions have on the wider community. This idea has given rise to the concept of triple-bottom-line accounting, which gets business to consider their contribution to not just economic prosperity, but also social justice and environmental quality. While the measurement of social justice and environmental quality is fraught with danger, the overall aim is to see that profits and net worth are just one measure of the performance of an organization. Triple-bottom-line accounting consequently provides for three measures of how a business contributes to society, with each measure being geared around the value-added concept. These measures are:

1. Economic value-added
2. Social value-added
3. Environmental value-added.

This way of measuring performance presents many challenges for sport organizations. It has already been noted that sport organizations are motivated by more than money. For a national sporting body, the growth of the sport may be equally important and, for a professional sports club, the dominant goal may be on-field success. However, despite the primacy of these goals, sport organizations can equally make decisions and produce outputs that have negative consequences for society in general. The heavy use of tobacco companies as sponsors may have secured a valuable source of funds, but the subsequent association of tobacco products with glamorous sport stars was instrumental in convincing young people that smoking was socially desirable, even if it might kill them in the long run. In some sports, heavy drinking of alcohol products is part of the club culture and, in these cases, no success is seen as complete without a long binge-drinking session. Similarly, in professional sport leagues, where neo-tribalism is strong, groups of rival supporters will often resolve their antagonism with a wild brawl. Football hooliganism in Britain is the archetypal model in this respect. All of these outputs have negative social consequences and it therefore makes senses to encourage sport clubs, associations and leagues to measure their overall performance in terms of their social and environmental impact as well as their participation impact, win–loss impact or revenue raising impact.

Recently, a number of global businesses with the support of the United Nations developed a CSR programme called the Global Reporting Initiative (GRI). The mission of GRI is to design and promulgate sustainability reporting guidelines for each of the economic, social and environmental outputs identified above. Organizations that sign up to GRI are expected to enact reporting systems that are transparent and accessible, provide quality and reliable information and include information that is relevant and complete. GRI has also compiled a list of factors under each of the economic, social and environmental headings that indicate specific issues that require addressing. A sample of factors particularly relevant to sport organizations is provided in Table 13.5.

While the GRI model of performance management is complex, it will encourage sport organizations to be more

Continued

systematic in the way they build their stakeholder relations. It will also enable them to go beyond revenue growth and on-field success and evaluate the contribution they are making to the wider society and monitor their impact on the physical environment. This can only be a good thing.

Nike's CSR Transformation

Nike is world leader in sport clothing and footwear production and supply and has become one of the world's most prominent brands. At the same time, its reputation was tarnished during the 1990s when it was accused of using Asian sweat-shop labour to produce its sports footwear. In other words, it produced its products in low cost third world countries, sold then at massive mark-ups to consumers in affluent first world nations and pocketed the profits.

There was a global backlash against this strategy and a number of international aid agencies were highly critical of Nike's corporate behaviour. While Nike was performing outstandingly well from a financial perspective, it was seen as performing poorly from a social and environmental perspective. As the 1990s proceeded, the backlash turned into a boycott of its products and Nike's reputation for good global citizenship fell alarmingly. To counter this serious image problem, which was also translating into a fall in sales and profits, Nike set out to change its behaviour, actively engaged in a programme of social responsibility and began to measure its performance against a range of social and environmental indicators as well as the more conventional financial indicators like net profit and return on investment.

Re-inventing Nike through Broadening Measures of Performance

Nike now acknowledges that CSR is good for its broad community image. It also concedes that it can also be good for its long-term sustainability. It decided that it must change its credo. Among other things, Nike is now projecting the following values and using them to frame their strategic direction:

- The opportunity is greater than ever for corporate responsibility principles and practices to deliver business returns and become a driver of growth, to build deeper consumer and community connections and to create positive social and environmental

impact in the world. Nike believes it has made tremendous progress over the past few years in more deeply integrating corporate responsibility into its business model.

- Corporate responsibility is not only a catalyst for growth and innovation, but is also an integral part of how Nike can use the power of its brand, the energy and passion of its people and the scale of its business to create meaningful change. This expanded mindset evolved from an intense review of how corporate responsibility operated at Nike and it translates into leadership, team building, accountabilities and skill sets.

- As a result of the organizational and strategic changes made in 2005, corporate responsibility at Nike has grown beyond its role as a tool to define, discover and address compliance issues and manage risk and reputation. It no longer exists on the planning periphery as a check on business activity, but now assumes a pivotal role as a source of innovation within Nike's core business. Corporate responsibility is no longer a staff function. It is a design function, a sourcing function and a consumer experience function.

- Incremental progress isn't good enough any more. Nike admits it is a highly competitive organization and, to that extent, it does not want just to get better financially, it wants to win at all levels of its operation. Moreover, if real change is to occur in the supply chain and contract factories around the world and in the communities in which it operates, then small, conservative steps will always fall short of Nike's potential.

At the same time, Nike now believes that broad-based CSR goals are needed to realize positive and globally significant achievements. So, it has set a series of strategic business targets that, while on one hand, are very ambitious are, on the other hand, at least in its eyes, achievable. Nike now aims to focus its CSR efforts in three areas:

- Improve working conditions in its contract factories through a holistic, integrated business approach to its supply chain

- Minimize its global environmental footprint through sustainable product innovation and supply chain innovation – both in its direct operations and in its contract factories.
- Using the power of its brand to give excluded and marginalized youth around the world greater access to the social and health benefits of sport participation.

This is an excellent strategic model from a CSR perspective, but it begs the question as to how these initiatives can be measured and how Nike knows when it is being successful. To this end Nike has fashioned the following performance indictors and targets:

- Implement freedom of association education programme in all contract factories
- Develop programmes that empower workers and improve job satisfaction
- Ensure all products meet minimum design standards
- Reduce footwear and apparel material waste
- Reduce amount of volatile organic compounds in machinery
- Use environmentally approved materials in manufacture processes
- Reduce carbon emissions from manufacture processes
- Increase funding of programmes that increase youth participation in disadvantaged communities.

It is now a matter of setting some specific and measurable targets and working toward their attainment. This is the challenge facing Nike. Can it provide an appropriate financial return to its shareholders while also delivering its sporting apparel to its customers in a fair, equitable and environmentally friendly way?

Case Study Questions

1. Nike is a publically owned business whose shares can be bought and sold on the stock exchange. How does this private enterprise style organizational and legal structure differ from that of a sport governing body?

2. How might these differences impact on the goals and objectives of Nike, on one hand and a national governing body for sport, on the other?

3. What are the implications of Nike's primary need to make profits for its day-to-day operations?

4. Is profit making of any relevance to a sport national governing body?

5. How does the concept of CSR impact on the performance measures of profit making enterprises like Nike, on one hand and sport development agencies like a national sporting body, on the other?

6. What has Nike done to strengthen its CSR programme?

7. How would you use a model of CSR to extend the performance measures of a sport organization that has responsibility for the national development of the sport? Give specific examples.

Table 13.5 GRI Performance Indicators	
Performance Category	**Performance Measures**
Direct economic impacts	Sales to satisfied customers
	Purchases from suppliers
	Employees hired
	Taxes paid
	Dividend and interest paid
Product responsibility	Safety and durability
	Truth in advertising and product labelling
Work practices	Health, safety and security
	Training, education and consultation
	Appropriate wages and conditions
Social practices	No bribery and corruption
	Transparent lobbying
	Free from collusion and coercion
Human rights	Non-discriminatory hiring practices
	Free from forced labour
Environmental impacts	Efficient energy use
	Appropriate water recycling
	Controlled carbon and other emissions
	Waste management
	Maintenance of biodiversity

References

Allison, M. (2002). *Sports clubs in Scotland summary: Research Digest no. 59.* Sports Scotland, Edinburgh.

American Marketing Association (2004). *Code of ethics*, revised edition. American Marketing Association, Chicago.

Amis, J. and Cornwell, T.B. (2005). *Global sport sponsorship*. Berg, Oxford.

Amis, J. and Slack, T. (1996). The size-structure relationship in voluntary sport organizations. *Journal of Sport Management*, 10, 76-86.

Anthony, R. and Young, D. (2003). *Management control in nonprofit organizations*, 7th edn. McGraw Hill, New York.

Atkinson, A., Waterhouse, J.H. and Wells, R. (1997). A stakeholder approach to strategic performance measurement. *Sloan Management Review, Spring*, 25-37.

Atrill, P., McLaney, E., Harvey, D. and Jenner, M. (2006). *Accounting: an introduction*. Pearson Education Australia, Frenchs Forest.

Australian Bureau of Statistics, (2005). *Involvement in organised sport and physical activity, Australia, Cat. No. 6285.0.* Australian Bureau of Statistics, Canberra.

Australian Sports Commission. (2000). *Committee management, active Australia club/association management program*. Australian Sports Commission, Canberra.

Australian Sports Commission, (2003). *Independent soccer review: report of the independent soccer review committee into the structure, governance and management of soccer in Australia*. Australian Sports Commission, Canberra.

Australian Sports Commission, (2004). *Sport innovation and best practice – governance at* http://www.ausport.gov.au/ibp/governance.asp. Australian Sports Commission, Canberra.

Australian Sports Commission, (2007). *Report of the steering committee into the structure and governance review of basketball in Australia* (November 2007). Australian Sports Commission, Canberra.

Australian Sports Commission, (2008). *Review of high performance pathways in Australian basketball* (January 2008). Australian Sports Commission, Canberra.

Baldwin, R. and Cave, M. (1999). *Understanding regulation: theory, strategy and practice*. Oxford University Press, Oxford.

Bass, B. M. (1985). *Leadership and performance beyond expectations*. The Free Press, New York.

Bass, B.M. (1990). *Bass & Stogdill's handbook of leadership: theory, research, and managerial applications*, 3rd edn. Free Press, New York.

Bass, B.M. and Avolio, B.J. (1994). *Improving organisational effectiveness through transformational leadership*. Sage Publications, London.

Beech, J. and Chadwick, S. (eds). (2004). *The business of sport management*. Prentice Hall, Harlow.

Bellamy, R. (1998). The evolving television sports marketplace. In L. Wenner (ed.), *MediaSport*. Routledge, London, pp. 73-87.

Berger, P. and Luckmann, T. (1967). *The social construction of reality: a treatise on the sociology of knowledge*. Penguin, London.

Bettinger, C. (1989). Use corporate culture to trigger high performance. *Journal of Business Strategy*, 10, 38-42.

Block, S.R. (1998). *Perfect nonprofit boards: myths, paradoxes and paradigms*. Simon & Schuster, Needham Heights.

Bloomfield, J. (2003). *Australia's sporting success: the inside story*. University of New South Wales Press, Sydney.

Bouckaert, G. (1995). Improving performance management. In A. Halachmi and G. Bouckaert (eds), *The enduring challenges in public management*. Jossey-Bass, San Francisco.

Bouckaert, G. and van Doren, W. (2003). Performance measurement and management in public sector organisations. In T. Bovaird and E. Lofler (eds), *Public management and governance*. Routledge, London.

Boyle, R. and Haynes, R. (2000). *Power play: sport, the media and popular culture*. Longman, Sydney.

Brohm, J. (1978). *Sport: a prison of measured time*. Ink Links, London.

Carver, J. (1997). *Boards that make a difference: a new design for leadership in non-profit and public organizations*, 2nd edn. Jossey-Bass, San Francisco.

Cashman, R. (1995). *Paradise of sport*. Oxford University Press, Melbourne.

Chalip, L., Johnson, A. and Stachura, L. (eds.). (1996). *National sports policies: an international handbook*. Greenwood Press, Westport.

Chappelet, J. and Bayle, E. (2005). *Strategic and performance management of Olympic sport organisations*. Human Kinetics, Champaign.

Chelladurai, P. (2006). *Human resource management in sport and recreation*. Human Kinetics, Champaign.

Clarke, T. (ed.) (2004). *Theories of corporate governance*. Routledge, Oxford.

Cook, R.A. and Szumal, J.L. (1993). Measuring normative beliefs and shared behavioral expectations in organizations: the reliability and validity of the organizational culture inventory. *Psychological Reports*, 72, 1290-1330.

Colyer, S. (2000). Organizational culture in selected Western Australian sport organizations. *Journal of Sport Management*, 14, 321-341.

Cousens, L. and Slack, T. (2005). Field-level change: the case of North American major league professional sport. *Journal of Sport Management*, 19, 13-42.

Cuskelly, G. (2004). Volunteer retention in community sport organisations. *European Sport Management Quarterly*, 4, 59-76.

Cuskelly, G., Hoye, R. and Auld, C. (2006). *Working with volunteers in sport: theory and practice*. Routledge, London.

DaCosta, L. and Miragaya, A. (eds) (2002). Sport for all worldwide: a cross national and comparative research. In *Worldwide experiences and trends in sport for all*. Meyer and Meyer, Oxford.

Dejonghe, T. (2001). Sport in de wereld: ontstaan, evolutie en verspreiding. Academia Press, Gent, p. 117.

Deming, W. (1993). *The new economics for industry, government, education*. MIT, Cambridge.

Denison, D. and Mishra, A. (1995). Toward a theory of organizational culture and effectiveness. *Organizational Science*, 6, 204-224.

Dess, G. and Lumpkin, G. (2003). *Strategic management: creating competitive advantages*. McGraw-Hill Irwin, Boston.

Doherty, A. (1998). Managing our human resources: a review of organizational behaviour in sport. *Journal of Sport Management*, 12, 1-24.

Downward, P. and Dawson, A. (2000). *The economics of professional team sports*. Routledge: London.

Dressler, G. (2003). *Human resource management*. Prentice Hall, Englewood Cliffs.

Drucker, P.F. (1990). Lessons for successful nonprofit governance. *Nonprofit Management and Leadership*, 1, 7-14.

England Netball. (2007a). *Student pack*. England Netball, Hertfordshire.

England Netball. (2007b). *Annual Report 2006–2007*. England Netball, Hertfordshire.

Euchner, C. (1993). *Playing the field: why sports teams move and cities fight to keep them*. Johns Hopkins University Press, Baltimore.

Fan Hong. (1997). Commercialism and sport in China. *Journal of Sport Management*, 11, 343-354.

Fiedler, F. E. (1967). *A theory of leadership effectiveness*. McGraw-Hill, New York.

Fielding, L, Miller, L. and Brown, J. (1999). Harlem Globetrotters International, Inc. *Journal of Sport Management*, 13, 45-77.

Fletcher, K. (1999). Four books on nonprofit boards and governance. *Nonprofit Management and Leadership*, 9, 435-441.

Football Association (FA). (2008). *The FA's Vision 2008–2012*. FA, London.

Football Governance Research Centre (2004). *The state of the game: the corporate governance of football clubs 2004*, Research paper 2004 No. 3. Football Governance Research Centre, Birkbeck, University of London.

Foster, G., Greyser, A. and Walsh, B. (2006). *The business of sports: text and cases on strategy and management*. Thompson South-Western, Mason.

Friedman, M., Parent, M. and Mason, D. (2004). Building a framework for issues management in sport through stakeholder theory. *European Sport Management Quarterly*, 3, 170-190.

Frisby, W. (1986). The organizational structure and effectiveness of voluntary organizations: the case of Canadian national sport governing bodies. *Journal of Park and Recreation Administration*, 4, 61-74.

Frosdick, S. and Walley, L. (eds). (1997). *Sport and safety management*. Butterworth-Heinemann, Oxford.

Goffee, R. and Jones, G. (1996). What holds the modern company together? *Harvard Business Review*, 74, 133-149.

Goldman , R. and Papson, S. (1998) *Nike culture*, Sage, Thousand Oaks.

Graaff, A. (1996). Service quality and sport centres. *European Journal for Sport Management*, xx/2.

Gratton, C. and Taylor, P. (1991). *Government and the economics of sport*. Longman, London.

Green, M. (2006). From 'sport for all' to not about 'sport' at all: interrogating sport policy interventions in the United Kingdom. *European Sport Management Quarterly*, 6, 217-238.

Green, M. and Houlihan, B. (2005) *Elite sport development*. Routledge, London.

Greenfield, S. and Osborn, G. (2001). *Regulating football; commodification, consumption and the law*. Pluto Press, London.

Hanlon, C. and Cuskelly, G. (2002) Pulsating major sport event organizations: a framework for inducting managerial personnel, *Event Management*, 7, 231–243.

Harvard Business Review. (1998). *On measuring corporate performance*. Harvard Business Review Press, Boston.

Hart, L. (2006). *Accounting demystified: a self teaching guide*. McGraw Hill, New York.

Heimovics, R.D. and Herman, R.D. (1990). Responsibility for critical events in nonprofit organizations. *Nonprofit and Voluntary Sector Quarterly*, 19, 59-72.

Henry, I. and Lee, P.C. (2004). Governance and ethics in sport. In J. Beech and S. Chadwick (eds), *The business of sport management*. Prentice Hall, London.

Henry, I., and Uchium, K. (2001). Political ideology, modernity, and sport policy: a comparative analysis of sport policy in Britain and Japan. *Hitotsubashi Journal of Social Studies*, 33, 161-185.

Herman, R.D. and Heimovics, R. (1990). The effective nonprofit executive: leader of the board. *Nonprofit Management and Leadership* 1, 167-180.

Herman, R.D. and Heimovics, R. (1994). Executive leadership. In R.D. Herman & Associates (eds), *The Jossey-Bass handbook of nonprofit leadership and management*. Jossey-Bass, San Fransisco, pp. 137-153.

Herman, R.D. and Renz, D.O. (1997). Multiple constituencies and the social construction of nonprofit organizational effectiveness. *Nonprofit and Voluntary Sector Quarterly*, 26, 185-206.

Herman, R.D. and Renz, D.O. (1998). Nonprofit organizational effectiveness: contrasts between especially effective and less effective organizations. *Nonprofit Management and Leadership*, 9, 23-38.

Herman, R.D. and Renz, D.O. (2000). Board practices of especially effective and less effective local nonprofit organizations. *American Review of Public Administration*, 30, 146-160.

Hersey, P. and Blanchard, K. (1977). *Management of organizational behaviour: utilizing human resources*. Prentice-Hall, Englewood Cliffs.

Hess, R. Nicholson, M., Stewart, B. and de Moore, G. (2008). A *national game: the history of Australian rules football*, Viking/Penguin, Melbourne.

Hess, R. and Stewart, R. (eds). (1998). *More than a game: an unauthorised history of Australian football*. Melbourne University Press, Melbourne.

Hillary Commission. (1998). *The growing business of sport and leisure: the impact of the physical leisure industry in New Zealand*. Hillary Commission, Wellington.

Hindley, D. (2003). *Resource guide in governance and sport*. Learning and teaching support network in hospitality, leisure, sport and tourism at http://www.hlst.ltsn.ac.uk/resources/governance.html.

Hockey Canada (2007). *Annual Report 2007*. Hockey Canada, Calgary.

Hofstede, G. (1991). *Cultures and organizations: software of the mind*, McGraw Hill, London.

Hofstede, G. (2001). *Culture's consequences: comparing values, behaviors, institutions and organizations across nations*. Sage, Thousand Oaks.

Hofstede, G., Neuijen, B., Ohayv, D. and Sanders, G. (1990). Measuring organizational cultures: a qualitative and quantitative study across twenty cases. *Administrative Science Quarterly*, 35, 286-316.

Hoggett, J., Edwards, L. and Medlin, J. (2006). *Accounting*, 6th edn. Wiley, Milton.

Houle, C.O. (1960). *The effective board*. Association Press, New York.

Houle, C.O. (1997). *Governing boards: their nature and nurture*. Jossey-Bass, San Francisco.

Houlihan, B. (1997). *Sport policy and politics: a comparative analysis*. Routledge, London.

Houlihan, B. and Green, M. (2007). *Comparative elite sport development. Systems, structures and public policy*. Elsevier, London.

Houlihan, B. and White, A. (2002). *The politics of sport development: development of sport or development through sport?* Routledge, London.

House, R.J. (1971). A path-goal theory of leader effectiveness. *Administrative Science Quarterly*, 16, 321-338

House, R.J. and Mitchell, T.R. (1974). Path-goal theory of leadership. *Contemporary Business*, 3, 81-91.

Howard, L. (1998). Validating the competing values model as a representation of organizational cultures. *International Journal of Organizational Analysis*, 6, 231-251.

Howard, D. and Crompton, J. (2004). *Financing sport*, 2nd edn. Fitness Information Technology, Morgantown.

Hoye, R. and Cuskelly, G. (2003). Board-executive relationships within voluntary sport organisations. *Sport Management Review*, 6, 53-73.

Hoye, R. and Cuskelly, G. (2007). *Sport governance*. Butterworth-Heinemann, Oxford.

Hoye, R. and Inglis, S. (2003). Governance of nonprofit leisure organizations. *Society and Leisure*, 26, 369-387.

Hoye, R., Nicholson, M. and Smith, A. (2008). Unique aspects of managing sport organizations. In C. Wankel (ed.), *21st century management: a reference handbook*. Sage, Thousands Oaks, pp. 499-507.

Hughes, H. (1981). *News and the human interest story*. Transaction Books, London (reprint of the 1940 University of Chicago Press edition).

Human Kinetics National Intelligence Council (2000). *Global trends 2015: a dialogue about the future with non government experts*. National Foreign Intelligence Board, Washington DC.

Hylton, K. and Bramham, P. (eds) (2007). *Sports development: policy, process and practice*, 2nd edn. Routledge, London.

Hylton, K., Bramham, P., Jackson, D. and Nesti, M. (ed.). (2001). *Sport development*. Routledge, London.

Institute for Volunteering Research. (2008). *Management matters: a national survey of volunteer management capacity*. Institute for Volunteering Research, London.

Institute for Volunteering Research and Volunteering England. (2008). *A winning team? The impacts of volunteers in sport*. Institute for Volunteering Research, London.

International Monetary Fund. (2000-2005). *Globalization: Threat or opportunity?* http://www.imf.org/external/np/exr/ib/2000/041200.htm Retrieved March 1, 2005.

Jensen, R. (1999). *The dream society*. McGraw-Hill, New York.

John, G. and Sheard, R. (1997). *Stadia: a design and development guide*. Architectural Press, Oxford.

Johnson, G. and Scholes, K. (2002). *Exploring corporate strategy*, 6th edn. Prentice-Hall, London, pp. 4–11.

Kaplan, R. and Norton, D. (1992). The balanced scorecard: measures that drive performance. *Harvard Business Review* (January-February), 71-79.

Kaplan, R. and Norton, D. (1996). *The balanced scorecard*. Harvard University Press, Boston.

Kikulis, L.M., Slack, T. and Hinings, B. (1992). Institutionally specific design archetypes: a framework for understanding change in national sport organizations. *International Review for the Sociology of Sport*, 27, 343-367.

Kikulis, L.M., Slack, T. and Hinings, B. (1995). Toward an understanding of the role of agency and choice in the changing structure of Canada's national sport organizations. *Journal of Sport Management*, 9, 135-152.

Kikulis, L.M., Slack, T., Hinings, B. and Zimmermann, A. (1989). A structural taxonomy of amateur sport organizations. *Journal of Sport Management*, 3, 129-150.

Kotter, J.P. (1990). *A force for change: how leadership differs from management*. The Free Press, New York.

Kouzes, J.M. and Posner, B.Z. (2006). *A leader's legacy*. Jossey-Bass, Hoboken.

Leisure Industries Research Centre. (2003). *Sports volunteering in England 2002: a report for Sport England*. Leisure Industries Research Centre, Sheffield.

Lewis, G. (1993). Concepts in strategic management. In G. Lewis, A. Morkel and G. Hubbard (eds), *Australian strategic management: concepts, context and cases*. Prentice-Hall, Sydney, pp. 5–38.

Li, M., Hofacre, S. and Mahony, D. (2001). *Economics of sport*. Fitness Information Technology, Morgantown.

Locke, E.A. (1991). *The essence of leadership: the four keys to leading successfully*. Lexington Books, New York.

Lyons, M. (2001). *Third sector: the contribution of nonprofit and cooperative enterprises in Australia*. Allen & Unwin, Crows Nest.

MacLean, J. (2001). *Performance appraisal for sport and recreation managers*. Human Kinetics, Champaign.

Mason, D., Andrews, D. and Silk, M. (eds) (2005). *Qualitative methods for sports studies*. Berg, Oxford.

Mechikoff, R. and Estes, S. (1993). *A history and philosophy of sport and physical education*. Brown and Benchmark, Madison.

Miles, R.E. (1975). *Theories of management: implications for organizational behaviour and development*. McGraw-Hill, New York.

Miller, T., Lawrence, G., McKay, J. and Rowe, D. (2001). *Globalisation and sport*. Sage, London.

Nicholson, M. (2007). *Sport and the media: managing the nexus*. Butterworth-Heinemann, London.

Norman, W. and MacDonald, C. (2004). Getting to the bottom of 'triple bottom-line accounting'. *Business Ethics Quarterly*, 14, 243-262.

O'Brien, D. and Slack, T. (2003) An analysis of change in an organizational field: the professionalization of English rugby union. *Journal of Sport Management*, 17, 417-448.

Ogbonna, E. and Harris, L.C. (2002). Organizational culture: a ten year, two-phase study of change in the UK food retailing sector. *Journal of Management Studies*, 39, 673-706.

Organization for Economic Cooperation and Development. (2004). *Principles of corporate governance*. OECD, Paris.

Oriard, M. (1993). *Reading football*. University of North Carolina Press, Chapel Hill.

Parent, M., O'Brien, D. and Slack, T. (2003). Strategic management in the context of sport. In L. Trenberth (ed.), *Managing the business of sport*. Dunmore Press, Palmerston North, pp. 101-122.

Pattavino, P. and Pye, G. (1994) *Sport in Cuba: the diamond in the rough*. University of Pittsburg Press, Pittsburg.

Perryman, M. (ed.). (2001). *Hooligan wars: causes and effects of football violence*. Mainstream Publishing, Edinburgh.

Pettigrew, A.M. (1979). On studying organizational cultures. *Administrative Science Quarterly*, 24, 570-581.

Pfeffer, J. and Salancik, G. (1978). *The external control of organizations: a resource dependence perspective*. Harper & Row, New York.

Porter, M. (1980). *Competitive strategy*, The Free Press, New York.

Porter, M. (1985). *Competitive strategy: creating and sustaining superior performance*. Simon & Schuster, New York.

Porter, M. (1996). What is strategy? *Harvard Business Review*, November-December, 61-78.

Productivity Commission. (2003). *social capital: reviewing the concept and its policy implications*. Commonwealth of Australia, Canberra.

Putnam, R. (2000). *Bowling alone: the collapse and revival of American community*. Simon and Schuster, New York.

Quinn, R. and Rohrbaugh, J. (1983). A spatial model of effectiveness criteria: towards a competing values approach to organizational analysis. *Management Science*, 29, 363-377.

Quirk, J. and Fort, R. (1992). *Pay dirt: the business of professional team sports*. Princeton University Press, Princeton.

Rein, I., Kotler, P. and Shields, B. (2006). *The elusive fan: reinventing sports in a crowded marketplace*. McGraw-Hill, New York.

Riordan, J. (1977). *Sport in Soviet society*. Cambridge University Press, Cambridge.

Riordon, J. (ed.). (1978). *Sport under communism: the USSR., Czechoslovakia, the GDR., China, Cuba*. Australian National University Press, Canberra.

Robbins, S. (1990). *Organization theory: structure design & applications*. Prentice Hall, Englewood Cliffs.

Robbins, S. and Barnwell, N. (2002). *Organisation theory*. Pearson Education Australia, Frenchs Forest.

Robbins, S.P., Bergman, R., Stagg, I. and Coulter, M. (2004a). *Management*, 3rd edn. Pearson Education, Sydney.

Robbins, S.P., Millett, B. and Waters-Marsh, T. (2004b). *Organizational behaviour*, 4th edn. Pearson Education, Sydney.

Robinson, L. (ed.) (2004). Human resource management. In *Managing public sport and leisure services*. Routledge, London.

Rowe, D. (1999). *Sport, culture and the media: the unruly trinity*. Open University Press, Buckingham.

Sandy, R., Sloane, P. J. and Rosentraub, M. (2004). *The economics of sport: an international perspective*. Palgrave Macmillan, Basingstoke.

Sashkin, M. (1996). *Organizational beliefs questionnaire: pillars of excellence*. Human Resource Development Press, Amherst.

Schein, E. (1984). *Coming to a new awareness of organizational culture*. Jossey-Bass, San Francisco.

Schein, E. (1985). How culture forms, develops and changes. In R.H. Kilman, M.J. Saxton, R. Serpa & Associates (eds), *Gaining control of the corporate culture*. Jossey-Bass, San Francisco, pp. 17-43.

Schein, E. (2004). *Organizational culture and leadership*, 3rd edn. Jossey-Bass, San Francisco.

Schermerhorn, J.R., Hunt, J.G. and Osborne, R.N. (1994). *Managing organizational behaviour*, 5th edn. John Wiley & Sons, Inc., Brisbane

Schudson, M. (1978) *Discovering the news: a social history of American newspapers*. Basic Books, New York.

Senge, P. (1990). *The fifth discipline*. Currency Doubleday, New York.

Shilbury, D., Quick, S. and Westerbeek, H. (2003) *Strategic sport marketing*, 2nd edn. Allen & Unwin, Sydney.

Shropshire, K. (1995). *The sports franchise game*. University of Pennsylvania Press, Philadelphia.

Slack, T. (1997). *Understanding sport organizations: the application of organization theory*. Human Kinetics, Champaign.

Slack, T. and Parent, M. (2006). *Understanding sport organizations: the application of organization theory*, 2nd edn. Human Kinetics, Champaign.

Slesinger, L.H. (1991). *Self-assessment for nonprofit governing boards*. National Centre for Nonprofit Boards, Washington, DC.

Smith, A. (2008). *Introduction to sport marketing*. Elsevier Butterworth-Heinemann. Oxford.

Smith, A. and Shilbury, D. (2004). Mapping cultural dimensions in Australian sporting organizations. *Sport Management Review*, 7, 133-165.

Smith, A. and Stewart, B. (1999). *Sports management: a guide to professional practice*. Allen & Unwin, Sydney.

Sport England. (2007). *Clubmark factsheet*. Sport England, London.

Standing Committee on Recreation and Sport Working Party on Management Improvement. (1997). *Report to the standing committee on recreation and sport July 1997*. Standing Committee on Recreation and Sport, Canberra.

Statistics Canada. (2004). *Cornerstones of community: highlights of the national survey of nonprofit and voluntary organizations*. Statistics Canada, Ottawa.

Statistics Canada. (2008). *Sports participation in Canada, 2005*. Statistics Canada Ottawa.

Stevens, J. (2006). The Canadian hockey association merger and the emergence of the amateur sport enterprise. *Journal of Sport Management*, 20, 74-101.

Stensholt, J. and Thomson, J. (2005). Kicking goals. *Business Review Weekly*, March 10-16, 38-42.

Stewart, B. (2007a). *Sport funding and finance*. Butterworth-Heinemann, Oxford.

Stewart, B. (ed) (2007b). *The games are not the same: the political economy of football in Australia*. Melbourne University Press, Melbourne.

Stewart, R. (1989). The nature of sport under capitalism and its relationship to the capitalist labour process. *Sporting Traditions*, 6, 43-61.

Stewart, R. and Smith, A. (1999). The special features of sport. *Annals of Leisure Research*, 2, 87-99.

Stewart, R., Nicholson, M., Smith, A. and Westerbeek, H. (2004). *Australian sport: better by design? The evolution of Australian sport policy*. Routledge, London.

Szymanski, S. and Kuypers, T. (1999). *Winners and losers: the business strategy of football*. Viking, London.

Taylor, T., Doherty, A. and McGraw, P. (2008). *Managing people in sport organizations: a strategic human resource management perspective*. Butterworth-Heinemann, London.

Theodoraki, E.I. and Henry, I.P. (1994). Organizational structures and contexts in British national governing bodies of sport. *International Review for the Sociology of Sport*, 29, 243-263.

Thibault, L., Slack, T. and Hinings, B. (1991). Professionalism, structures and systems: the impact of professional staff on voluntary sport organizations, *International Review for the Sociology of Sport*, 26, 83-97.

Thomas, R.J. (2008). *Crucibles of leadership*. Harvard Business School Publishing Corporation, Boston.

Tricker, R.I. (1984). *Corporate governance*. Gower, London.

Tricker, R.I. (1993). Corporate governance – the new focus of interest. *Corporate Governance*, 1, 1-3.

UEFA. (2007). Financial Report 2006–2007. UEFA, Nyon.

Van der Post, W. and de Coning, T. (1997). An instrument to measure organizational culture. *South African Journal of Business Management*, 28, 147-169.

Viljoen, J. and Dann, S. (2003). *Strategic management*, 4th edn. Prentice Hall, Frenchs Forest.

Volunteering Australia. (2004). *Snapshot 2004: volunteering report card*. Volunteering Australia, Melbourne.

Westerbeek, H. and Smith, A. (2005). *Business leadership and the lessons from sport*. Palgrave Macmillan, London.

Westerbeek, H.M. and Smith, A.C.T. (2003). *Sport business in the global marketplace*. Palgrave Macmillan, London.

Wexley, K.N. and Yukl, G.A. (1984). *Organizational behaviour and personnel psychology*, revised edn. Richard D. Irwin, Inc., Homewood.

Williams, R. (1998). *Performance management: perspectives on employee performance*. Thomson Business Press, London.

Whitson, D. (1998). Circuits of promotion: media, marketing and the globalization of sport. In L. Wenner (ed.), *MediaSport*. Routledge, London, pp.57-72.

Index

315